Sport Policy:
a comparative analysis of stability and change

Sport Policy: a comparative analysis of stability and change

Nils Asle Bergsgard,
Barrie Houlihan,
Per Mangset,
Svein Ingve Nødland and
Hilmar Rommetvedt

AMSTERDAM • BOSTON • HEIDELBERG • LONDON •
NEW YORK • OXFORD • PARIS • SAN DIEGO •
SAN FRANCISCO • SINGAPORE • SYDNEY • TOKYO
Butterworth-Heinemann is an imprint of Elsevier

Butterworth-Heinemann is an imprint of Elsevier
Linacre House, Jordan Hill, Oxford OX2 8DP, UK
30 Corporate Drive, Suite 400, Burlington, MA 01803, USA

First edition 2007

British Library Cataloguing in Publication Data
A catalogue record for this book is available from the British Library

Library of Congress Control Number:
A catalogue record for this book is available from the Library of Congress

ISBN: 978-0-7506-8364-7

For information on all publications visit our web site at
http://books.elsevier.com

Typeset by Charon Tec Ltd (A Macmillan Company), Chennai, India
www.charontec.com

Printed and bound in the Great Britain

Contents

Preface

In recent years there has been a substantial increase in the number of books that deal with aspects of sport politics and policy. In large part the increased output is a reflection of the growth in interest from governments in sport both as a focus for public policy in its own right and as an instrument that can support the achievement of other non-sport policy objectives in areas such as social welfare, economic development and international relations. The growth in academic interest in sport has produced a number of valuable single country studies of sport policy and politics or studies of particular aspects of sport policy such as elite development or mass participation. There have been significantly fewer studies which seek to compare across national boundaries. Indeed, in contrast to areas such as education, welfare and housing comparative studies in the area of sport policy are thin on the ground.

The rationale for our study is that comparative analysis offers insights into sport policy that are not available from the conduct of individual country studies. The purpose of this study is to analyse sport policies in four economically developed countries: Anglo-American Canada and England, and Continental/North European Germany and Norway. The special merit of this book is that it compares sport policies with the application of typologies and dimensions of analysis developed for comparative politics in general. The book discusses the relevance and implications for sport policies of welfare regimes and state systems, executive–legislative and government-interest group relations, and general late modern social transformation processes. This study is intended to provide an insight into the sport policy of the four countries and also to stimulate and contribute to the debate about the practice of comparative policy analysis.

Acknowledgements

The book is based primarily on a comparative research project sponsored by the Research Council of Norway. The project has been coordinated administratively by Telemark Research Institute, Bø, Norway, in cooperation with the International Research Institute of Stavanger (IRIS), Norway, and the Institute of Sport and Leisure Policy at Loughborough University, UK. The book has also benefited from earlier and ongoing research projects about Norwegian sports policy, conducted by the two Norwegian research institutes.

The book is the product of collective authorship, but there has been a certain division of labour. Bergsgard was centrally involved in the fieldwork in England and Germany and wrote the first draft of Chapter 5; Houlihan and Rommetvedt had the major responsibility for the first draft of Chapter 1 and Houlihan prepared the first draft of Chapter 3. Houlihan also undertook substantial editorial work on all chapters; Mangset and Nødland undertook the fieldwork in Canada and Mangset wrote the first draft of Chapter 6; Nødland was heavily involved in the fieldwork not only in Canada, but also in England and Germany and wrote the first drafts of Chapters 4 and 7; and finally, Rommetvedt participated in some of the fieldwork in Germany, had the major responsibility for the first drafts of Chapters 2 (with Houlihan) and 8, and completed editorial work on several chapters.

We are indebted to many persons and institutions in several countries for their help in providing the information and analytical perspectives that are reflected in this book. We are particularly grateful to about 50 anonymous interviewees in the sports fields of Canada, England and Germany. We are also indebted to several contacts in public institutions and sport institutions in Norway that have provided information in connection with earlier studies. We are finally indebted to about 20 sports policy researchers who attended a seminar about comparative sport policy research in Bø, Norway in February 2006. We have special reasons to thank warmly seven international sport policy researchers, who offered extensive and rigorous comments and criticisms on drafts of chapters of the book during the seminar, namely, Fred Coalter, the University of Sterling, Scotland; Peter Donnelly, the University of Toronto, Canada; Mick Green, Loughborough University, England; Ilse Hartman-Tews, the German Sport University, Cologne, Germany; Bjarne Ibsen, the University of Southern Denmark, Odense, Denmark; Ørnulf Seippel, the Institute for Social Research, Oslo, Norway; and Jan Ove Tangen, Telemark University College, Bø, Norway.

Despite all this valuable assistance, comment and criticism it is, of course, the authors that are responsible for the final content of the book.

List of figures

List of tables

List of abbreviations

ACF	Advocacy coalition framework
ASAA	Alberta School Athletics Association
BMI	*Bundesministerium des Innern* (Ministry of Interior)
BOA	British Olympic Association
BRD/FRG	*Bundesrepublik Deutschland*/Federal Republic of Germany (former West Germany)
CAC	Coaching Association of Canada
CCPR	Central Council of Physical Recreation
CMSSC	Culture, Media and Sport Select Committee
COC	Canadian Olympic Committee
CODA	Calgary Olympic Development Association
DCMS	Department for Culture, Media and Sport
DDR/GDR	*Deutsche Demokratische Republik*/German Democratic Republic (former East Germany)
DfES	Department for Education and Skills
DSB	*Deutscher Sportbund* (the German Sports Confederation)
GDP	Gross Domestic Product
IAAF	International Association of Athletics Federations
IOC	International Olympic Committee
KKD	*Kultur- og kirkedepartementet* (the Ministry of Culture and Church Affairs); before 2001 *Kulturdepartementet* (KD, Ministry for Culture Affairs)
LSB	*Land Sportbund* (the Land Sports Confederation)
MSO	Multi-sport/service organisations
NGB	National Governing Body (Britain)
NGO	Non-government organisation
NIF	*Norges Idrettsforbund* (before 1996) (the Norwegian Confederation of Sports)

NIF/NOC	*Norges Idrettsforbund og Olympiske komité* (from 1996) (the Norwegian Olympic Committee and Confederation of Sports)
NOC	National Olympic Committee
NOK	*Nationales Olympisches Komittee* (National Olympic Committee in Germany)
	Norwegian Kroner
NRW	Nordrhein-Westfalen
NSO	National Sports Organisation (Norwegian: *Særforbund*; German: *Spitzenverbände*)
OECD	Organisation for Economic Co-operation and Development
PE	Physical Education
PESSCL	PE, School Sport and Club Links
QCA	Qualification and Curriculum Authority
SDO	Sport development officer
SEEM	Sport England East Midlands
STUI	*Statens ungdoms- og idrettskontor* (the State Office for Youth and Sport)
TASS	Talented Athlete Scholarship Scheme
UKSI	UK Sport Institute
UN	United Nations
UNESCO	United Nations Educational, Scientific and Cultural Organization
YMCA	Young Men's Christian Association

German names and English translations

Deutscher Bundestag	German Parliament
Sportausschuss der Bundestages	Standing Committee for Sport of the Bundestag
Länder	Land/region/provinces/state
Olympiastützpunkte	Olympic training centres

CHAPTER 1

Introduction

In recent years a number of studies have been published which have charted the extensive changes in the nature and context of sport that have taken place over the last 50 years or so. Studies have variously examined the interconnection between sport and internationalisation and globalisation (e.g. Maguire, 1999; Houlihan, 2003), commercialisation (Amis and Cornwell, 2005; Slack, 2004), the growth of state involvement (Riordan, 1978; Goksøyr, 1992; Houlihan, 1992, 1997; Mangset and Rommetvedt, 2002; Bergsgard, 2005) and the expansion of media interest in sport (Bernstein and Blain, 2003; Rowe, 2003). Although focusing on different aspects of the contemporary context they collectively attest to the dynamism of that context for sport and sport policy. The pace of change has prompted debate and expressions of concern in many countries and regions about the place of sport in the spectrum of public policy and the vulnerability of distinctive national models of sport to erosion by powerful global forces or particularly dominant countries. For example, in Canada the impact of the US on the domestic sports system is viewed by many as undermining the distinctiveness of Canadian sport and weakening the relationship between sport and broader welfare and diplomatic policy objectives. In Germany following reunification there was considerable concern to ensure that the highly centralised, highly politicised, corrupt and elite-focused sports system of the former German Democratic Republic (GDR) should be dismantled in favour of the more decentralised, club-based and welfare-oriented system established in the Federal Republic. The European Union has attempted to define a European model of sport (European Commission, 1998) in contradistinction to the heavily commercialised model typified by the US and, to a lesser extent, by England. Finally, the concern with the impact of commercialisation on sport in the European Union is one that is substantially shared by many sports administrators and politicians in Norway where there is a long tradition of sport being a decommodified practice deeply rooted in the every-day culture of the community.

Sport and sport policy

The range of interpretations of sport across the four countries we have selected for our study, Canada, England, Germany and Norway, reflects not only the adaptability of sport as a policy resource, but also the problems in identifying the essence of the practice and its boundaries with related practices such as recreation, games and physical activity. There has been a number of practitioner and academic attempts to define the scope of the policy field. The Council of Europe's European Sports Charter, as revised in 2001, defines sport as 'all forms of physical activity which, through casual or organised participation, aim at expressing or improving physical fitness and mental well-being, forming social relationships or obtaining results in competition at all levels'. Among the many academic attempts at definition is that by Jay Coakley who views sport as 'institutionalised competitive activities that involve vigorous physical exertion or the use of relatively complex physical skills by participants motivated by intrinsic and extrinsic rewards' (2003, p. 21). While both these definitions are useful reference points our primary concern is to explore how policy-makers in each of the four countries operationalise the concept of sport and translate it into policy outputs and outcomes.

The increased salience of sport to governments reflects: first, its strong cultural significance; second, its malleability as a resource to help deliver non-sport government objectives; and third, its multi-dimensional character. The increasing cultural significance of sport is indicated not only by the growth in evidence that the public see sports opportunities and facilities to be significant aspects of their quality of life, but also by the intense attention given to sporting success or failure by national teams and athletes, and by clubs in international competitions (see e.g. DCMS/Strategy Unit, 2002). The malleability of sport was most dramatically and systematically demonstrated by the former communist governments in Europe who used sport, and international sporting success in particular, as a lever to make progress towards recognition of sovereignty (former East Germany, GDR), to generate a sense of national identity in culturally, ethnically and linguistically diverse states (former Soviet Union and Yugoslavia), and to demonstrate the ideological superiority of socialism over capitalism (Soviet Union and GDR). While the richer capitalist governments were initially reluctant to emulate communism they soon began to invest in the preparation of their elite athletes, especially for the Olympic Games, and to acknowledge and utilise the capacity of sport to address a range of social problems (such as social exclusion, juvenile delinquency, childhood obesity and community fragmentation), economic problems (including urban and rural regeneration) and diplomatic issues (such as the indication of approval or disapproval of the actions of other countries in ways that were highly visible, low cost and low risk). The final factor explaining increased government interest in sport is its multi-dimensional character insofar as sport is not only a distinct public service and, in many countries, an important aspect of overall welfare provision, but is also an important element of the economy in terms of job creation, capital investment and balance of payments. The malleability of sport and the range of different policy objectives to which it contributes further reinforce the problematic nature of defining the scope of the policy area. As such sport has the potential to stimulate interest across a wide range of policy sectors.

Exploring the contemporary context and dynamics of sport policy[1] has generally been approached through analyses which focus on the extent to which the policy of individual countries has been insulated from, or permeated by, exogenous influences, or which focus on the dynamics of globalisation, the extent of its reach into individual countries and cultures, and the response that it generated. By contrast there are relatively few studies that adopt an explicitly comparative approach to explaining the stimulus for, and character of, policy change. This is surprising as comparison is at the heart of all social science whether it is comparison over time, across countries, between policy areas or with other cases. But comparison, especially in the field of social policy, is challenging and problematic at both the theoretical and methodological levels. At the theoretical level too many multi-country studies are simply parallel single country reviews of policy which, though insightful, fail to take advantage of the opportunities that comparison offers. Theoretically informed research design is, unfortunately, all too often conspicuous by its absence. Ironically, the neglect of theory has resulted in an over concentration on the debates concerning comparative methodology consequently giving matters of *research process* precedence over questions of *research purpose*. Thus, while acknowledging that methodological questions are important in comparative analysis there is the risk that, as Keman notes, 'the domain of [the] discipline is defined by its method, rather than by its substance' (2002: p. 33).

The selected countries and their socio-economic profiles

The aims of the present study are to identify the characteristics of sport policy in four countries, namely Canada, England,[2] Germany and Norway, to determine whether, and to what extent, sport policy reflects the characteristics of the broader welfare regime and whether, and in what ways, sport policy is affected by key attributes of the domestic political system and transnational influences such as globalisation and commercialisation. The associated objectives are to review and analyse changes in the role of government and public agencies in sport and to suggest the causes of any changes; to examine the development of public policy in relation to *sport for all* (mass participation) and high-performance sport (both non-commercial/publicly subsidised and commercial) and to identify the extent to which changes in public policy represent shifts in more deeply embedded values in relation to sport.

In selecting the four countries we have followed Lijphart who recommends the selection of countries that are similar 'in a large number of important characteristics (variables) which one wants to treat as constants, but dissimilar as far as those variables are concerned which one wants to relate to each other. If such comparable cases can be found they offer particularly good opportunities for the application of the comparative method because they allow the establishment of relationships among a few variables while many other variables are controlled' (Lijphart, 1971, p. 687).

All four countries are broadly similar in terms of economic development, per capita wealth and the proportion of the population in higher education (see Table 1.1). However, where they differ, in addition to size and population, is in the pattern of values and policies that define and shape their welfare regimes.

Table 1.1 Socio-economic profile of the four case study countries

Variable	Canada	England[*]	Germany	Norway
Population (m) 2005	31.6	50.1	82.5	4.6
Life expectancy (years, male/female) UN 2005	77/84	76/81	76/81	77/82
Average annual per capita income (US$) World Bank 2004	31,930	29,600	28,700	40,000
Gross domestic product (GDP) composition 2004 (%):				
Agriculture	2.3	1.0	1.0	2.2
Industry	26.4	26.3	31.0	36.3
Services	71.3	72.7	68.0	61.6
Household income or consumption by percentage of share:	(1994)	(1999)	(1997)	(1995)
Poorest 10%	2.8%	2.1%	3.6%	4.1%
Richest 10%	23.8%	28.5%	25.1%	21.8%
GINI index[3]	33.1	36.0	28.3	25.8
Higher education participation (%) (1992):				
18–21 year olds	23.9	14.2	7.4	8.4
22–25 year olds	13.9	4.7	15.2	15.3
26–29 year olds	5.6	1.8	9.6	6.5

Sources: OECD Factbook 2005; UN (http://unstats.un.org/unsd/mi/mi_series_quick.asp); Human Development Reports (UNDP) http://hdr.undp.org/statistics/data/indicators.cfm?x=148&y=1&z=1
*Note that apart from the figures for population and life expectancy all figures refer to the UK

Welfare state regimes and sport

In his analysis of welfare states, Esping-Andersen (1990) distinguished between three welfare regimes: liberal, conservative and social democratic. The distinction is based on the private–public mix, the degree of de-commodification and modes of stratification or solidarities. *Liberal welfare regimes* 'reflect a political commitment to minimise the state, to individualise risks, and to promote market solutions'. It is 'residual' in the sense that 'social guarantees are typically restricted to "bad risks"', due to its 'narrow conception of what risks should be considered "social"', and its 'encouragement of the market' (Esping-Andersen, 1999, p. 74ff). Liberal welfare regimes include Canada and the UK.

According to Esping-Andersen (1999, pp. 78ff) the *social democratic welfare regime* is 'virtually synonymous with the Nordic countries', including Norway. The social democratic welfare regime is 'committed to comprehensive risk coverage, generous benefit levels, and egalitarianism'. It is distinct for its active 'effort to de-commodify welfare', for the 'fusion of universalism with generosity' and its 'comprehensive socialisation of risks'. The social democratic regime is 'inevitably a state-dominated welfare nexus'.

Our final case, Germany, represents what Esping-Andersen (1999, pp. 81ff) labels a *conservative welfare regime*. The 'essence' of this regime 'lies in its blend of status segmentation and familialism'. Social security systems are based on occupational schemes and corporatist status divisions. The 'accent on compulsory social insurance' means that 'purely private market provision of welfare remains marginal'. In some countries 'a significant part of health care is […] non-state but this is chiefly due to the role played by non-profit, "voluntary" associations, frequently affiliated with the Church'. The family is the central care-giver and 'ultimately responsible for its members' welfare'.

Esping-Andersen's research remains a landmark in the development of the comparative analysis of welfare/social policy, as much for the stimulus it gave to similar research as for the initial identification of the three distinct types of welfare systems. The tripartite categorisation between liberal welfare regimes, conservative corporatist welfare states, and social democratic welfare states has been criticised on a number of grounds and has led to a series of refinements of, and extensions to, his initial model. Some of the critics have challenged the allocation of countries to particular categories. For example, Castles and Mitchell (1990) argued that the UK should not be placed in the liberal category as they considered that it embodied an unresolved tension between economic liberalism and welfare collectivism. Similarly, Liebfried (1990) argued that southern European welfare states constituted a separate category – the Latin Rim. Others directed their criticism towards the methodological assumptions that underpinned Esping-Andersen's typology.

Siaroff (1994), who developed a cluster analysis of welfare states in developed countries based on the extent to which they met women's needs, provided one of the most interesting critical re-analyses of Esping-Andersen's work. Women's needs were defined in relations to three criteria: the general family welfare orientation of policy, the desirability of female work (e.g. the extent to which the state supports women's employment with subsidised child care facilities) and which parent receives child benefits. Interestingly, Siaroff's analysis produced clusters very similar to Esping-Andersen's except that there was also a distinct category similar to the Latin Rim identified by Liebfried and that countries such as Spain and Switzerland were also placed in a distinct category. Siaroff labelled his categories the Protestant liberal welfare states (e.g. the UK), the advanced Christian democratic welfare state (e.g. Germany), the Protestant social democratic welfare states (e.g. Sweden) and the late female mobilisation welfare state (e.g. Spain and Switzerland) (see Table 1.2).

Table 1.2 Welfare regimes in OECD countries and Eastern Europe

Welfare regime type	Typical country	Entitlement basis of benefits	Distributional impact of benefits	Extent of meeting women's needs
Liberalism (Protestant liberal)	US,UK Australia Canada	Commodified	Inequality	2
Conservatism (advanced Christian democratic)	Germany France	Semi-decommodified (insurance)	Status differential maintained	2
Social democratic (Protestant social democratic)	Sweden Denmark Norway	Decommodified (citizenship)	Redistribution	3
Late female mobilisation	Japan Spain	Semi-commodified (insurance)	Status differential maintained	0
State bureaucratic	Bulgaria Russia	Decommodified (work loyalty)	Proletarianised but privileges	2/3

Source: Adapted from Deacon *et al.*, (1997, p. 42).

What is most notable about the typology summarised in Table 1.2 is the extent to which the initial identification of regime types by Esping-Andersen remains intact. However, the debate about classification of welfare regimes and particularly the contribution from Siaroff, has emphasised the importance of considering the distributional consequences (i.e. impact) of different regimes. Using the Esping-Andersen's typology it is possible to ask a series of research questions focused on outputs and impacts designed to establish whether sport policy conformed to the pattern evident for the general welfare regimes. On the basis of Esping-Andersen's typology one would expect, in liberal welfare regimes like Canada and England, the state to play a limited role and to leave welfare supply to the market. In social democratic welfare regimes like Norway we would expect the state to play an active role and to take responsibility for citizens' welfare. Indeed, there is an established tradition of close cooperation between the Norwegian state and voluntary associations and numerous comparative studies rank Norway as one of the most corporatist countries in the world (cf. Rommetvedt, 2005 and Chapter 2). In conservative welfare regimes like Germany we would expect non-state but non-profit associations and the family to take care of matters related to welfare.

It is not obvious that welfare policy should include sport. Sport can hardly be said to belong to the core concerns of the welfare state and consequently, we might expect the state to play a relatively passive role with regard to sport. However, especially since Second World War the welfare state has expanded in most western countries. The development of modern welfare states is characterised by a stepwise expansion of government responsibilities, from the basic and 'state-defining' tasks of defence and policing via core welfare state issues, for example social security, to what could be considered to be secondary welfare state issues like leisure policy. It is not self evident how to regard sport in this connection. Sport and physical fitness could be seen as a prerequisite for effective defence, and thus a basic responsibility for the state. Emphasis could be placed on sport's effect on health, one of the core issues of the welfare state. Finally, sport could be viewed as leisure activity and a welfare state responsibility of secondary order. The question of what sport is and the related question of what the government responsibilities with regard to sport should be, are *political* questions. Consequently – and especially when we compare countries – we would not expect *one* answer, but several answers at variance with each other. Accordingly we would expect the state in a social democratic welfare regime like Norway to play an active role with regard to sport policy. In liberal regimes like Canada and England we would expect the state to be more passive and to encourage commercialisation of sport. Finally, in conservative welfare regimes like Germany we would expect voluntary associations to play the most important role with regard to sport policy.

Sport profiles

The hypothesis that state policy towards sport is shaped by welfare regime type needs to be set in a context where sport has deep cultural roots particularly at the elite level (see Table 1.3) where involvement in elite competition has a long history and where success at this level is strong.

However, it is not just success and enthusiasm for elite level sport that are common to the four countries as they also exhibit a number of common characteristics in relation to involvement in recreational sport and physical activity as indicated in Table 1.4.

The first thing to note is that sport and recreation activities are an important part of everyday activity for many people, although there are some differences between the countries. In Germany and Norway almost one-third of the population engage actively in sport and recreation on an average day. In Canada about one-fourth is active, and in Great Britain a little less than one-sixth. The European countries with the highest activity levels are Finland and Sweden. This pattern of higher Scandinavian participation levels and lower British levels is consistent with the findings of the Compass project (Gratton, et al., 1999; see also Van Bottenburg et al., 2005). Time use data indicate moreover that the number of people active in sport and recreation activities in Canada is lower than in Germany and Norway, but higher than in Britain, although it needs to be borne in mind that the Canadian data cover a wider age range and include the generally more active, 15–19 year olds.

There is little agreement about what constitutes a definition of physical activity, but it is broadly accepted that it refers to a range of physical pursuits that would not be included in a conventional definition of sport. However, the problematic nature of the concept of physical activity results in data limitations that do not permit exact comparison among countries. With this caveat in mind the data collected by Vaage (2004) and through the Compass survey (Gratton et al., 1999) indicate that 66% of the Norwegian population took part in physical exercise at least once a week in 2001, with walking, cycling, skiing, swimming, jogging and weight training being the most popular activities. According to the Compass survey the percentage in UK exercising regularly, which is defined as at least 12 times a year, was 47%. A more recent household study of UK participation (Fox and Richards, 2004)

Table 1.3 Selected sport profile for the case study countries

Variable	Canada	England/ Great Britain	Germany	Norway
Recognition of National Olympic Committee	1907	1905	1895	1900
Hosted or scheduled to host the Olympic Games	Montreal 1976 Calgary 1988 Vancouver 2010	London 1908 London 1948 London 2012	Berlin 1936 Garmisch-Partenkirchen 1936 Munich 1972	Oslo 1952 Lillehammer 1994
Olympic medals–gold–silver–bronze (total):				
Sydney 2000	G3–S3–B8 (14)	G11–S10–B7 (28)	G13–S17–B26 (56)	G4–S3–B3 (10)
Salt Lake City 2002	G7–S3–B7 (17)	G1–S0–B1 (2)	G12–S16–B8 (36)	G13–S5–B7 (25)
Athens 2004	G3–S6–B3 (12)	G9–S9–B12 (30)	G13–S16–B20 (49)	G5–S0–B1 (6)
Turin 2006	G7–S10–B7 (24)	G0–S1–B0 (1)	G11–S12–B6 (29)	G2–S8–B9 (19)
Position in the medals table (number of gold medals):				
Sydney 2000	24th	10th	5th	19th
Salt Lake City 2002	4th	18th	2nd	1st
Athens 2004	21st	10th	6th	17th
Turin 2006	5th	21st	1st	13th
World Athletics Championships (Helsinki 2005)	33rd	16th	12th	26th
FIFA Football World Ranking (July 2006)	54th	5th (England)	9th	52nd
Other world class performances	Ice Hockey Federation world ranking 1st (men and women 2005)	2003 Rugby Union World Champions (England)	Ice Hockey Federation world ranking 8th (men) and 6th (women) in 2005	World Ski Championships 1st (Obersdorf 2005)

Source: International Olympic Committee (IOC) (www.olympic.org/uk/games/index_uk.asp).

Table 1.4 Time spent on sport and recreation (European countries, 20–74 years; Canada, 15 years and over[4])

	Average time devoted to sport and recreation (hours) per day			Share of population who spend time on sport and recreation on any particular day (%)	
	All	**Men**	**Women**	**Men**	**Women**
Canada	0.5	0.6	0.4	26	22
Germany	0.32	0.32	0.32	29	33
Great Britain	0.21	0.24	0.17	17	13
Norway	0.34	0.37	0.31	30	31

Sources: Vaage (2005) and Canada Statistics (www.statcan.ca).

indicates that in 2002 59% participated in some kind of sport, game or physical activity in the last 4 weeks before the interview. If walking is excluded the percentage declines to 43%. Besides walking the most popular activities were swimming, keep fit/yoga, snooker/pool/billiards and cycling.

As regards Germany it is important to distinguish between the former western and eastern parts of the country. The stronger focus on elite sport and the much weaker emphasis on mass activity in former East Germany than in former West Germany continue to affect current participation rates. In 1999, in the former West Germany, about 53% of adults said they were active in sport, while the corresponding percentage in the former East Germany was 43% (Erlinghagen, 2003).

In Canada the most useful data source for physical exercise patterns does not use the number of sport and recreational sessions or time use but adopts a different unit of measurement, namely the amount of energy used roughly equivalent to one half hour of walking every day.[5] Using this measure it is estimated that 49% of the population reached this physical activity level in 2002 (Cameron et al, 2004). Another Canadian study focusing on sport in its narrower sense and therefore excluding walking, fitness activities and the like, estimated that 34% of the adult population participate in sport activities regularly, that is participated at least once a week during the sporting season (Sport Canada, 1998). According to this study the most popular activities were golf, ice hockey, baseball and swimming.

To sum up these different studies, the evidence points to substantially higher levels of participation in sport and physical activity in Norway and Germany than in Canada and England. It is probable that of the four countries the participation level is lowest in England. How the participation levels in Canada compare to those Norway and Germany is less clear, but it would appear that Canada is closer to English levels than to those in the other two countries.

The overall pattern that emerges from this brief review of available data is that in each of the four countries sport is significant at both the elite level and at the participation level where sport merges with less distinct forms of physical activity. In addition, although data are collected according to different protocols the collection of data by government or its agencies is, in itself, an indication that sport/physical activity is an area of social life of increasing interest to government.

Political systems and policy change

While the four countries have many clear economic and social characteristics in common it is important not to ignore the limits of their similarity. The countries vary not only by geographic size and population density, but also, as the discussion of Esping-Andersen's typology of welfare regimes demonstrates, in terms of history and the cultural context of policy. The impact of historical and cultural development on sport policy is explored in more detail in Chapter 3 where particular attention is paid to the differential impact of four forces: globalisation, politicisation, governmentalisation and commercialisation. It is the cultural and historical variables, along with a series of political variables discussed in the next chapter, that provide the framework for analysis. Suffice to say at this stage that our point of departure is the general characteristics of, and recent and ongoing changes in, the four political systems of Canada, England/UK, Germany and Norway. Sport politics and policy-making will be thrown into relief with general political characteristics and trends. On the one hand it seems natural to assume that variations with regard to sport politics and policy-making can be related to, and explained by variations in political systems, institutions and processes in general. On the other hand many sports are indeed globalised phenomena with common rules of play, world-wide associations, competitions and media coverage. Consequently, one might assume that sport politics and policy is 'homogenised' across country borders.

To take a global perspective would be too ambitious. In our comparative study we have chosen to concentrate on four industrialised states in the western hemisphere, two Anglo-American countries Canada and the UK or more precisely England, and two Continental/Northern European countries Germany and Norway. The labels attached to the two pairs of countries indicate cultural and political differences. In general terms we will assume that the Canadian and English political cultures are more liberal and individualistic than the German and Norwegian cultures which are assumed to be more collectivistic and socially oriented. However, these assumptions are interrogated in Chapters 2 and 3.

In the subsequent chapters we examine closely the political systems and the implications for sport politics and policy. On the one hand we will focus on variations with regard to welfare state regimes, federal and unitary states, concentrations of private and public power and corporatism versus lobbyism, executive–legislative relations, coalition building and values and interests: on the other hand we will look for variations with regard to central and local government support of elite sport and *sport for all*.

Methods of comparison and research design

Although the research strategy for this study is based on a small sample of cases and the use of largely qualitative techniques the aims and objectives of this study could possibly have been achieved by the adoption of a research strategy which was designed around a large sample and the use of mainly quantitative techniques. However, our concern is to produce what Geertz (1973) referred to as 'thick description' rather than seek the higher level of abstraction that a large n sample would encourage (Ragin, 1994). Yet the clear virtues of large n comparisons are that they encourage the specification of a parsimonious set of explanatory factors and a focus on a limited number of control variables. For example, elite development systems might be categorised as 'systematic' or 'asystematic' (Fisher and Borms, 1990) or sports systems as centralised or decentralised, autonomous or state dependent. The main advantages of large n comparison, in addition to the coverage of an extensive range of cases, are that deviant cases can be identified with greater confidence and that stronger inferences can be made and more confident theory building undertaken. However, the frequent reliance on aggregate national level data and the prioritising of a limited number of variables is generally unsatisfactory in capturing the more nuanced differentiation between policy processes and between the policies themselves. In the area of sport it is notoriously difficult to obtain accurate data about the level of government expenditure on sport largely because of the problem of disaggregating sport expenditure from more general leisure, youth services, education or cultural services budgets. In addition, as has already been made clear data are often collected using different definitions of key concepts. For example, sport is not defined consistently across different countries (some countries include walking and camping for example, while others do not) and 'regular participation' is also defined very differently meaning once in the last 4 weeks in some countries and once in the previous 2 months or even previous year in others. Finally, participation data are often collected for different age ranges thus making comparison difficult (Gratton *et al.*, 1999). Important non-sports concepts are equally problematic. For example, attempts to explore the level of wealth of a country and its pattern of sport provision would usually rely upon per capita indicators of wealth and ignore the distribution of wealth in a country.

Given the nature of our research aims and the weaknesses of large *n* comparisons our preference is to select a small number of countries. The comparison of a small number of countries, roughly three to eight, has generated a substantial literature and is characterised by a middle level of conceptual abstraction. Breadth and extent of comparison is sacrificed for depth of understanding. The focus for this type of comparison is often on identifying and explaining similarities and differences between cases rather than establishing analytical relationships between variables. However, despite its popularity there are weaknesses with the 'similar cases' approach the first of which is the danger that the researchers express an undue degree of confidence that they have identified key variables and the second is the assumption that correlation is also causality. Despite these words of caution Przeworski and Teune (1970) agree that the 'most similar systems' design is especially well suited to area/regional comparative studies where assumed inherent major similarities (culture, religion, language, economic status, etc) enable an analysis of the distinctive factors that account for perceived variation in response to similar or common problems such as poor cardiovascular health, poor international sporting performance and pressure on physical education in the school curriculum. The attractiveness and, one would hope, the proven explanatory capacity of this approach is reflected in the large number of studies of policies in areas other than sport that have focused on groups of Scandinavian, western European and Anglo-American countries with their broadly similar legal–political and socio-economic profile and background.

As regards research design the analysis began with the identification and review of the secondary academic literature and primary documentary sources from the public sector and national level sports organisations. The period of desk study helped to determine and refine the research focus and questions, and also to define the areas where additional information was required. The analysis of documents also helped to identify the levels and units of government that were considered important to the study and also the policy actors to be interviewed. The fieldwork strategy was broadly similar in each of the four countries with a series of interviews undertaken with senior policy actors at both national and sub-national levels of administration and, as appropriate, in both the public and voluntary sectors. In addition, interviews were also conducted with academic observers of the sport policy area.

The design of the fieldwork in Germany was typical. Due to the importance of the sub-national level in Germany it was considered essential to undertake interviews and other forms of data collection at the national (*bundes*), the state (*land*) and local levels. At the national level four people in different positions in the German Sport Confederation were interviewed as well as two officers in two national sport organisations, gymnastics and table tennis. A representative from the National Olympic Committee was also interviewed. Two civil servants from the ministry for domestic affairs as well as a member of the Bundestag's sports committee were interviewed in connection with the investigation of elite sport policy. At the state (*land*) level two representatives from the largest *land* level sport confederation in Nordrhein Westfalen were interviewed in relation to general sport policy issues and aspects of policy especially concerned with youth and women. Within the state government, interviews were conducted with two officers with responsibility for general sport policy issues. In addition, an interview was conducted with an officer within the state of Brandenburg, in the former East Germany. At the local level two municipalities were selected, one each from Nordrhein Westfalen and Brandenburg, where a series of interviews were conducted with administrators and also with representatives of the local sports council. Finally, interviews were conducted with two representatives from the national research institution, *Bundesinstitut für Sportwissenschaft*, which is linked to the Ministry of Domestic Affairs, and with two academics with an interest in sport policy. Twenty-two interviews were conducted in total with the interviews being recorded and partially transcribed before analysis. Most of the fieldwork was carried out during 2004.

The pattern of fieldwork was similar in England and Canada. As regards England the interviewees were identified in part prior to the commencement of the first phase of fieldwork and in part through the snowball method of asking interviewees to suggest additional candidates for interview. Interviews were conducted at national level with policy actors in the relevant central government department, the Department of Culture, Media and Sport, the two main government agencies, Sport England and UK Sport and with non-governmental national organisations, the Central Council of Physical Recreation (CCPR) and the British Olympic Association (BOA). At the regional level interviews took place with officers within the East Midlands region and at the local level within Nottinghamshire County Council. In total, 13 interviews were conducted. In Canada six interviews were conducted with sports administrators within Sport Canada and a further two interviews took place with chief officers of the National Olympic Committee (NOC) and a major domestic sports federation. The provincial level interviews took place within Alberta and Quebec where 10 policy actors were interviewed drawn from the provincial government and a range of non-governmental/not-for-profit organisations. The local level interviews took place in Quebec City and Edmonton. In total 21 interviews were conducted.

Material on Norway was drawn from earlier and continuing research by some of the authors into various aspects of Norwegian sport policy. The Norwegian studies include quantitative data and surveys in addition to data collected using essentially the same strategy of document analysis and qualitative interviews as adopted in Canada, England and Germany (Mangset and Rommetvedt, 2002; Bergsgard, 2005).

Structure of the book

Chapter 2 presents the framework for analysis and also explores the underlying rationale for comparative study. After an examination of the epistemological debates that surround comparative analysis the chapter identifies the frameworks for analysis that offer the greatest potential in relation to the study of sport policy. Institutional approaches, network approaches and the advocacy coalition framework are all briefly discussed. Within the institutional approach a number of useful dimensions for analysis are identified and explored in addition to social policy regime type and include concentration of power, government system and executive–legislative relations.

Chapter 3 examines the significance of historical context and cultural patterns for current sport policy. Taking each country in turn the emergence of public policy for sport is related to the history of sport in the countries over the last one hundred years or so. Four factors emerge as important in shaping sport and the public policy for sport, namely globalisation, commercialisation, politicisation and governmentalisation, although the significance of each varies substantially between countries.

In Chapter 4 the infrastructure for sport in each country is delineated and analysed. Particular attention is paid to the identification and exploration of the role of the voluntary/not-for-profit sector within the policy-making and delivery systems for sport in general and for provision at the participation/*sport for all* level in particular. Chapter 5 examines the development of public policy for sport and the administrative structures that have been developed to deliver public policy. The analysis is informed by reference to four dimensions namely: the concentration or dispersion of power; executive–legislative relations; corporatism versus lobbyism and the generalisation of interest and coalition building.

Chapter 6 explores the variable emphasis on elite sport in the four countries while Chapter 7 undertakes a similar exploration of *sport for all* policy. Both chapters trace the emergence of policy objectives, the framework for delivery and the development of policy priorities. Finally, Chapter 8 returns to the analytical framework developed in Chapters 1 and 2 and examines the development of sport policy in relation to the dominant welfare regime type and the other dimensions for analysis.

Notes

1 The term sport policy, rather than sport policies, will be used except where there is a need to refer to a set of policies which can be viewed as discrete, for example, by being tailored to the needs of particular sports (such as the regulation of boxing or horse racing), objectives (such as elite success or mass participation) or client group (such as young people or people with disabilities), by being discrete temporally, or when we wish to refer to variations between policies of the countries in our study.

2 The focus for this study is England rather than the UK. Northern Ireland has had, at times, substantial autonomy in areas of social and sport policy and recently both Wales and Scotland have been granted substantial discretion in a number of areas of public policy including sport and recreation. The divergence in policy between the four home countries is encouraged by the long history of separate representation in many major sports such as rugby, football and hockey. As a result generalisation about UK sport policy has become increasingly difficult. However, while this study takes England as its focus reference is made to Britain or the UK where it is either not appropriate or not possible to identify the distinct English dimension.

3 The GINI index measures the extent to which distribution of income (or consumption) among individuals or households within a country deviates from equal distribution. A value of 0 represents perfect equality and a value of 100 represents perfect inequality.

4 Although there may be some differences with regard to activity definitions it is interesting to compare the different European countries as much work has been done to make surveys and numbers comparable across different countries (Vaage, 2005).

5 Inactivity for adults is defined as a daily energy expenditure of less than 1.5 KKD: 1.5 kilocalories of body weight/day, roughly equivalent to walking one-half hour every day.

CHAPTER 2

Comparing sport policies in economically developed countries

Introduction

Among the reasons given for undertaking a comparative study is the suggestion that it will generate policy-related benefits. One possible benefit derives from the opportunity that comparison offers for policy learning and policy transfer. As countries are increasingly faced with similar policy problems, for example, stimulating increased participation in sport and physical activities, controlling the use of drugs in sport and achieving elite sporting success, it is commonsense to look to the experience of other countries, especially those considered successful, as a way of informing domestic policy choices (Dolowitz and Marsh, 2000; Rose, 2005). A second possible benefit for domestic policy-making is that a heightened awareness of the policy process and practices in other countries can sharpen sensitivity to those in one's own and thus avoid culture-bound solutions/policies (Heidenheimer *et al.*, 1990).

Although the use of comparative study as a means of improving policy-making is a valuable endeavour our concern is less with comparative analysis *for* policy and more concerned with comparative analysis *of* policy and with the emphasis on the identification and explanation of differences between domestic policy infrastructures, processes and outcomes. One frequently used approach to the identification and explanation of differences between domestic policy regimes is through the use of typologies which not only stimulate discussion of the relative importance of particular regime characteristics, but also enable the formulation and testing of hypotheses. Finally, one of the most compelling arguments in favour of comparative domestic policy analysis is that there are some aspects of policy regimes that can best be explored through the adoption of a comparative approach. As Keman observes 'the goal of comparative politics is to explain those "puzzles" which cannot be studied without comparing' (2002, p. 34). Comparative policy analysis may therefore be justified as an approach that seeks to establish and validate its conclusions as a result of theoretically informed comparison between domestic policy regimes.

Comparative sport policy studies

Over the last 35 years or so there has been a steady, but very slow, increase in the number of comparative studies of sport policy although they vary greatly in terms of focus, theoretical basis, and methodology. Rodger (1978) and Szalai (1972) were pioneers adopting a comparative approach in their studies of the use of leisure time. Rodger's study was commissioned by the Council of Europe, as indeed were many subsequent comparative studies concerned with sport, and was designed to provide information and analysis for policy-makers rather than provide an analysis of the leisure policy process. A similar priority to inform policy-making underpins many of the analyses of physical education and school sport. Bennet *et al.* (1975) Simri (1979) and, more recently, Hardman and Marshall (2000) and Hardman (2002) provided much valuable data regarding patterns and trends in curriculum time allocated for physical education. All four studies were focused on the evaluation of policy outputs rather than on analysing the policy process that produced the outputs or the pattern of interaction between policy actors that generated the policy inputs. The work of Vrijman (1995), Chaker (1998) and van Bottenburg (2005), dealing with the legal and administrative infrastructure for doping control, the general legal framework for sport, and sports participation levels respectively, are typical of much of the policy-related comparative research insofar as they are large n surveys/reviews which produce valuable baseline data or snapshots of current provision in a particular area. While these studies are analytical there is no explicit theoretical comparative framework and the analysis tends to focus on policy outputs and outcomes rather than inputs and policy process. The recent studies of high-performance sports systems by Digel are similar in many respects although there is a stronger focus on model building. Digel's review of the elite sports system in eight countries has an explicit policy orientation insofar as the objective is to 'develop a resources model for successful top level sport' (2002, p. 37). As such these valuable studies, like the earlier work of Rodger and Simri, are more concerned with contributing to the policy process than analysing it.

The body of comparative literature on sport which is not explicitly concerned to provide analysis *for* policy, or which has not been commissioned by a particular policy actor is small. Arbena's (1988) study of sport in Latin America, Wilson's (1988) comparison of sport structures and policy in the UK, United States and in a number of totalitarian regimes, Riordan's (1978) study of sport in five communist states, Houlihan's (1997) study of sport policy in five countries, and Green and Houlihan's (2005) analysis of three elite sports development systems all provide useful insights into a wide range of countries and regime types but are generally concerned to identify patterns of difference and similarity rather than use the comparative data to develop theoretical explanations of policy change and regime type. The study by Stamm and Lemprecht (2001) of the impact of a range of socio-economic factors on the success of countries participating in the Olympic Games is one of the few large n studies which aims to generate data for use by policy-makers and also connect to debates within the study of policy processes. Finally, the two volumes by Bramham *et al.* (1989, 1993) also go some way towards combining description, analysis and explanation. However, both books explicitly eschew comparative analysis as the organising framework for their city and country-based case studies. In the study of leisure policy in selected western European cities they note that 'each [study] deals predominantly with aspects of policy development in a single nation-state' (1989, p. 4). The more recent volume gives greater emphasis to comparison as it examines the motives of government. However, the case studies focus on the identification of 'the variety of "local" features of ... national leisure policy' (1993, p. 5) with the consequence that although the studies contain a wealth of empirical data there is little explicit reference to comparative theory.

As this brief review indicates the comparative sport policy literature is modest and much of the literature that has been produced is substantially concerned to fulfil the important but narrow functions of, on the one hand, providing information on policy trends and impact and, on the other hand, providing data for actors involved in the sport policy process. However, the paucity of comparative literature in sport policy is less a reflection of the limited value of comparison and more the result of the practical constraints on comparative research arising from inadequate funding and an insufficient core of interested researchers. There is no reason to expect that the comparative study of sport policy would not yield the same rich insights into the policy process that have been generated in other areas, especially those of education policy, industrial policy and social welfare policy.

Policy processes and approaches to comparison

It is a truism that while empirical case studies that eschew theoretical questions 'can be interesting in themselves the possibilities of explanation, generalisation and analysis is limited' (Higgins, 1981, p. 16). In this study we are concerned to identify and analyse similarities and differences in both policy processes and in policy outputs in order to fulfil the primary aim of examining how sport policy is affected by the characteristics of domestic political system, the welfare regime type, and global pressures. More specifically, we need a framework that will facilitate investigation of these aspects of the policy process that offer the sharpest insights into the factors that shape sport policy. Consequently, rather than just focus on one aspect of the policy process – policy outputs for example – we will examine: the sources of policy inputs; the mediation of policy inputs; and policy outputs. The second aspect, the mediation of policy inputs, refers to the role of a variety of institutions in shaping access to the policy agenda and the way issues are presented and interpreted and would include the impact of culture, political parties, advocacy coalitions and administrative structures and traditions. The third aspect is concerned with the nature of policy outputs – that is the balance between active and passive responses to issues and, where action is initiated, the particular mix of instruments (sanctions, incentives and information) that are selected.

As is the case across the social sciences the identification of the empirical focus of the research is inseparable from debates on epistemology. Lichbach (1997) provides a typology identifying three broad approaches to comparison – rationalist, structuralist and culturalist – each of which is based on a distinctive set of epistemological assumptions. Rationalist perspectives stress the importance of studying the intentional features of choices made by individuals as the basis of aggregate policy processes and outputs. In contrast to rationalist and individualist perspectives structuralists focus on the holistic aspects of the policy process and the interdependence between institutions, organisations and human agency. The key assumption is that, over time, institutions become reified and consequently constrain or facilitate policy-making activity (Blom-Hansen, 1997). Culturalist perspectives also emphasise the importance of an holistic approach, but one that seeks to uncover the shared meanings and understandings ('deep structure' to use Benson's (1982) phrase) which define and bind communities and shape their perception of policy issues and solutions (Lichbach, 1997; Ross, 1997). Landman sums up the differing emphases of these three approaches as follows, 'Rationalists focus on the *interests and actions* of individuals, culturalists focus on the *ideas and norms* of human communities, and structuralists focus on the *institutions and relationships* that constrain and facilitate political activity' (2000, p. 205).

The research communities identified by Lichbach reflect the long-standing tension in social science between those researchers who emphasise the significance of structure and those who emphasise agency (see e.g. Giddens, 1984; Hay, 1999; Sibeon, 1999; Lewis, 2002; Scambler, 2005). Those who give priority to structural factors in explaining policy outputs and impact would emphasise, for example, the significance of the institutional and funding relationship between government and sports organisations, the administrative arrangements of government, the allocation of responsibility for sport between central and sub-national levels of government, and whether particular functions of government are statutory or discretionary. Thus the frequent calls in the UK for sport to be made a statutory responsibility of local government or that sport should have a separate minister at Cabinet level are often based on the perceived effectiveness of these institutional/structural arrangements in other countries. However, the concept of an institution covers not only the allocation of functions between departments and the arrangement of departments and agencies within the machinery of government, but also the interconnected pattern of rules and informal routines that provide the ideological structure of a political and social system.

There are a number of overlapping bodies of literature from within policy analysis and broader political analysis which provide specific concepts and analytical frameworks that recognise the importance of the relationship between structure and agency that can be utilised for our study. Analyses of welfare state regimes as well as institutional approaches, network analysis and the advocacy coalition framework (ACF) are drawn from debates on meso-level policy analysis and provide a series of insights into the significance of structure and agency in initiating policy debates and, more significantly, in mediating policy inputs and decision-making within the political system.

Analytical dimensions

Among the institutional features and associated analytic dimensions offering potential insights for an analysis of sport policy are: state systems (federal or unitary, decentralised or centralised) and executive-legislative relations (strength of government/administration versus parliament/opposition); concentration of private and public power (corporatism/corporatist representation versus pluralism/lobbyism and degree of segmentation and the nature of policy networks); and strategic implications for political actors (alliance and coalition building and generalisation of interests).

Interest in institutions was stimulated by growing dissatisfaction with the behavioural emphasis in much of American political science of the 1960s which, it was argued, obscured the deeply entrenched socio-economic and political structures that shaped behaviour. Institutions include not only the formal apparatus of government, but also, and arguably more importantly, the established patterns of norms and conventions found within a policy field. For Ostrom *et al.* (1994) policy is made within 'action arenas' that develop operational rules which are nested within other more deeply rooted rules namely, collective choice rules and, at a deeper level, constitutional choice rules which are more resistant to change. As will be discussed in more detail in Chapter 3 an understanding of sport policy requires an acknowledgement of the significance of institutional arrangements which operate at different levels in the political system. For Thelen and Steinmo, institutions 'shape how political actors define their interests and ... structure their relations of power to other groups' (1992, p. 2). As Olsen comments 'Political institutions are the building blocks of political life. They influence the available options for policy-making ... They also influence the choices made among available options' (1998, p. 95), while for Keman (2002, p. 11) they are the 'conditions under which policy-making takes place ... [they] define the room for manoeuvre for each actor involved in policy-making'. To suggest that there is a causal relationship between institutional/administrative arrangements and a particular policy impact would be to overstate the case, but institutions, such as federalism, corporatism, the allocation of functions at central/federal government level and the arrangements for local government, constitute important intervening variables. As intervening variables institutions are recognised as links between policy inputs (agenda-setting activities) and policy outputs.

While state institutions are seen as significant constraints and mediating factors in politics, which 'leave their own imprint' (Thelen and Steinmo, 1992, p. 8), they are not the only or even the dominant constraints and, as such, fit comfortably with neopluralist theories of interests and power which stress the influence of non-state actors such as sports businesses or governing federations of sport. One of the clear strengths of this framework is that it directs attention to both the behaviour of actors (both individuals and interest groups) and the structures within which they operate. In addition, it is a powerful corrective to those who are too ready to ignore the significance of state institutions, as well as ministers and public officials in the policy process. Moreover, the institutional framework has the capacity to explain temporal continuities within policy arenas and also address differences across countries.

Where the institutionalist framework is weaker is in its treatment of policy dynamics which are, at best, indistinct often relying on an implicit rational model of actor behaviour. A further related weakness concerns the treatment of interests – the tendency to substitute ideas for interests, and the assumption that institutions strongly influence interests (Pontusson, 1995). Attempts to suggest sources of institutional dynamics – such as previously latent institutions becoming more prominent, exogenous changes in wider socio-economic environment, or the breakdown, replacement and creation of new institutions go some way to overcoming this weakness but are still not wholly satisfactory.

Although the institutional framework is far from being a completely persuasive explanation of the policy process it is important in emphasising the need to take account of the institutional context within which policy is made. Sport policy, in particular, is often made in a variety of institutional settings, for example within tourism or education policy areas, at multiple levels of government, and with the involvement of a mix of public, not-for-profit and commercial organisations, the combination of which will affect how issues are defined, objectives are set, and impact assessed. However, of particular importance is the extent to which the deeply-rooted policy orientations and rules of collective choice become institutionalised to the extent that they can be identified as distinct and stable regime types. The identification and specification of regime types has been most fully explored in the area of welfare policy as outlined and discussed in Chapter 1.

State systems and executive-legislative relations

Within the overall framework of different welfare regimes we would expect government responsibilities with regard to welfare policies and sport policy to vary with regard to other aspects of the government systems. The four countries we have chosen for our study include two *federal* systems, Canada and Germany, and two *unitary* states, Norway and England/the UK. The Canadian provinces and German *länder* play far more important roles than the English counties and Norwegian *fylker*. Furthermore a distinction may be drawn between *centralised* and *decentralised* versions of federalism and unitary states, as is done by Schmidt (2002, p. 177). He depicts Canadian federalism as decentralised, German federalism as centralised, the Norwegian unitary state as decentralised, and finally the British unitary state as centralised.[1] Lijphart (1999, p. 189) agrees that Norway and the UK are decentralised and centralised unitary states respectively. He does not distinguish between Canada and Germany, both are characterised as federal and decentralised. However, central government's tax share is a little higher in Germany than in Canada, thus indicating that Germany is slightly more centralised (Lijphart, 1999 p. 193) although the difference between the two countries is small.

It is not clear how we should rank a decentralised unitary state in comparison with a centralised federal state. Nevertheless, we would expect the differences to have an impact on the allocation of responsibilities between the national/state level, the sub-national/province/county level, and the local/municipal level of government. Combining welfare regimes with the federal–unitary and decentralised–centralised dimensions produces the following expectations:

- English sport policy is expected to be limited in scope, but dominated by the state. Local government is expected to play a minor role, and sport is expected to be commercialised.
- Norwegian sport policy is expected to be comprehensive, but less dominated by the state. Local government should play an important role and sport is expected to be less commercialised. With the modification of the Esping-Andersen model mentioned in Chapter 1 in mind, we would also expect Norwegian voluntary sport associations to play an important role.
- German sport policy is expected to be dominated by the *länder*. Voluntary sport associations are expected to play an important role and an intermediate degree of commercialisation of sport is expected.
- Canadian sport policy is expected to be limited and dominated by the provinces and local government. Sport is expected to be commercialised.

Another important aspect of the political system is the power of legislatures relative to that of executives. Numerous scholars and political observers, including Lord Bryce as early as 1921, have subscribed to the 'decline of legislatures' thesis (Norton, 1990). In the case of Norway in the 1960s, Rokkan (1966, p. 107) found that crucial decisions were 'rarely taken in the parties or in Parliament'. Kvavik (1976, pp. 118f) observed that 'legislation was shaped in the administration; once in parliament, the lines were fixed' and that parliamentary institutions received 'an exceedingly weak evaluation' among leaders of Norwegian interest groups. However, according to Olsen (1983, p. 72), during the last part of the 1970s the Norwegian Parliament 'became a more rather than a less significant institution'. More recent studies clearly indicate that during the 1980s and 1990s the Norwegian Parliament strengthened its position vis-à-vis the executive (Rommetvedt, 2003, 2005). According to the World Bank Institute, 'We are living in an "age of parliaments" with a revitalisation of legislatures that make them stronger and more relevant today than ever before' (WBI 2001, p. 32).

Analysing the influence of legislatures, Polsby (1975/1990, p. 148) distinguished between 'transformative' legislatures and legislatures as merely 'arenas', thus indicating that the former has more policy-making power than the latter. He characterises the US Congress as 'highly transformative', the Swedish *Riksdag* as 'modified transformative', the German *Bundestag* as a 'modified arena', and the British Parliament as an 'arena'. Unfortunately, Canada and Norway were not included in the examples given by Polsby. However, all four countries in our study are included in Lijphart's analysis (1999, pp. 132f). He has constructed an index of 'executive dominance' on the basis of cabinet duration. The calculations show that executive dominance is most pronounced in the UK followed by Canada. Germany followed by Norway has the lowest score on the index of executive dominance.

The per cent of government time in office for minimal winning cabinets and single party cabinets may also tell us something about the strength of the executive. Lijphart (1999, pp. 110f) has calculated mean percentages for minimal winning and single party cabinets from 1945 to 1996. Among our cases, UK gets the highest score, closely followed by Canada. We find Norway in third place, mainly due to the frequent occurrence of single party governments, and Germany in forth place due to the lack of such cabinets.

In government systems based on the principle of parliamentarianism, the government has to be supported, or at least accepted, by the majority of the parliament. The parliamentary branch of governing parties is supposed to make sure that the government's proposals are adopted by the parliament. Consequently it may be difficult to distinguish between the government and the majority of the parliament. Arguably the parliament should not be viewed as a single entity, but rather as two (or more) entities: government and opposition. Accordingly, instead of measuring the strength of parliament we should measure opposition strength.

Forestiere (2005) has measured opposition strength as a function of various party system attributes and institutional resources. Her calculations show that in 'our' countries we find the strongest opposition in Norway followed by Germany. The weakest opposition is found in the UK. In fact, the UK occupies the last position on a list of thirteen countries. Norway is number four and Germany number six. Unfortunately, Canada was not included in Forestiere's calculations.

Taking executive-legislative relations into consideration, we may also ask whether the lobbying efforts of various interest groups are directed at the civil service or parliament. In the case of Norway (and Denmark), organised interests have more frequent contacts with the public administration than with parliament. However, parliamentary contacts have increased more than administrative contacts with regard to both frequency and importance. This may be interpreted as a reflection of the strengthening of parliaments vis-à-vis executives (Christiansen and Rommetvedt, 1999). Is this a general trend? And what are the implications with regard to sport policy?

Taken altogether, the various assessments of the strength of legislatures and/or oppositions clearly indicate that in general the parliaments of Norway and Germany play a more central role in policy-making than the parliaments of Canada and the UK. The question we ask in our context is whether this is also the case with regard to sport policy. If so, we should expect Norwegian and German sport policy-making to be dominated by the parliament, and Canadian and English sport policy-making to be dominated by the executive.

Corporatism versus pluralism – segmentation and policy networks

Organised interest and voluntary associations play important roles in the four countries we have chosen for our study. Among all the voluntary associations and interest groups that exist, sport associations can show some of the highest membership figures. Interest groups may be more or less integrated into the processes concerned with formulating and implementing public policies. In the previous sections we have mentioned briefly the importance of voluntary associations and corporatism (especially in relation to conservative welfare regimes). *Corporatism* and *pluralism* are frequently used terms for highly integrated and institutionalised government-interest group relations and less integrated and institutionalised relationships respectively. Corporatism includes the representation of selected interest groups in governmental boards, committees and councils. Pluralism on the other hand is characterised by a multiplicity of interest groups and associations competing for members and lobbying for political influence.

In his path-breaking study Schmitter (1979) differentiated between two forms of corporatism: state corporatism and societal corporatism. The 'stronger' version – state corporatism – is found in countries with 'singular, noncompetitive, hierarchically ordered, sectorally compartmentalised, interest associations exercising representational monopolies and accepting (...) governmentally imposed or negotiated limitations on the type of leaders they elect and on the scope and intensity of demands they routinely make upon the state' (Schmitter, 1979, p. 18). Such interest associations have attained a quasi-legal status and a prescriptive right to speak for their segments of the population. They influence the process of government directly, bypassing parliament. Societal corporatism, on the other hand, 'is found embedded in political systems with relatively autonomous, multi-layered territorial units; open, competitive electoral processes and party systems; ideologically varied, coalitionally based executive authorities' (Schmitter, 1979, pp. 21f).

Corporatism and pluralism are also important categories in the description of government systems given by Heinz *et al.* (1993, pp. 395f). Combining two dimensions, the degrees of *concentration of private power* and *concentration of government power* respectively, they attain a fourfold typology of government systems. *Corporatist* and *pluralist* systems are characterised by respectively high or low concentrations of both private and government power. Low concentration of government power and high concentration of private power paves the way for *private* government. Finally, *state directed* systems are based on low concentration of private power and highly concentrated government power.

With the exception of the state directed government system in the former German Democratic Republic, we consider corporatism and pluralism to be the relevant categories for the countries we have selected for our study. Furthermore we believe that concentrations of power are matters of degree – not categorical variables. For the purpose of this study, we may treat corporatism versus pluralism as a continuous dimension or variable.

In comparative studies Norway is commonly ranked at – or close to – the top of the list of corporatist countries. Schmitter mentioned Norway, together with Sweden, Switzerland, the Netherlands, and Denmark, as one of the best examples of societal corporatism. In Siaroff's presentation of the 'agreed' rankings of 23 different analyses, Norway is considered to be 'strongly corporatist', surpassed only by Austria. (West) Germany is categorised as 'moderately-to-strongly corporatist' and the UK as 'weakly or only somewhat corporatist'. Finally, Canada is characterised as 'not at all corporatist, but rather pluralist' (Siaroff, 1999, p. 184).

The corporatist ranking of Norway is based on what we may call conventional wisdom. However, in recent years important changes have taken place. Norway has moved in a pluralist direction (Rommetvedt, 2005). On the private side of the coin the number of interest groups and associations has increased substantially and on the public side the number of corporatist arrangement like governmental boards and councils has been significantly reduced. Consequently the corporatist channel has been 'overcrowded' and corporatist representation replaced by less institutionalised forms of lobbyism.

What then about sport politics? To what degree is sport policy-making and policy implementation characterised by corporatism and corporatist representation or pluralism and lobbyism?

According to the conventional wisdom we should expect to find Norway and Germany in the corporatist category, and Canada and England in the pluralist position. However, in line with the general trend we may also expect Norwegian and perhaps also German sport and sport policy to be moving in the pluralist direction. But what about Canada and England – are they moving in a corporatist direction? Or is sport rather a clearly demarcated political segment or policy community?

The typology of Heinz *et al.*, (1993) has been elaborated in order to distinguish between two types of concentration of power: public as well as private power may be concentrated in a monolithic or in a sectorised or segmented way thus constituting a fifth type of government systems: the *segmented state* (Rommetvedt, 2005). The term 'segmented state' was introduced by Egeberg *et al.* (1978). Political segments may be found within particular economic areas such as agriculture, fisheries and industry, or around functions like health care, communications, education and defence. Members of a segment come from various institutions such as ministries, parliamentary committees, interest organisations, research institutions, the mass media etc. They 'are assumed to share certain basic values and perceptions, such that their models of the world coincide more with one another than with those of representatives of other segments' (Christensen and Egeberg, 1979, p. 253). A simplified interpretation of general trends in Norway indicates that after periods with high degrees of corporatism in the 1950s and 1960s and segmentation in some sectors in the 1970s, Norway has become more pluralist and less segmented since the 1980s. The pattern of contacts between organised interests and public authorities in the 1990s and at the beginning of the twenty-first century seems to be less segmented than suggested by the thesis of the segmented state (Rommetvedt, 2003).

The segmentation of the policy process described above has led to considerable theorising regarding the characteristics and dynamics of sectorised policy-making. Political segments bear a clear resemblance to concepts like 'sub government' and 'policy communities' in the family of 'policy network' concepts covering the spectrum from strong and closed 'policy communities' to loose and more open 'issue networks' (see König, 1998 for an overview).

From the late 1970s academic attention focused on the utility of the metaphor of networks as a starting point for concept development and theory building. The metaphor draws attention to the role of informal networks (or communities) in shaping policy agendas and decision-making, and also in facilitating policy implementation. The metaphor also draws attention to the interaction between informal networks and the formal policy-making procedures of government. Influenced by the work of Heclo (1978) and Benson (1982) in the United States and Richardson and Jordan (1979) in Britain Rhodes (1981) described a sectorised or segmented polity where policy-making was best explained through the pattern of exchange and resource dependency (see also Marsh and Rhodes, 1992; Smith, 1993). The room for manoeuvre that organisations have to make policy is circumscribed by the need to develop resource dependency relationships which, over time, coalesce into relatively stable policy networks. For Rhodes there are a variety of types of policy network including issue networks which have loose, more open and shifting memberships and policy communities which are characterised by more stable and restricted membership. It was the concept of the policy community, rather than issue network, which seemed especially useful in understanding the policy process in many European countries. The policy community, particularly when it included members from state agencies and departments, proved attractive at an intuitive level but was also supported by a body of empirical research which seemed to confirm both the existence and influence of policy communities and the robustness of the network metaphor (Marsh and Rhodes, 1992). Not only was the metaphor useful in capturing the sectorised natured of the policy process, but it was also an effective tool for identifying differences between policy outcomes by reference to differences in their characteristics (the strength and exclusiveness of relationships in particular).

However, the utility of the network metaphor has been challenged at both the theoretical and empirical levels. At the theoretical level the concept has been criticised for being: too vague (all policy-making is about relationships) (John, 1998); descriptive rather than explanatory (Sabatier, 1999); and redundant due to the core importance of resource dependency relations rather than any distinctive features of community (Dowding, 1995). At the empirical level it was argued that definition of community membership and community boundaries was extremely difficult (Kassim, 1994) and that in many policy sectors there seemed to be multiple clusters of allied organisations rather than a simple community with recognisable members and non-members.

Strategic implications: generalisation of interests and alliance building

A development towards an increasingly pluralistic society characterised by dispersion of power among a multiplicity of organised interests, political parties, and public institutions, downsizing of the corporatist apparatus and strengthening of the parliament vis-à-vis the cabinet have certain strategic implications for political actors who seek to influence policy-making. We have already mentioned restricted corporatist representation and increased lobbyism, especially targeted at the parliament. Furthermore, we will pay attention to the need for alliance building and the related strategy of generalisation of interests.

In a pluralist society, political power is divided and there are no actors with a monopoly of power. Political actors cannot simply resort to force and rely on their own power in the pursuit of self-interest. They need to gain support from a majority – literally as well as figuratively speaking. In other words, political actors have to build *alliances*. The more numerous the participants and interests in the political process, the broader the alliances need to be. Consequently, political actors have to widen their appeal. General or public interests have a wider appeal and basis of legitimacy than self-interests, and *generalisation of interests* is thus a way to enhance legitimacy and win more support. Actors who are able to show, or to argue convincingly, that their viewpoints and suggestions promote the public good have better chances of obtaining general acceptance or of acquiring support from the necessary number and kinds of alliance partners.

In a highly segmented state, each political segment or policy community may 'live its own life' more or less independent of other segments. A limited number of members of a segment may, on the basis of shared values and perceptions, obtain a dominant position with regard to defining relevant expertise, problems and possible solution within their domain. The members constitute an alliance *within* the segment or community. Strong segments are closed and do not need to pay much attention to other interest and concerns. However, in modern societies efficient communications and communication technologies and critical mass media enhance contact, openness and transparency and 'everything depends on everything'. Consequently, there is an increasing need for coordination and specialised interests need to build alliances *across* sectors and segments (Rommetvedt, 2002). In the process of building broad alliances it becomes more likely that 'one has to phrase one's argument in impartial terms, as if one were arguing for the public good and not for one's own self-interest' (Elster, 1992, p. 18). In a modern pluralist society there is, in other words, a need for generalisation of interests in order to gain the necessary support.

Naturally, in appealing to the public good one has to take into account the general cultural and political values of the society concerned. In a comparative perspective we would expect variations in basic cultural and political values to have an impact on the various activities of social actors, including policy-making. We have already indicated some differences between our Anglo-American and North and Continental European cases. Broadly speaking, we would expect the cultures of England and Canada to be characterised by individualist, elitist and commercialist values and the cultures of Germany and Norway to be more oriented towards collectivist, egalitarian and non-commercial values.

In line with this, we would expect English and Canadian sports to be competitive, elite oriented and commercialised and German and Norwegian sports to be less competitive, more sport-for-all oriented and less commercialised. Correspondingly, sport policies in Canada and England on the one hand and Germany and Norway on the other should be expected to give priority to competitive elite sport and less competitive sport-for-all respectively. Furthermore, we would expect governments in Germany and Norway be more involved with sport while the governments of Canada and England should be expected to leave sport to market actors.

Following this line of reasoning, what kind of general interests exogenous to sport should we expect sport to appeal to in order to get support? In highly commercialised societies specialist sport's interests may underline the potential of sport to contribute to business development, job creation and economic profits. Competitive elite sports may accentuate national prestige and the reputation associated with gold medallists in World Cups and Olympic Games. In egalitarian societies sport may underline the importance of physical training and *sport for all's* contribution to fitness and improvement of defensive power, public health, social integration etc.

So far, we have emphasised differences. However, in the age of globalisation pluralism and neo-liberalism seem to be more widespread. Ideas of 'New Public Management' seem to have a strong impact on public sector reforms in many countries. Market and market-like mechanisms are implemented in areas that were formerly taken care of by public monopolies, either through privatisation of public institutions or through the introduction of free choices of service suppliers and competition between public schools, hospitals and the like. As a consequence, over time we should expect decreased variation between sports practices and sport policies in the countries we are studying.

One meso-level analytical framework which has been applied across a range of political systems and which has the capacity to take into account the impact of sustained globalising pressures as well as constitutional and administrative complexity is the ACF which has emerged as a highly regarded basis for policy analysis. The framework is based on five assumptions: first, a time perspective of at least 10 years is required for the analysis of policy change; second, a focus on policy sub-systems/policy communities, which for, Sabatier, consist 'of actors from a variety of public and private organisations who are actively concerned with a policy problem or issue ... and who regularly seek to influence public policy in that domain' (1998, p. 99); third, sub-systems involve actors from different levels and units of government and increasingly from international organisations and other countries; fourth, the possession and use of technical information is important; and finally, public policy incorporates implicit 'sets of value priorities and causal assumptions about how to realise them' (Jenkins-Smith and Sabatier, 1994, p. 178).

Within each policy sub-system there would normally be between two and four coalitions competing for influence although there might be one dominant coalition. Belief systems provide the primary source of cohesion within coalitions and 'policy-brokers' play an important role in facilitating policy design and in mediating conflict between coalitions. Inter-coalition conflict is seen as a source of policy outputs and policy dynamics although change can occur as a result of medium to long-term 'policy-oriented learning' (Sabatier, 1998, p. 104). Policy-oriented learning describes relatively long-term changes in beliefs that result from 'experience and/or new information' (Sabatier, 1998, p. 104).

The ACF is of interest not only as an analytic framework in its own right, but also for its capacity to balance institutional explanations of policy stability and change through a sensitivity to the importance of agency. In relation to the capacity of the ACF to take account of the peculiarities of the sports policy process the conceptualisation of the policy area as comprising a number of competing advocacy coalitions has not only an intuitive appeal, but also a growing body of empirical support which suggests the emergence and consolidation, in both the UK and Canada, of competing coalitions around elite sport, *sport for all*, physical activity and health, and school sport (Houlihan and White, 2002; Green, 2003; Green and Houlihan, 2005). In addition, the concept of the 'policy broker' has potential value given the extent of administrative dispersal found in many countries and the degree to which coalitions are in competition for the same resources.

Summary

According to Heidenheimer *et al.* (1990, p. 3) the study of comparative public policy is defined by its concern to determine 'how, why and to what effect different governments pursue particular courses of action or inaction'. The concern to identify

Table 2.1 Summary of analytical dimensions and their suggested implications for sport policy

Analytical dimension	Canada	England	Germany	Norway
State structure	Decentralised federalism *Strong role for the provinces*	Centralised unitary *Policy dominated by central government; minor role for municipalities*	Centralised federalism *Strong role for the länder*	Decentralised unitary *Substantial local policy discretion*
Executive-legislative relations	Executive dominance *Sport policy shaped by the executive*	Executive dominance *Sport policy shaped by the executive*	Stronger role for the legislature *Sport policy shaped by the legislature*	Stronger role for the legislature *Sport policy shaped by the legislature*
Relationship between organisations and government	Pluralist *Loose policy networks for sport*	Pluralist *Loose policy networks for sport*	Weakly corporatist *Closer to a policy community than a looser network*	Strongly corporatist, but moving in a pluralist direction *Relatively closed policy community*
Generalisation of interests and coalition building	Dominant interests: elite, commercial and competitive sport *Appealing to the public good in terms of business opportunities, job creation, national prestige and profit*	Dominant interests: elite, commercial and competitive sport *Appealing to the public good in terms of business opportunities, national prestige, job creation and profit*	Dominant interests: sport for all, and sport and community *Appealing to the public good in terms of health, fitness and community development*	Dominant interests: sport for all, and sport and community *Appealing to the public good in terms of health, fitness and community development*

'how' governments decide to act draws attention not only to the pattern of institutional arrangements in a country and to the extent and pattern of interest group interaction, but also to the structure of deeply-rooted values and beliefs in societies. Furthermore it also directs attention to the significance of transnational actors and the permeability of domestic policy processes. Asking 'why' governments act in the way that they do requires an understanding and analysis of the cultural, historical and ideological context of policy-making. The concern expressed by Heidenheimer *et al.* also to explore the 'effect' of policy decisions is a timely reminder of Lasswell's succinct definition of politics as the study of the distributional consequences of policy decisions, in other words 'Who gets what, when and how'.

While there has been little theoretically informed comparative analysis of sport policy there has been, as shown in this chapter, substantial comparative analysis involving the four countries that form the basis for this study. In particular, there has also been considerable theorising of the implications of the mix of constitutional and political characteristics of their political systems for policy in general and welfare policy in particular. This body of literature and analysis, summarised in Table 2.1, consequently provides an important reference point for the present study. The table includes expectations regarding sport policies based on general characterisations of the four countries in our study.

The research framework that we propose draws on a series of overlapping bodies of literature to allow the investigation and comparison across the four countries of individual aspects of the policy process as well as of the process as a whole. Institutional analysis and the ACF share a concern with inputs and with the mediation of policy in the decision-making process and complement each other in their respective emphasis on structure and agency and the well established typologies of welfare regimes provides a strong framework for comparing sport policy impacts. However, in order to recognise and appreciate the significance of structure and the scope for agency in particular countries it is important to understand the historical context within which the current arrangements of government and characteristics of political life have developed and also to identify the societal trends of especial importance to an analysis of sport policy. It is to these questions that we turn in the next chapter.

Note

1 While Schmidt refers to Britain other researchers, such as Forestiere and Lijphart, refer to the UK. In reporting their conclusions we have retained their terminology.

CHAPTER 3

Political and historical context

Deep structures and policy paradigms

As was argued in the previous chapter, in order to understand the contemporary landscape and salience of sport policy it is important to acknowledge the specific institutional context in which it developed and continues to operate. One way of constructing a framework for the analysis of the significance of institutional arrangements is through the use of the metaphor of levels of cultural embeddedness (Benson, 1982; Sabatier, 1998; Jenkins-Smith and Sabatier, 1993) where each level is partially autonomous, but embedded in a deeper level which sets limits on the degree of autonomy. While each level is rooted in the culture and history of a country, policy predispositions have a longer history and are more deeply embedded in culture than, for example, the location of responsibility for sport in the machinery of government. Consequently, it is especially important to identify deep-seated policy predispositions or 'storylines' (Fischer, 2003), but it is also necessary to acknowledge that while the historical and ideological (or mythological) context of policy will be significant so too will be factors such as the structure of the machinery of government and the pattern of interest group activity.

At the shallower, but still significant, level is the pattern of administrative arrangements for a service which refers to the organisational location of a function (among government departments and between levels of government for example), the extent of division of labour between units and the form of control exercised over subordinate units. While institutional/administrative arrangements are located at the shallower level they do become embedded over time (Granovetter, 1985) and are 'nested within an ever-ascending hierarchy of yet more fundamental, yet more authoritative rules and regimes, and practices and procedures' (Goodin and Klingemann, 1996, p. 18). Administrative units therefore affect policy as a consequence of their tendency, over time, to develop a distinctive culture which tends to institutionalise relatively stable preferences for policy tools, perceptions of problems and modes of working which constrain the response to new issues.

Closely related to the pattern of administrative arrangements and also located at the shallower level, is the pattern of inter-organisational resource dependencies which is concerned with questions of the distribution among organisations of resources such as expertise, finance, facilities, potential elite athletes, authority and administrative capacity. The complex pattern of resource dependency between national sports organisations (NSOs), voluntary sports clubs and public agencies has substantial implications for the process of policy-making (due, for example, to the increase in the number of clearance points in decision-making) and for the role and influence of the state. While the greater complexity of resource dependency relationships is a symptom of the emergence of a 'congested state' it may also be an indication of an 'extended state' which has steadily retreated from direct service delivery, but which has enhanced its capacity to steer policy sub-systems due to its strategic control over resources.

Operating within the matrix created by administrative structures is a set of interest groups. Adapting Benson's classification it is possible to identify at least four types of interest groups that are relevant to the study of sports policy namely, demand groups (consumers of policy outputs such as facility users, clubs and elite athletes), provider groups (the delivers of services such as physical education (PE) teachers, coaches, sports development officers and voluntary and commercial clubs), direct support groups (those groups upon which organisations depend for systems support, such as NSOs, commercial sponsors, municipalities and schools), and indirect support groups (related local authority services such as land use planning). It is the interaction between these interest groups that provides the policy process with an important dynamic. However, it also needs to be noted that analysing the interaction between these groups and the machinery of government is also significant for policy analysis as, in many countries, the network of groups is both a source of demands and also a significant element in the government's infrastructure for implementation.

What prevents this broadly neo-pluralist model of the policy process drifting towards pluralist utopianism is an acknowledgement of the significance of the facilitative and constraining impact of the dominant policy paradigm, the service-specific core policy paradigm, and what Benson refers to as the rules of structure formation. The dominant policy paradigm is the set of values and assumptions that influence policy choice and administrative practice across a range of services. In the UK, during the Thatcher years, privatisation was the dominant policy paradigm just as social inclusion and modernisation are for the Labour governments of Tony Blair. Nested within the dominant policy paradigm will be a service-specific policy paradigm which, in sport in a number of countries, has shifted between an emphasis on *sport for all*, social inclusion, elite development and fitness and health.

It is at the levels of the dominant policy paradigm and the service-specific policy paradigm that ideas have their most obvious impact. Strategies for elite development, using sport to tackle youth disaffection, strategies to promote physical activity and *'sport for all'* are all subject to extensive policy transfer and policy-oriented learning between countries (Rose, 2005; Dolowitz and Marsh, 2000). However, while substantial policy-oriented learning is a key assumption of some influential frameworks such as the Advocacy Coalition Framework this emphasis on the medium-term rationality of the policy process needs to be tempered with an acknowledgement that policy actors do not always refer to evidence and the weight of expert opinion. Very often actors turn to, what Fischer refers to as, 'discursive storylines' which are decision-making short cuts which 'function to condense large amounts of factual information inter-mixed with normative assumptions and value orientations that assign meaning to them' (2003, p. 87).

Establishing and maintaining dominant storylines is a contemporary struggle between interests but is also a reflection of deeply entrenched and longer established biases within the policy process and as such are part of the rules of structure formation which set the limits to policy action by defining activities that are acceptable and those that are not. Benson's notion of 'deep structure' corresponds broadly to the ideas of the cultural institutionalists and relates to the biases inherent in the fabric of the political process. At this deeper level would be found those beliefs and values that are both taken for granted and very slow to change and would include beliefs about the appropriate/acceptable involvement in sport by men and women, attitudes towards amateurism in sport, and acceptable behaviour by sportsmen and women on the field of play.

Forces of change

While different explanatory frameworks emphasise different triggers for policy change, for example lobbying activity, policy learning, and the accumulation of evidence there are four major overlapping forces that have routinely permeated domestic policy processes in all advanced industrial countries over the last 50–100 years and affected all levels from the shallowest to the most deeply rooted, namely globalisation, commercialisation, governmentalisation and wider politicisation (see Figure 3.1). However, while these forces are evident in all four countries their manifestation varies considerably as does the domestic response. Moreover, the response to these forces will, to vary extents, become institutionalised and form part of the fabric of institutional constraints within which sport policy is made. Consequently, while the discussion that follows is intended to identify the differing patterns of impact and response over the medium- to long-term the discussion also fulfils a sensitising

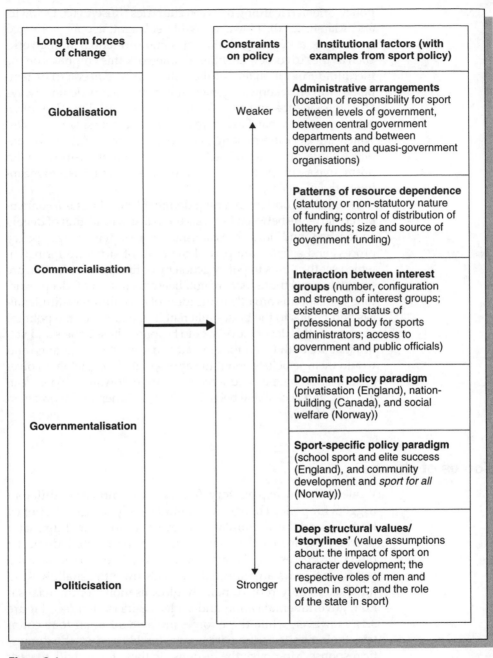

Long term forces of change	Constraints on policy	Institutional factors (with examples from sport policy)
Globalisation	Weaker	**Administrative arrangements** (location of responsibility for sport between levels of government, between central government departments and between government and quasi-government organisations)
		Patterns of resource dependence (statutory or non-statutory nature of funding; control of distribution of lottery funds; size and source of government funding)
Commercialisation		**Interaction between interest groups** (number, configuration and strength of interest groups; existence and status of professional body for sports administrators; access to government and public officials)
		Dominant policy paradigm (privatisation (England), nation-building (Canada), and social welfare (Norway))
Governmentalisation		**Sport-specific policy paradigm** (school sport and elite success (England), and community development and *sport for all* (Norway))
Politicisation	Stronger	**Deep structural values/ 'storylines'** (value assumptions about: the impact of sport on character development; the respective roles of men and women in sport; and the role of the state in sport)

Figure 3.1
Forces of change, institutional constraints and sport policy

function in relation to the analysis of contemporary sport policy and policy processes.

As regards *globalisation* Hechter noted that comparative research assumes that 'the causes of development were located within units defined by political boundaries, such as sovereign states' (1975, p. 217). While this assumption is still appropriate for some policy areas, it is becoming less satisfactory as an increasing number of formerly domestic policy issues are now embedded in a series of supranational policy networks. The problem for the comparative policy analyst is to determine whether actors external to the domestic political system are participants in a national policy process or whether the proper focus should be on the global policy arena to which national actors seek entry and influence. For Andersen and Eliassen, in their study of policy-making in the European Union (EU), the answer is clear, 'Europeification of policy-making implies a need for a new way of delineating the policy context, where the European political system becomes the unit of analysis' (1993, p. 12).

Yet it is not just within formalised supranational policy arrangements, such as the EU, that one is obliged to acknowledge the impact of globalisation on public policy. According to Deacon with Hulse and Stubbs (1997) the relative decline in the power of national governments as a result of globally mobile finance capital has altered the traditional approach to welfare policy analysis in a number of ways. First, supranational policy actors can no longer be ignored. Although institutions such as the International Monetary Fund, the Organisation for Economic Cooperation and Development, and the World Bank have for many years impacted upon the domestic policy of poorer countries they are now, even if only at the ideological level, influencing debates about the future of welfare programmes in the richer countries of Western Europe. Second, Deacon suggests that greater account needs to be taken of the 'globalisation of social policy instruments, policy and provision' (1997, p. 20) which takes three distinct forms – supranational regulation, supranational redistribution and supranational provision. Supranational regulation refers to 'those mechanisms, instruments and policies at the global level that seek to regulate the terms of trade and operation of firms in the interests of social protection and welfare objectives' (1997, p. 2). Examples from within the area of sport would include the regulation by international sports federations of the transfer market, and of eligibility rules for national teams, the role of the World Anti-Doping Agency in shaping national anti-doping policy and the growing importance of the Court for Arbitration for Sport in settling sports-related disputes.

Welfare-related supranational redistribution policies already operate within the EU and at a much lower level of effectiveness through the United Nations and key agencies such as UNESCO. In sport the closest examples would be the operation of sports development aid bodies such as Olympic Solidarity and the IAAF sports development programme where the spread of the Olympic diet of international sport is supported with some very modest redistribution of resources. Supranational provision refers, according to Deacon, 'to the embryonic measures ... whereby people gain an entitlement to a service or are empowered in the field of social citizenship rights by an agency acting at the supranational level' (1997, p. 3). The UN High Commission for Refugees and the Council of Europe Court of Human Rights provide two examples while in the area of sport the Court of Arbitration for Sport is beginning to fulfil a similar role for athletes. At the very least the wealth of research on globalisation requires that any comparative analysis of sport policy-making is sensitive to the increasing significance of supranational organisations for domestic policy.

The evidence that domestic social policy is increasingly affected by non-domestic policy actors is strong but this phenomenon in itself does not clarify the long-term particular impact of globalisation. As Scholte (2003) argues homogenisation of culture, and by implication sport policy, is only one of a number of possible outcomes of the increasing permeability of the domestic policy process. As Rommetvedt (2000) has argued, an important aspect of globalisation seems to be an increased degree of pluralism at the national level. He notes the paradox that 'the pluralisation that occurs at the national level is paralleled by homogenisation at the global level' (2000, p. 130).

In evaluating the utility of the concept of globalisation Scholte (2003) identifies five common uses of the term: internationalisation, liberalisation, universalisation, Westernisation/Americanisation and deterritorialisation. Each usage of the term is based on the different weight given to economic, political and cultural processes. Some definitions give priority to one process: liberalisation gives clear priority to economic forces whereas universalisation gives greater emphasis to the role of culture in globalisation. Other conceptualisations of globalisation, such as Westernisation/Americanisation, reflect a combined emphasis on economic, political and cultural factors. The five usages of the concept of globalisation are not mutually exclusive, but highlight the interweaving of cultural, economic and political dimensions of the process of globalisation. While an extended discussion of the nature of globalisation is not appropriate here there is a substantial degree of agreement that (1) seeing globalisation as a coherent and unidirectional process would be misleading, (2) that an acknowledgement that the significance of cultural change must be conceptualised in terms of depth of social embeddedness and that we must be wary of granting too much importance to shifts in the popularity of particular teams, sports or events, (3) that the impact of globalisation on policy within individual countries will vary due to the differential 'reach' of global influences and the variability in 'response' in different countries (Houlihan, 2003) and (4) that while the political and cultural dimensions have a degree of autonomy from economic processes it is economic interests that have become much more prominent in sport in the last 25 years as major sports and sports events have become increasingly a focus for private profit rather than state subsidy (see Hirst and Thompson, 1999; Held and McGrew, 2002; Houlihan, 2003; Scholte, 2003).

There are three interrelated elements to the *commercialisation* of sport: first, the transformation of many sports events, clubs and athletes into valuable brands and commodities; second, the growth of sport as a source of profit for non-sports businesses through, for example, sponsorship and broadcasting and third, the growth of sports-related businesses such as sportswear and equipment manufacture (Slack, 2004; Amis and Cornwell, 2005). The growth in the commercial value of sport has been spectacular. In the United States the sport industries were valued at $47 billion in 1986 increasing to $152 billion in 1995 and $213 billion by 1999 (Slack, 2004). In the United Kingdom there has also been rapid growth with the value of sport to the economy rising from £8.9 billion in 1990 to £15.2 billion in 2000 (Gratton and Taylor, 2000). Both countries are part of an estimated $324 billion global sports industry (Silk *et al.*, 2004). While the growth in the size of the sports industrial sector is significant in its own right it is the implications of this growth for the development of sport, for those involved in sport and for the state that is of especial concern.

Of particular importance is the extent to which governments acknowledge sport as an economic sector that they need to foster and also the extent to which the buoyancy of the sports sector is a resource that they can use to help achieve other non-sporting objectives. The perception of sport (along with other cultural services) as part of a cultural industrial sector rather than simply as a recipient of public subsidy has taken a long time to work its way into the consciousness of governments, especially those of a more neo-liberal persuasion. Recognition has come most obviously in respect of bids to host major sports events. For Norway (1994 Lillehammer Olympics and proposed bid for the 2018 winter Olympic Games), Germany (World Cup hosts in 2006), Canada (winter Olympic hosts in Vancouver in 2010) and the UK (hosts of Euro'96 and of the 2012 Olympic Games) the economic benefits to the national balance of payments and to the local and regional economy have featured prominently in the rationales for government support of bids.

Commercialisation has also affected the way in which athletes relate to their sports with the most obvious impact being the increasing number who see sport as a career. The rapid decline in elite level amateur sport in track and field, tennis and, most recently, in rugby union, and the steady increase in the number of national Olympic committees which routinely give financial rewards to their medallists are both indicative of this trend. Countries, especially in Scandinavia, and organisations, such as the EU, in which there is a lobby to retain, what the EU refers to as, the 'European model of sport' in contrast to the commercial model typified by the United States, face an uphill struggle to hold back the neo-liberal commercialisation of sport. Canada (in relation to football, track and field, and hockey) and Norway (particularly in relation to soccer) have both tried to resist, or at least manage, commercialisation but with only limited success and have consequently seen many of their elite players move abroad and, in the case of Canada, their domestic leagues taken over by the more powerful neighbour as well as seen the standard of play in their domestic competitions fall.

Finally, commercialisation has had an impact upon the ethos and management practices in sport and demonstrates the extent of overlap with *governmentalisation*. In Canada the sometimes painful transition from 'kitchen table to boardroom' for NSOs has been well documented (see e.g. Slack and Hinings, 1992; Kikulis *et al.*, 1995; Auld and Godbey, 1998). In the UK the Labour government's modernisation agenda has had significant consequences for how national governing bodies of sport are managed and, more importantly, manage themselves (Green and Houlihan, 2006). In order to access sponsorship funding and develop their sports, events and teams as brands and marketable commodities NSOs have increasingly had to import business practices and expertise of the corporate sponsors they are trying to impress. Although there is an element of mimetic isomorphism in relation to commercial corporations governments are increasingly putting pressure on NSOs to adopt a more 'business-like' approach to running their sports and events. For example, targets and performance indicators are imposed from the centre. Audit and inspection regimes now proliferate, and are supported by sanctions imposed on those organisations that 'fail' to meet these centrally imposed targets. One recent example of such a value for money review is the National Audit Office report which recommended that UK Sport should 'be prepared to take tough decisions based on performance about whether sports merit funding and on what scale' (Houlihan and Green, 2005, p. 6) if it was 'to maximise its return on investment in the future' (2005, p. 34). This form of governmentalisation clearly reinforces and legit-imises the value system of commercialisation in privileging 'the values of self-sufficiency, competitiveness and entrepreneurial dynamism' (Slack and Hinings, 1992, p. 11). As Raco and Imrie comment, 'increasingly, government seeks not to govern society *per se*, but to promote individual and institutional conduct that is consistent with government objectives' (2000, p. 2191).

Governmentalisation consequently overlaps with and rein-forces many of the pressures exerted through commercialisation. However, the most important aspect of governmentalisation is the development of a state apparatus for the delivery and man-agement of sport. In all four countries in this study government involvement has generally expanded, often with the government working in conjunction with voluntary sports associations, but also with the steady accrual of functions to itself and the conse-quent development of specialist administrative units and agen-cies at national and sub-national levels, and the allocation of responsibility for sport policy at ministerial level. By the early part of the twenty-first century sport has become so well estab-lished within the machinery of government and within the port-folio of government responsibilities that governments are able to influence significantly the pattern of sporting opportunities within communities, success at elite level and the scope and activ-ities of both the commercial and voluntary sectors.

The extent of governmentalisation overlaps substantially, and not surprisingly, with the fourth force, *politicisation*. However, politicisation refers to the use of sport to achieve non-sporting objectives not only by governments, but also by non-governmental interests. The instrumental attitude towards sport by govern-ments has a long history. For example, for Hitler the 1936 Olympic Games was an opportunity to showcase National Socialism while 20 years later Manfred Ewald used sport and his 'diplomats in tracksuits' to further the GDR's claims to sov-ereignty and diplomatic recognition (Houlihan, 1994; Peppard and Riordan, 1993). But instrumentalism was not limited to totalitarian regimes. Trudeau, in the 1960s, hoped that inter-national sporting success would enhance the development of Canadian national unity and undermine the Quebec separatist movement. Throughout the 1970s and 1980s actual or threatened boycotts of the Olympic Games and Commonwealth Games were prompted by Cold War rivalry or by the persistence of apartheid in South Africa. In summary, sport is a well estab-lished, high visibility, low cost and low risk political resource in global diplomacy.

The politicisation of sport by non-governmental interests also has a long history. In 1968 Tommy Smith and John Carlos used the Olympic medal ceremony as an opportunity to protest against the treatment of black Americans in the United States, and in the 1972, at the Munich Olympic Games, terrorists took a number of Israeli team members hostage in protest at Israeli government policy in the Middle East. More recently, major sports events such as the Olympic Games have been used as a focus for campaigns on a range of issues including the environment, minority rights and anti-globalisation.

The four countries in the study

In the historical review of the four countries that follows all four forces are evident, but with differing degrees of intensity and in different combination. However, what is clear is that these forces leave a unique imprint on the structural context within which sport has developed and within which contemporary sport policy is made.

Canada

Over the last 100 years or so the dominant theme in Canadian sport has been national identity, followed by race and commercialisation. Prior to that Canadian sport mirrored many of the features found in England with, for example sport being promoted in the schools for the rich because of its assumed 'character-forming' qualities. As Metcalfe noted attitudes towards sport were affected by the English Victorian 'muscular Christianity' movement whose influence on 'Canadian sport and physical education cannot be over-emphasised' (1974, p. 69). However, as access to education expanded beyond the rich the Christian justification for including sport in the curriculum was augmented by the growing concern among the settlers to define themselves relative to the native people and, somewhat later, in relation to the imperial power.

In parallel with the dismissal of native people's territory rights Canadian settlers expropriated and redefined their sporting heritage and granted them only a marginal role in organised and commercial sport. Cosentino, examining the history of commercial sport in Canada noted that native people's sports such as lacrosse and snowshoe racing were adopted by settlers and redefined as EuroCanadian sports (see also Salter, 1977; Paraschak, 1989).

Until the late nineteenth century Canadian culture was unproblematically derived from Britain, France and the US.

It was only from the 1880s onwards that sustained debates took place about the nature of Canadian identity and, particularly, how that identity might be manifest in sport. Brown, reflecting on the emergence of NSOs towards the end of the nineteenth century, commented that 'while the moral theory of games was unquestionably British in its association, there is no doubt that in actual form, sport was illustrative of an emerging sense of Canadianism. Ice hockey, lacrosse and Canadian football were games which extolled the individuality of a people in search of their own identity' (1984, p. 132). However, just at the time that Canada was beginning to distance itself culturally from Britain it was being drawn into the orbit of commercialised American ice hockey, football and later basketball and baseball. The Americanisation and commercialisation of Canadian sport gathered pace throughout the twentieth century. For example, Kidd and Macfarlane (1972) trace the gradual undermining, by American business interests, of an autonomous Canadian sports structure for ice hockey and its progressive absorption into a US-dominated professional league. The gradual dominance of professional sport in Canada had the effect of reducing the quality of national amateur teams. However, the decline in the success of ice hockey teams in Olympic and World Championship events made Canadians more receptive to Prime Minister Trudeau's proposal in the 1960s to use federal funds to improve international success.

Apart from modest contributions to the cost of attending major sports events such as the Olympic Games the Canadian state had displayed only a limited interest in sport. However, Trudeau recognised sport as a potentially valuable vehicle in defining and enhancing a sense of Canadian identity and, more specifically, helping to undermine the separatist movement in Quebec. From the early 1970s the government became increasingly interventionist not only providing substantial funding primarily to support elite sport development, but also seeking to reshape NSOs as effective conduits for government policy. The 1970s and 1980s saw a substantial growth in federal government grant to NSOs and the effective 'seduction of amateur sport' (Carlson, 1992, p. 30). In addition, the government was also providing direct funding for elite athletes through the Athlete Assistance Program undermining a key role of NSOs. As Franks and Macintosh concluded the overall effect of federal policy in the 1960s and 1970s was that 'the relative autonomy from government which sport had enjoyed for 100 years in Canada was lost' (1984, p. 206).

Throughout the 1980s, at least until the Ben Johnson doping scandal at the 1988 Seoul Olympics, there was a steady centralisation of state control over elite sport underpinned by increasing public subsidy. Mass participation was largely pushed to the margin of political debate at the federal level and was increasingly left to the provinces and municipalities to administer and finance as they saw fit. The impact of the Ben Johnson affair was to initiate a period of prolonged introspection within the federal government regarding the objectives of its sport policy in general and elite sports policy in particular. The high profile government inquiry in 1989 into Johnson's positive drug test, chaired by Justice Dubin, was highly critical of the federal government's manipulation of NSOs for state purposes and of the emphasis given to elite achievement. Since the publication of the report of the Dubin Inquiry there has been a decline in the volume of public funds directed towards elite sport, but no clear reduction in the emphasis given to Olympic success.

The period from 1990 to 2005 has been one of uncertainty in federal policy against a background of reduced funding. Government not only reduced the overall volume of funding given to sport in the mid-1990s, but became increasingly selective about which sports would receive public funding. As the typical NSO relied on the federal government for 70% of its funding the loss of public finance has been traumatic (Green and Houlihan, 2005). The continuing uncertainty and tension regarding public policy towards sport in Canada is exemplified by the direction that policy took following the relatively poor performance by Canadian athletes at the Sydney Olympics where 14 medals were won. Denis Coderre, Secretary of State for Amateur Sport at the time, stated, 'Following the Sydney Games the need was identified for a funding programme focused on high performance sport with the specific objective of achieving medal-winning results' (quoted in Canadian Heritage 2001). Coderre's statement is in stark contrast to the recommendation that 'it is inappropriate to target medals/medal counts as goals or policy determinants for the federal government' which was made by the Task Force on Federal Government Sport Policy (Sport: The Way Ahead, 1992, p. 210).

Canada provides evidence of the significance of all four forces discussed above. For well over 100 years Canadian sport has been shaped by globalisation, as post-colonialism and, more recently, as Americanisation. Politicisation also has a long history and is deeply entrenched in the tensions between the Anglophone and Francophone communities. Overlapping with these forces is the more recent impact of governmentalisation, though now possibly in retreat, and commercialisation. While resistance to the commercialised sport structures of the United States contributed to the development of a sense of Canadian identity and unity, the growing separatist movement and the incorporation of sport symbolism into separatist politics provided a strong countervailing and fissiparous pressure. Attempts to utilise sport for nation-building purposes has been hampered not only by the separatist movement in Quebec, but also by the decentralist federal system in Canada and the strength of the provinces in relation to the federal government. The dominance of commercialisation as the most powerful force shaping Canadian sport was to an extent modified, if not checked, by the surge in government interest in sport that lasted for roughly 25 years from the mid-1960s to the late-1980s. Since then the decline in the clarity of purpose and intensity of government involvement has resulted in public policy drift and has allowed commercial interests to reassert their dominance by default in the policy field.

England

The major historical factors shaping sport in modern England were a mix of class-based policies, neo-liberal commercialisation and increasing government intervention. The connection between class and sport was at its most transparent in the mid-nineteenth century and is best illustrated by the distinction between amateurs and professionals. Social exclusivity was achieved in two ways: first, by the fostering of a distinctive set of expensive sports, such as hunting, game-fishing and shooting, among the affluent and higher social groups and defining these sports as confirmatory of elite social status and, second, by the domination of the organisation of many sports through the establishment of elite social control over the newly established national governing bodies.[1] The British system of public (fee-paying) schools and the universities of Oxford and Cambridge played a key part in defining and refining the culture of athleticism which emphasised the intrinsic rewards of participation and also in establishing and developing the organisational framework for the promotion and control of individual sports. For example, the formation of both the Football Association in 1863 and the Rugby Football Union in 1871 was both inspired by former pupils of public schools.

Although the division between amateurs and professionals was at its most bitter and divisive in the nineteenth century the debate over amateurism continued well into the twentieth century. While only a few sports, and often only for a limited time, used the rules governing amateurism as a way of excluding manual workers, much more common was the use of governing body rules to exclude those who sought to make a living from the sport rather than treat it, in the words of the Amateur Athletic Association President, the Marquess of Exeter, as a 'happy recreation' (quoted in Holt and Mason, 2000, p. 45). Athletics (see Lovesey, 1979) and rowing (Holt, 1989) fought protracted battles to resist any dilution of amateurism and rugby split into two codes, union and league, over the issue. Where the rules allowed amateurs and professionals to compete in the same team social divisions were often maintained through the use of separate changing rooms, different forms of address and, in the case of cricket, a division of labour where the professionals undertook the more arduous task of bowling.

During the second half of the twentieth century amateurism was steadily forced to retreat partly because of the increasing commercialisation of sport, but also because of the clear under-mining of amateurism by the making of unofficial payments to competitors in athletics, rugby union and tennis, and by the advent of competitors from communist countries who, while notionally amateur, clearly trained full time. In 1963 cricket dropped its distinction between amateurs and professionals, tennis became open to professionals in 1967 and in 1995 rugby union abandoned amateurism. However, as Holt and Mason (2000) make clear with regard to the Wimbledon tennis com-petition, while amateurism might have been abandoned, the class-ridden nature of some sports and their associated events continues to linger.

One of the key contributory factors to the eventual collapse of amateurism in many English sports was the powerful tide of commercialisation that developed in the early 1960s. The arrival of commercial television in 1955 and the expansion of live satel-lite broadcasting of international sports events began to generate the explosion in sports broadcasting and commercial sponsor-ship that has still not peaked. Golf, one of the first sports to receive extended television coverage, saw its prize money increase tenfold in the 20 years from the mid-1950s. But golf's income was dwarfed by comparison to that available in football especially during the period between the mid-1970s and mid-1980s when English clubs were very successful in international competition. The momentum behind commercialisation received a further boost with the arrival of satellite and cable broadcast-ers such as Sky. Not only did the scale of income to national governing bodies and individual clubs increase substantially, but it also led to growing friction within national governing bodies and clubs regarding the division of the increasing televi-sion and sponsorship income. The formation of the football Premiership in 1992 was in part an attempt by the Football Association to maintain some authority over a set of clubs whose combined wealth and earning potential dwarfed that of their governing body. Similarly, within football clubs (and to a lesser extent within cricket, and rugby union and league clubs) the power of players has grown substantially as players compete for a share of commercial income. With the growth in commercialisation has come demands for closer regulation by the state and, consequently, in recent years, the government and the EU have intervened, for example, to ensure that culturally important sports events are available for broadcast 'free to air', that players have the same right of free movement between employers as other employees, that the purchase of Manchester United by Sky was not acceptable, that stadiums needed to be licensed by local government and that anti-doping regulations apply in wealthy commercial sports as effectively as in the less commercial sports.

The role of government is the third defining theme in shaping English sport policy. Up until the early 1960s government intervention in sport could best be described as haphazard and infrequent. There is, nevertheless, a degree of consistency: first, in the paternalistic attitude towards the 'lower classes'; second, and closely related to the first, a concern that too much undisciplined sport and leisure for the urban lower classes constituted a potential danger to social stability; and third, a concern to use government power to defend class privilege. While these concerns were much discussed there was relatively little government action as the general preference was to avoid direct government involvement in the use of leisure time. By the early 1960s there were clear signs from both the Conservative and Labour parties that sport was slowly being acknowledged as a legitimate concern of government. The change in attitude was due to a recurrence of the concern with the potential for disorder by increasingly affluent young urban working class males, the maturation of the post-war welfare state which accepted leisure time as an important aspect of social welfare, and a growing concern with England's declining success at international level in sport.

Three years after the establishment of the Sports Council in 1972 the White Paper, *Sport and Recreation*, confirmed the place of sport and recreation as a legitimate aspect of the welfare state while also endorsing the intervention on the grounds of social order, international success and individual health. Despite this public endorsement of sport as a formal concern of government and the establishment of the Sports Council as an executive agency governmental involvement was erratic. It is possible to identify four reasonably discrete phases of government involvement in sport in England. The first, from the mid-1960s to the late-1970s, was characterised by an emphasis on investment in facility construction and service development at the municipal level, with central government maintaining a broadly non-interventionist stance. The period from the late 1970s to the early 1990s was one of relative neglect by the neo-liberal governments of Margaret Thatcher whose personal attitude towards sport at all levels was a mix of incomprehension and disdain. A more interventionist phase began in the early 1990s. Following the government's publication of a national curriculum for physical education in 1991, the government of John Major signalled, in the policy statement, *Sport: Raising the Game*, that the salience of sport to government had increased, especially in relation to school and elite sport. Funding from the newly established National Lottery was to be used to underpin substantial investment in facilities and services for young people and elite athletes. The loss of power by the Conservatives in 1997 heralded the beginning of a period of prolonged and intense intervention by government as New Labour not only confirmed its predecessor's policy priorities but showed far less deference towards national governing bodies of sport and other sports organisations. Using the rhetoric of modernisation the government, through its agencies Sport England and UK Sport, aimed to refashion clubs, schools and above all national governing bodies to be effective 'partners' in achieving the government's policy objectives for participation, elite success and health improvement.

In summary, the two dominant long-term forces shaping the contemporary sports landscape in England have been politicisation and commercialisation: politicisation, manifest in the persistence of the association between social class and participation in particular sports, and commercialisation, particularly evident at the elite level of major team sports since the late 1960s. In many respects the initial reluctance of governments, whether Conservative or Labour, up to the 1990s to intervene in order to influence the development of sport gave commercial interests the opportunity to shape substantially the development of elite sport. The relatively recent enthusiasm of the government of John Major and those of Tony Blair was stimulated less by a desire to temper the excesses of commercialisation than by a desire to harness what was increasingly recognised as a significant political resource that could be deployed to aid the achievement of a series of non-sporting policy objectives such as improved behaviour among the young, community integration, urban regeneration and strengthened national morale. An instrumental perception of sport dominates, not surprisingly, within business which sees sport as a significant source of profit, but also within government which sees sport as a relatively cheap, yet high profile tool for contributing to the achievement of a broad range of social policy objectives.

Germany

The historic ruptures that mark Germany have created a particular mix of continuity and change. The rise and fall of the Nazi regime and the reunification of East and West Germany were dramatic breaks with the past, but the Nazi and Communist legacies have left strong imprints on subsequent developments. Distancing themselves from the past Germans sometimes move from one extreme to another.

The dominant motif in the history of German sport is the depth of political involvement in sport. From the late eighteenth century onwards the content and organisation of school physical education and sport and of community physical activity and sport has been the subject to intense political debate and sporting practices have been laden with weighty political symbolism. Much of the nineteenth century was dominated by debates over the particular form of gymnastics that should be promoted among German youth and the underlying purpose of participation in the sport. In the early nineteenth century the popularity of Gutsmuth's system of gymnastics, based on 'pan-European ideas' was challenged by Jahn who sought to develop a 'more patriotic system of German gymnastics' (Naul, 2002, p. 15). In the middle of the century there was a debate within the army over the relative merits of the Swedish Ling gymnastic system and the Jahn-inspired alternative with the latter's combination of marching, floor and apparatus exercises gaining preferment. A similar debate arose regarding the growing popularity of English sport such as football, rowing and athletics. Many educators admired the English 'cult of athleticism and ideas on muscular Christianity' (Naul, 2002, p. 18) and while there was some attempt to resist this early example of globalisation through the development of 'Turner-games' English sport continued to grow in popularity with the result that two of the earliest NSOs to be formed in Germany were for football (1890) and rowing (1883).

The interconnection between German nationalism and sport continued and intensified in the twentieth century. Following the end of First World War military training for young Germans was outlawed by the Treaty of Versailles. One consequence of this prohibition was to intensify the debate concerning the content of the school physical education curriculum with more right-wing politicians wanting schools to introduce military-style physical training while the newly elected social democrat government sought to introduce a more liberal curriculum which emphasised sport and games rather than training. However, the liberalisation of sport did not last long as the rise of the National Socialists reinforced the right-wing critique of school sport. Perhaps the most significant change was that the locus of debate over the nature of sport in German society moved away from schools and into clubs. The National Socialists created a centralised unitary state and tightened their grip on German society. Federal sports associations lost their independence and were incorporated into the German National Socialist Reichsbund of Physical Activities and all sports clubs linked to political parties other than the National Socialists were required to close. The Hitler Youth organisation became the focal point for developing a programme of sport and physical training suitable, according to the 1937 physical education curriculum, for a 'hygienic Aryan race' and the development of the qualities required of soldiers. The intense politicisation of sport was accompanied by the rapid governmentalisation of sport through the disbandment of independent regional sports associations and their alignment with state administrative boundaries which in turn were co-terminus with Nazi Party districts.

Although initially reluctant to bear the expense of the 1936 Olympic Games which had been awarded to Berlin in 1931, 2 years before Hitler came to power, the National Socialists quickly realised the propaganda potential of the event. The Berlin Olympics were a lavishly funded showcase for the carefully managed image of Germany that the Nazis wanted to project. Integral to that achievement was the complete subordination of all sport and sports organisations to National Socialist control (Krüger, 1999). The depth of subordination of sport to National Socialism and the longer-term association between German nationalism and sport made the allied powers in 1945 suspicious of the unregulated re-establishment of sports clubs and activities. Sports clubs in the Soviet occupied zone (which later became the GDR) remained closed due to fears that they might act as cover organisations for Nazi sympathisers (Krüger, 2003). When sports clubs were eventually permitted they had to operate under the aegis of Communist-dominated trade unions and the communist party youth organisations mirroring, in many ways, the Nazi system they were replacing. In the three other occupied zones sports clubs emerged rapidly and as independent organisations.

As the division between East and West Germany hardened the two countries developed quite different sports systems. In the Federal Republic of Germany (FRG) *länder* retained significant responsibility for funding sport, especially the rebuilding of facilities while strong national sports federations were also established. At the heart of the FRG system was the network of largely independent clubs whose combined membership totalled almost 26 million in 1995. While clubs receive on average 10% of their income from the state in the form of grants as well as substantial indirect subsidies such as low cost hire of facilities and equipment, by far the most significant source of direct income is from membership fees which accounts for 55% of total income (Heinemann, 1999). The limits on the independence of Olympic sports federations were amply illustrated by the call by President Carter for a boycott of the Moscow Olympic Games in protest against the recent Soviet invasion of Afghanistan. As Krüger notes 'The sports movement did not have the strength of will to resist government pressure. Sport was receiving too much public funding to give that up for something as "trivial" as the rights of athletes to take part in "their" Olympics' (2003, p. 80).

Despite the dependence of FRG sports organisations on state funding the degree of direct control exercised over sport was slight by comparison to that found in the GDR where sport remained tightly under state management. Tight control was deemed essential for three reasons: first, because it was seen, as in the Federal Republic, as important in the de-Nazification process in the immediate post-war years; second, because the GDR soon recognised the value of elite level sporting success in furthering its claim for sovereignty and third, because the GDR shared the same fear and contempt for the institutions of civil society as its predecessor regime.

Following reunification in 1990 most of the institutions that comprised the GDR sports system were dismantled and the volume of funding enjoyed by East German athletes was drastically cut as was the funding made available to their West German counterparts. As Krüger notes 'now that the immediate competitor [had] gone, there [was] far less money being put into elite sport' (2003, p. 85).

In summary, the dominant themes in German sports history are the intense politicisation of sport and physical activity and the extent of government intervention and control. The long-term association between sport and nationalism, the organisation of sports clubs along political and religious lines, and the periods of totalitarian rule created a lasting legacy that, at a deep structural level, continues to shape current policy. The sports system that was established in West Germany in the post-war period was designed to contrast with the earlier Nazi system and with the emerging East German system. The considerable role of states (länder) in providing sports facilities and support for clubs was a deliberate contrast with the highly centralised systems of the Nazis and the East Germans.

The extent of politicisation of sport was also affected by Germany's interaction with global developments. The suspicion and eventual rejection of Swedish forms of gymnastics in favour of a Jahnian model and the attempts to exclude English sports from communities and schools both indicate the importance of global influences in affecting domestic policy. The attitude of German sports organisations and politicians to the Olympic movement is also indicative of the ambiguous relationship with globalisation. The suspicion among more right-wing sports administrators of the proposed revival of the Olympics in 1896 organised by the Frenchman de Coubertin and the value of continuing to host the 1936 Olympic Games in Berlin soon gave way to a recognition of the value of the Games. For Hitler the Games provided a global platform for promoting the virtues and achievements of the National Socialists.

In 1972 the West German government considered hosting the Games in Munich as an opportunity to signal the FRG's political rehabilitation and to demonstrate the recovery of the West German economy. Both the embrace of the Olympic movement and the compromises that were made with Swedish gymnastics and especially the English conceptualisation of sport illustrate the permeability of the domestic policy system.

German authorities are still closely involved with sport, but sport organisations and government emphasise the autonomy of the sports movement. The emphasis on autonomy should be seen in the light of a wish to re-establish the independence of voluntary associations after the heavy politicisation of German sport and civil society during the Nazi and communist periods.

Norway

Since the early part of the nineteenth century there has been a close association between sport and nationalism in Norway and also between sport and the state. Although 400 years of Danish rule ended in 1814 it was replaced by union with Sweden which, far from satisfying Norwegian aspirations for autonomy, fuelled nationalist sentiment especially as the Swedish king tried on a number of occasions to undermine the Norwegian constitution. Challenges to the constitution were resisted publicly through the celebration of the constitution each 17th May. The defence of the constitution and fostering of Norwegian nationalism was expanded beyond the growing urban middle class partly through the incorporation of sports competitions in climbing, wrestling and running for example, into the Constitution Day festivals. As Goksøyr notes, 'Sport was used as a deliberate instrument for extending the popular basis of the celebration' (1996, p. 130). Sports competitions were also a useful vehicle for the popularisation of Constitution Day and therefore the geographic diffusion of nationalism.

Although tensions with Sweden lessened in the middle years of the nineteenth century they stirred again in the 1880s and thus coincided with the establishment of NSOs across much of Europe and also with the revival of the Olympic Games in 1896. During this period there was a much more vigorous debate about the type of sports that best symbolised the strengthening Norwegian nationalism (Goksøyr, 1996). The various interpretations of sport familiar in Norway at the time provided an important reference point for discussing and defining the distinctiveness of Norwegian identity. The sports that best reflected this developing sense of national self among the middle class were those that had clear roots in the countryside such as skiing and skating, those that had strong associations with Norwegian day to day work culture (outrigger deep-water rowing rather than English shallow-water rowing), and those that had associations with military preparedness, such as weapons training and elements of Jahnian and Lingian gymnastics which were particularly favoured by the more conservative strata in Norway (Augestad, 2003b). As Skirstad and Felde observe the legitimation for the practice of sport was extrinsic, 'the practical outcomes of military preparedness, nationalism, and improved public health' (1996, p. 320).

The turn of the century, when the separation from Sweden was imminent, was also the time of rapid growth in international competition. The first biennial Nordic Winter Games, intended to foster good relations between the two countries, were held in 1901 and were successful, as indeed were those in 1903. However, by 1905 tension between the two countries was such that the Norwegians boycotted the Games which were to be held in Stockholm. Later that year Norway declared its independence and its athletes did not return to Sweden until the 1912 Olympic Games.

The trend of governmentalisation began in the 1860s when the Ministry of Defence provided finance for military-related outdoor training. Public funding was provided for the 1901 Nordic Winter Games and then for the 1908 London Olympic Games despite reservations from conservatives that Olympic sport promoted 'specialisation, circus and fanaticism' (Goksøyr, 1996, p. 137). However, these conservative reservations were not shared by the government which increased financial support rapidly for the Olympic team. Indeed, for the Stockholm Games of 1912 the government provided sufficient funding for Norway to send the third largest national team to the event.

A major theme of the inter-war period was the ideological tension between the two national sports associations, the left-oriented

Workers Sports Movement (*Arbeidernes idrettsforbund*) and what was seen as a more bourgeoisie sports association, The National Confederation of Sport (*Landsforbundet for idræt*). In the 1930s there were several initiatives to bridge the gap between the two organisations. From the government side a Sport Commission was established in 1935 with members from the Ministry and also from the two organisations which resulted in an agreement regarding cooperation which came into force in 1936 (Goksøyr, 1992). At the end of the 1930s further talks were held concerning the possible merger of the two organisations. However, the planned merger was postponed due to the German occupation of Norway, but the two organisations formally united as the Norwegian Confederation of Sport (NIF) in 1946. The eventual merger was given additional impetus due to the German occupation which had the effect of unifying the sport movement ideologically, due to the so-called sport-boycott of the Nazi regime in Norway when all Norwegian sports organisations chose to disband rather than be directly controlled by the occupation administration. Not surprisingly, the combined effect of the Nazi politicisation efforts and the previous tension between 'workers' and 'bourgeois' sports organisations was to deepen the suspicion of direct state involvement in sport and to ensure that the statutes governing NIF required that the organisation be 'politically neutral' (Tønnesson, 1986).

However, despite the suspicion of state involvement in sport the welfare regime that developed in Norway after Second World War included sport which was seen as an important part of what, adopting Slagstad's terminology (1998, pp. 212–217, 336–343) could be called the Labour Party's 'regime of education and cultivation'. The sport policy at that time was a 'state planned, steered and controlled development project – a state socialistic project for the promotion of "a healthy culture"' (authors' translation, Slagstad, 1998, p. 341). Sport was, together with gymnastics in schools, an important factor in the 'hygienic logic' of the social functionalist ideology of that period (Augestad, 2003b).

Two events in 1946 became significant elements in the formation of sport as a discrete policy area: The establishment of a State Office for Sport, which 4 years later became part of the State Office for Youth and Sport (STUI) under the Ministry of Education and Church Affairs (Goksøyr *et al.*, 1996), and the approval by Parliament of the Money Game Act which allocated the profits from gaming to sport and research, and which established the National Gaming Corporation (*Norsk Tipping AS*) to oversee gaming in sport.[2] The gaming money was distributed to sport by STUI, primarily to enable the establishment of sport facilities in local communities all over the country. In addition to STUI, voluntary workers in local sports club and local government contributed to the building and funding of the sport facilities.

Interest intermediation and cooperation between voluntary associations and government have long traditions in Norway. After the Second World War, Norway developed a corporatist apparatus which has placed Norway on, or close to, the top of the ranking lists of corporatist countries (Rommetvedt, 2005). In 1957, a Norwegian Sport Council (*Statens idrettsråd*) was established with members from NIF and the Ministry. The Council was a typical example of the numerous corporatist bodies with representatives from organised interests and the civil service that were established in this period. However, in 1988, both NIF and the Ministry agreed to phase out the Sport Council on the grounds that the Council was no longer needed due to good and close relations between the government and NIF. In other words, they did not need a formalised corporatist body in order to cooperate. Government and voluntary sport associations developed an almost symbiotic relationship which has been characterised as a 'family relation' (Selle, 1995). On the one hand central and local government play an import role subsidising and funding sport facilities. On the other hand sports activities are organised by local sports clubs and NSOs. Sport organisations depend on public money, but they have great autonomy with regard to how they organise their activities.

Sport has played an important role in the social functionalist ideology of the post-war period. Sport was seen as a part of the welfare culture, as a contributor to the development of both body and mind in a modern welfare regime, as an important element in hygienic thinking in the widest sense (creating health, naturalness, discipline and so on). This was, however, mainly a governmental, or, more correctly, a Labour Party/social democratic way of looking at sport. Inside the sport movement itself it is arguable how deeply rooted these values were. It seems fair to say that the definition of sport as competitive sport, and the ideology of seeing sport as an end in itself, was growing stronger throughout the twentieth century (Bergsgard, 2005). Sport became increasingly part of a growing leisure time culture which emphasised the intrinsic value of sport, that is practicing sport for its own sake rather than for the social or moral benefits.

Despite this broad consensus tensions have surfaced, though generally causing ripples rather than storms, over the extent of public subsidy and, more controversially, over the provision of specific investment in elite athlete development for Olympic competition. Regarding the latter, Norway, like most other industrialised countries, has not been able or willing to resist the attraction of boosting medal chances by developing specialist programmes of support for its elite athletes. *Olympiatoppen*, which was introduced in 1988–1989 as joint venture between the Norwegian Olympic Committee and the NIF, provides facilities for elite training and other support programmes. *Olympiatoppen* is funded partly by sponsors and partly by gaming money (Augestad *et al.*, 2006).

In summary, as with Canada much of the development of sport in Norway has been shaped by the political issues of identity and nationalist ideology. Domination by Denmark and Sweden and occupation by Nazi Germany were crucial in constructing a distinctive symbolism for sport. A secondary factor shaping Norwegian sport was the various attempts to reconcile workers' and bourgeois conceptualisations of sports and culture. Although the extent of public subsidy (particularly at municipal level) and semi-public subsidy (through the national lottery) has steadily grown in recent years the level of autonomy of sports organisations from the state is a significant feature of the contemporary policy landscape in Norway. Throughout the period from roughly 1950 the overt politicisation of Norwegian sport has given way to a modest level of governmentalisation (more with regard to funding and less with regard to activities), but with commercialisation emerging as an increasingly insistent factor affecting the contemporary sport policy landscape.

Conclusion

In Chapter 2 attention was drawn to the importance of acknowledging the significance of the institutional context of policy and the scope allowed for agency in the competing conceptualisations of the policy process. In this chapter we have been concerned to locate the relationship between structure and agency in its broad cultural and historical setting particularly in relation to four major forces in sport policy namely, globalisation, commercialisation, politicisation and governmentalisation. Each of the four countries under review has experienced these pressures in different combination and in different degrees of intensity with, not surprisingly, highly varied impacts on the institutional infrastructure for sport and the scope for policy development. The ways in which the four countries have responded in more recent years to these global trends in sport is explored in detail in the following chapters.

Notes

1 While many countries refer to the organisations that oversee and organise individual sports as national sportsd organisations (NSOs) in England they are normally referred to as national governing bodies (NGBs).

2 We use the term 'gaming money' to emphasize that this is money from gaming on sport. However, from 1991/92 the bulk of money to sport came from the national lottery, and the term 'lottery money' is then used.

The structure of sport and the role of the voluntary sector

Introduction

One of the themes developed in the previous chapters was the importance of structure, both as institutional administrative arrangements and as embedded values and beliefs, for understanding policy and policy change. Consequently, this chapter begins with a review of the structure of the sports sector across the four countries with particular attention paid to the relationship between the structure of the sports sector (see Table 2.1) and the role of the voluntary/not-for-profit sector. An exploration of the character, size, scope and political significance of the voluntary sector will provide an insight into the extent to which the sport sector exhibits the characteristics of the broader welfare regime. The examination of the voluntary sector will also provide data relevant to the role of the government in sport policy and service provision and also the generalisation of interests.

The analysis is organised around three aspects: (i) the extent and nature of unity and/or diversity within the sport structure, (ii) the resource base of the voluntary sport sector and its pattern of resource dependency relationships and (iii) the character of the inter-relationships within the voluntary sport sector. The first aspect, unity/diversity of the sport sector deals with how united and concentrated, or alternatively how diverse and fragmented the sport structures of a country are. This is a multi-level aspect as the extent of uniformity or diversity may vary between national and sub-national levels. For example, the voluntary sport sector, which is of particular interest for us as a major independent actor in the policy process may be unified at the local or provincial levels while being fragmented at the national level. As regards the resource base of the voluntary sector the number of clubs and volunteers are the two key elements, but of substantial importance is the nature and pattern of resource dependencies within which the voluntary organisations operate, especially when those resource dependencies involve the state. The character of inter-relationships within voluntary sport can be described in terms of type of relationships as well as the content of those relationships. Of particular interest is the extent of closeness in the relationship, the degree of, and mechanisms for, co-ordination and concerted action, the nature of the policy agenda of the voluntary sports organisations and the direction and character of change.

The three aspects identified above can be linked to the earlier discussion of welfare regime types and also to two of the four analytical dimensions identified in Chapter 2. An examination of delivery systems for sport policy has a strong link to the type of welfare regime. Based on Esping-Andersen's (1990) description one might expect to find a strong voluntary sector in

Germany given its perception as a conservative welfare state, whereas the voluntary sector would be expected to be less important and the state to be more dominant in Norway. Within neo-liberal polities such as Canada and the UK one would expect a more limited role for the government and the voluntary sector and a more prominent role for commercial providers. However, these hypothesised relationships beg the question of whether sport policy and services are considered to be primarily elements of welfare provision or, as is the case in the UK, a hybrid service which is expected to fulfil both the welfare function and also feature as part of the new service economy.

The first analytic dimension that can be valuably explored in this chapter is the relationship between organisations, especially voluntary sports interests. Relationships between interest groups and the state may take different forms, depending on (i) the structures and power of the interest groups and (ii) the structures and power of related government institutions. In this chapter we focus mainly on the sport organisations, but to some degree we also consider the role of government even though this will be analysed in more detail in the next chapter. In general, it is suggested that Canada and England are known to have more pluralist systems, whereas Germany and especially Norway function within a more united and corporatist political system. Whether the degree of state pluralism is relevant for sport policy can be examined, for example, by looking for evidence of isomorphism among sports organisations. However, there is no necessary connection between features of the general political system, such as pluralism/corporatism and specific policy sectors.

The discussion of the voluntary sector is also relevant to the analytic dimension concerned with state structure. Each country has a distinctive state structure indicated by different political and administrative arrangements for managing territory and different patterns of distribution of function. Our four case study countries differ with regard to federal/unitary state and centralised/decentralised governing systems. In Chapter 2 it was suggested that the two federal states, Canada and Germany, are decentralised and centralised respectively, whereas the two unitary states, Norway and England, are decentralised and centralised, respectively. Do these different state systems affect the way voluntary sport is organised?

The organisational setting for voluntary sport

In this section we explore the organisational setting within which the voluntary sector operates. In particular, we examine the functional distribution of responsibility for sport within government, for example for youth sport and local facilities, and the impact that this might have on voluntary organisations. We also identify the scope and significance of the commercial sector and the extent to which this impacts on the activities of voluntary sports organisations.

Canada

The development of Canadian sport has been shaped by a combination of original, native sports (like lacrosse and snowshoeing), the traditions imported by various migrant groups (such as football and cricket) from Europe, and by its close geographical relationship to the USA (Horna, 1989; Macintosh, 1996). Within this diverse set of influences voluntary sport is the largest sector of the overall sport structure. Participation data indicate that, in 1998, 34% of the total adult population were engaged in competitive sport of one form or another, over half of whom belonged to a local club, community league or other local/regional amateur sport organisation (Sport Canada, 1998). The vitality of the voluntary sector is indicated by the increase in local club and league memberships. The overall trend shows a substantial increase, 20 percentage points, from 1992 to 1998, in the number of active Canadians belonging to a local club or community league. Taking into account that fewer people were active in sport in 1998, the increase in the proportion of adult Canadians having membership of a voluntary organisation was 4 percentage points (Sport Canada, 1998).

In terms of structure, the contemporary voluntary sector is more mixed with regard to type of units than in European countries. For example, YMCAs and scouts play an important part in the local delivery of recreation services. According to Slack (1999) sport clubs are not as common in Canada as in Europe, although their number is increasing. However, a significant feature of the voluntary sector in Canada is the local community sports league. Initiated in Edmonton in 1917 community sports leagues were established primarily for recreation, and are neighbourhood associations run by local volunteers and can now be found across the whole country. Although the format differs a typical community association might organise competitive leagues at 'minor' (junior) level for a number of sports, with football and ice hockey being among the most common (Searle and Brayley, 2000).

Although the voluntary club and league structures appear robust there are indications that informal sport activities have become increasingly important. On one hand, the number of physically active (broadly defined) adult (aged 20 or older) Canadians increased from 38% in 1994/1995 to 44% in 2000/2001 with a further increase to 49% recorded in 2002/2003 (Cameron *et al.*, 2004). On the other hand, the proportion of people engaged in competitive sport has decreased. A comparison of a survey in 1998 with a similar survey from 1992 shows a rather dramatic shift in the participation rate in competitive sport. In 1998 about one-third (34%) regularly participated in competitive sport, a figure that represented a decline of 11 percentage points on 1992 when the reported participation rate was 45% (Sport Canada, 1998). These studies defined sport as activities that involve two or more participants engaging for the purpose of competition and where formal rules and procedures are adhered to. This narrow definition excludes physical and leisure activities, such as aerobics, jogging and skate boarding, and consequently it is in areas of informal activity where most of the increase in participation is taking place. In other words, while organised competitive sport receives reduced interest, interest in general physical activity increases.

Of particular importance regarding youth sport is the role of municipalities in supporting (with access to facilities and sometimes with funding) and delivering activities. Sport programmes for youth are an important part of overall sport delivery and the number of children taking part is estimated to have increased from 2 million in 1978 to 2.5 million in 1991 (Coakley and Donnelly, 2004). However, it should be noted that while municipalities have an important role to play in facilitating youth programmes much of the actual delivery is undertaken by voluntary organisations (Slack, 2003). The programmes are often linked to a regional or provincial sport organisation which in turn may be linked to a national sport organisation (NSO) as is the case in football and ice hockey which have the largest number of participants. Although these voluntary organisations are mainly self-supporting through membership fees and fundraising, municipalities often provide additional financial support (Slack, 2003).

The commercial sector is an increasingly significant provider of sport and recreation services often through partnerships with municipalities (Thibault *et al.*, 2004), but also as a result of the privatisation of public sector sport and leisure services (Coakley and Donnelly, 2004). Although privatisation in some Canadian provinces is driven by ideology (as is the case in the UK) increasing pressure on local government finances is partly responsible. An illustration of the financial pressure was provided by a sport administrator in the province of Alberta who reported that not too long ago a town with 5,000 people would probably have had a recreation director and most would have had further recreation staff, whereas currently these resources were only available in the largest municipalities. For him sport was clearly one of the casualties of a tighter financial regime.

A further important element of the sport sector is the education system. In Canada education is a provincial responsibility and includes not only primary and secondary schools, but also colleges and universities. Through their control over curriculum, facilities and competitions they create major arenas for the introduction of young people to sport and for the development of sporting abilities. Various provincial organisations have a responsibility for educational sport at high school and post secondary levels. In Alberta, for example, there are Alberta School Athletics Association (ASAA) for high schools and the Alberta Colleges Athletic Conference which operates at the higher education level. The ASAA creates sport opportunities within 11 different activities and sponsors provincial championships involving 7,000 participants each year.

Provincial tournaments within the education system are held in many sports, but there are no national school championships. University sport, which is managed by paid personnel is more closely linked to the national level and is organised through four regional conferences and a national organisation, Canadian Interuniversity Sport. Member universities compete for conference and national championships in a number of disciplines. The colleges and universities in Alberta are typical insofar as they offer activities across a range of skill levels including the highly competitive as well as the less competitive and fun levels. College sport facilities may be open to, and have close relationships with, the local community prompted, in part, according to one interviewee, by the need to generate additional income and also to be seen to be part of the local community. Although higher education sport in Canada is closer to professional sport than in many European countries, it is far from being like the competitive, professionalised and commercialised university sport of the USA. Despite a significant proportion of the most talented Canadian student athletes obtaining scholarships at US universities, Canadian university sport has retained its strong links to educational goals (Slack, 2003; Coakley and Donnelly, 2004).

Professional sport has a long and strong history in Canada (Hall *et al.*, 1992; Kidd, 1996) and this element of the sport sector continues to expand. It is by far the most important type of sport activity as far as media and public interest are concerned. The most popular sports are baseball, basketball and especially ice hockey all of which have professional leagues, although the ice-hockey league is one that crosses the Canadian/US border (Macintosh, 1996). In the mid-1990s there were 149 professional sport clubs in the country. Turnover within the sector more than doubled from $Can 262 million in 1988 to $Can 527 million in 1994 (Mills report, 1998). Professional sport accounts for a substantial, but not dominating, part of the sport economy. For example, in 1995 employment in professional sport clubs accounted for 14% of the employment of the sport and recreation service industry (Mills report, 1998). The three major professional sports, baseball, basketball and ice hockey, are part of a large commercial sport and recreation industry. Total revenues from spectator sports including professional and semi-professional sport clubs and horse racing was, according to data from Statistics Canada, $Can 2.3 billion in 2004, a figure which had remained steady since 2000 (Statistics Canada, 2006). Fitness and recreation centres are also a large and expanding industry in Canada, reporting revenues of more than $Can 1.5 billion in 2004, up to 20.8% from 2003 which was an increase of 10.6% from the previous year. Golf courses and country clubs are an even larger industry with a turnover of $2.3 billion in 2004, and, as regards winter sports, the ski industry is also substantial with revenues of about $Can 800 million (*Statistics Canada*, 2004b, 2005, 2006).

In summary, the Canadian sport structure is characterised by three distinctive elements, the commercial, the educational and the voluntary sector, with the federal government's role remaining largely indirect and that of the municipal sector being substantially facilitative. It would therefore seem appropriate to refer to a threefold delivery system within which informal recreation is becoming increasingly important and in which the commercial sector continues to expand. As regards the Canadian voluntary sector it has maintained a prominent and stable position despite the growth of the commercial sector.

England

As arguably the cradle of modern competitive sport, England can trace a long history in school sport, voluntary sport and professional sport. In any review of contemporary sport in England each of these three traditions can not only still be clearly identified, but can also still be recognised as making a major contribution to provision.

Historically, one of the most important sources of modern English sport was the educational system and especially the organised physical activity at elite private schools. Today the education system remains a core focus for the delivery of sport for young people both within and beyond the curriculum. Over the last 5 years the government has invested heavily in an attempt to stop the steady decline in the time allocated to physical education (PE) and sport within the curriculum and also to increase the quality of curriculum physical education (QCA, 2004; DCMS/DfES, 2005). In addition, the government has designated almost 400 secondary schools as specialist sports colleges which enables the schools to obtain additional funding from central government. Specialist sports colleges have generally been very successful in working with schools in their local area in order to raise standards in physical education and sport and to create opportunities for increased participation in sport (Institute of Youth Sport, 2005a). Schools are also important in providing opportunities for participation in physical activity and sport outside the curriculum during lunch breaks, after school and at weekends. In 2002 in England 42% of all young people participated in extra school activities. Two in five participated in extracurricular sport in 2002, compared with about one-third in 1994 (Sport England, 2003). Much of the recent increase in the participation of young people in sport has been the result of substantial funding from government through the School Sport Partnership programme which provides staff and finance for the provision of extracurricular sport (Institute of Youth Sport, 2005b). Although schools are increasingly important in the pattern of opportunities for young people to participate in sport, other arenas are significant. In 2002 43% of the young participated in sport clubs outside school. This rate has remained fairly static since 1994. On the other hand, 55% in 2002 participated in sport in a youth club or other organisation, an increase of 4 percentage points since 1994 (Sport England, 2003).

Universities play an increasingly important role in the delivery of sports opportunities not only in offering sport for students and university staff, but also in making their facilities available to the surrounding community. Many higher education institutions run sport-related activities as part of a strategy to attract young people to higher education. There are more than 2,500 facilities of different kinds, such as grass pitches, tennis courts, squash courts and sport halls, available on university sites and close to 4,000 people are employed for the provision of sport in higher education in England (Sport England, 2002). Universities are an important source of employment for coaches and sports scientists, especially where a university has close links with local clubs, national governing bodies (NGBs), and elite sport programmes. With the current government committed to 50% of school leavers entering higher education, the role of universities and higher education colleges in maintaining and expanding opportunities for participation and competition at all levels will become increasingly significant.

Outside the education system the main vehicle for the development of sport is the voluntary club network. Volunteer resources retain a core position in sports delivery despite being challenged by the expansion of the commercial sector. Voluntary clubs are especially important for maintaining opportunities for competitive sport for adults. At the level of mass participation in almost all sports, particularly team sports are organised on a voluntary club basis (Dopson and Waddington, 2003). In UK the percentage of the active sports people who are members of a club increased from 34% in 1996 to 38% in 2002 (Fox and Richards, 2004). However, bearing in mind that the proportion of active sports people within the total population decreased the actual increase in club membership among the adult population was, at less than 1 percentage point, very small. Based on data from the 1990s, the club membership rate for the whole of the UK population has been estimated to be between 12.5% and 14% (Nichols, 2003). The recently published Carter Report (2005) gives an estimate of about 8.2 million sport club members in England. With a total population of around 50 million, and assuming some double memberships, it is reasonable to suggest that approximately 15% of the English population belong to a sports club.

As regards professional sports its roots are deep within English history. Despite the long held commitment to amateurism (Hill, 2002; Keech, 2003) which, for many sports, lasted until the 1960s or later, over the last 50 years cricket, tennis, rugby union and athletics have all embraced professionalism. The enthusiasm for commercial and professional sport is epitomised by football which has developed, both at the level of the individual Premiership club and the Premier League as a whole, brands that have a global reach. According to Deloitte & Touche (2006a) the English Premiership is the richest in the world with an annual turnover, in the 2004/2005 season, of £1.3 billion, a substantial increase from the 2000/2001 season when the equivalent figure was just under £1 billion. The Premier League's turnover compares with an estimated total income from all spectator sports in 2000 of £1.8 billion (Cambridge Econometrics, 2003).

The role of local authorities in sport and recreation delivery is probably more important in England than in most countries primarily through its role in the provision of sport and leisure facilities. According to the Carter Report (2005) England has 1,642 sport and leisure centres run or owned by local authorities, of which 679 are wet leisure centres, 569 dry leisure centres/ sport halls and 394 stand-alone swimming pools. Local authorities are also important for their investment (admittedly often supported by lottery funding) in sports development officers (SDOs) which have played a key role in delivering the government's sports development strategy. In 2000 it was estimated that there were roughly the same number of people in sports employment in the local government sector as there were in the voluntary sector (Cambridge Econometrics, 2003). As well as contributing to the direct delivery of sport services, via SDOs for example, local authorities also subsidise facility user costs. However, there is some evidence of a decline in the use of local authority facilities (Ravenscroft, 2004) with total admissions for the year ending April 2003 at 305 million, a reduction of 3.9% since 2000 (Carter Report, 2005).

The number of commercial sport clubs has increased rapidly in recent years totalling 1,757 in 2003 and commercial clubs have become an important arena for physical exercise. Almost 3 million people were members of a private health and fitness clubs in the UK in 2000 (DCMS/Strategy Unit, 2002), corresponding to about 5% of the population. Although the membership growth rate has slowed down recently (Carter Report, 2005) and indeed declined 8% in the 12 months to June 2006, the medium-term growth of the commercial sector indicates a trend towards increased commercialisation and individualisation of sport (Deloitte & Touche, 2006c). According to the Carter Report (2005) informal sport is estimated to account for 43% of all adult participation in sport (see Figure 4.1). Changes in participation patterns towards increased activity in swimming, keep fit, cycling, weights, and walking, also point towards individualisation (Coalter, 2004).

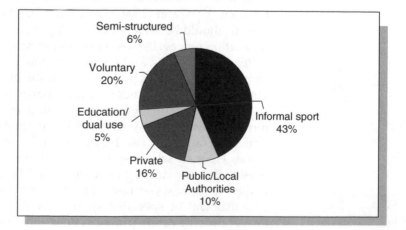

Figure 4.1
Estimated adult participation in England by setting (*Source*: Carter Report, 2005)

Summing up, as Figure 4.1 indicates, probably the most striking feature of the English sport structure as compared to that in many other countries is its strongly mixed character. Apart from informal and semi-structured activities one may possibly talk of a fourfold delivery system of private sector, voluntary sector, education sector and local government sector. In fact, the government, at local government level and through the education sector, sustains an important part of sport delivery services and makes a more substantial contribution than one would expect in a neo-liberal economy. The voluntary sector is maintaining a fairly stable position, although the modest level of club membership rates indicates that the voluntary sport clubs in England and UK are less important arenas for mass participation compared to many other countries.

Germany

History has left a strong imprint on German sport in two areas: the sport club and school sport. The sport club has for long been the basis of the German sport system. As an institution the club was tightly interwoven with the gymnastic movement and clubs were communities of like-minded people (Heinemann and Schubert, 1999) where social relations and identity creation were as important as sport. The club was the core organisation of supply and had the power to define the character of the sports experience. Approximately 29% of Germans have memberships in sports clubs. They are close to 23.6 million members (Deutscher Sportbund, 2004), although the net membership rate will be somewhat lower due to double counting. However, the sector has been growing with an increase in memberships of close to 2% (400,000) in the states (*länder*) sport confederations between 1998 and 2004 (Deutscher Sportbund, 2004). This growth should be understood as, in part, a consequence of the unification process between east and west.

PE also has a long and strong tradition in Germany, and like club sport has had an impact beyond the borders of Germany. The Federal Youth Games (*Bundesjugendspiele*), covering athletics, swimming and gymnastics, have been organised in the former West Germany since 1951 in collaboration with the respective associations. However, apart from these annual games German school sport is not as competitively oriented outside the curriculum as in Canada and England. By contrast, in the former East Germany the education system, through the establishment of specialist sports schools, was an important part of the elite development system and indeed has remained a part of the current educational and elite development infrastructure for sport.

Local government's primary involvement is with the construction and running of sport facilities often in close co-operation with voluntary sport, and with the extensive exploitation of the dual use of school facilities. Its role is facilitation of sport and not the organisation of sport activities.

The voluntary sport clubs are the main organised settings for sport participation outside the curriculum, a fact reflected in the high club membership rates among children and young teenagers. But the voluntary sports club is not the only arena for participation. In a survey of young adults active in sport, 50% were members of a voluntary sport club, 18% had membership in a commercial studio or sports arena, and 5% were members of both. People participating in sporting activities, but not members of voluntary or commercial sports clubs, accounted for 37% of the total (Veltins, 1999). According to statistics from DSSV[1] (*Arbeitsgeberverband Deutscher Fitness und Wellness-Anlagen*) the number of fitness and health-related commercial enterprises increased from 4,100 in the 1990 to 6,500 a decade later, and the membership increased from 1.7 to 4.6 million, corresponding to 5.6% of the population, for then to decrease somewhat. In 2006 the number of units had decreased to 5,554 and membership, after reaching a peak of 5.4 million in 2001, is now close to 5.05 million according to statistics from Deloitte & Touche (2006c).

Professional sport does not have the same long tradition in Germany as in Canada and England, although it is developing rapidly. As in most countries a professional sport of particular significance is football, but other important professional sports include handball, ice hockey, basketball, tennis and golf. The *Bundesliga* was established in 1963 and marked the entrance of professionalism in football. The economic size of the *Bundesliga* was calculated at DM 1.5 billion in 1999/2000 (Leibnitz Universität Hanover, 2000). In 2004 it had a turnover of more than €1.2 billion and was, with a growth in revenues of 17% in 2005 (mainly from broadcasting and commercial income), the fastest growing league of the 'big five' in Europe according to Deloitte & Touche (2006b). In terms of revenues the German *Bundesliga* has about 60% of the turnover value of the English Premier League.

Summing up, the German sport sector approximates to a dual system with voluntary sport being the largest sector and commercial sport (professional as well as private) rapidly expanding. Informal sport is, as elsewhere, also an important part of the picture. PE and school sport outside the curriculum operate on a relatively small scale by comparison to the UK.

Norway

Esping-Andersen (1990) emphasised the role of the state in social-democratic welfare regimes like Norway. However, Norwegian sport cannot be understood without reference to a strong volunteer tradition. The voluntary-based sport club has been a major local arena for sport and physical exercise in Norway since the dawn of modern sport and currently retains its dominant position in the national structure of sport. In a survey in 1998 it was estimated that there were 1.2 million members in Norwegian sport clubs (Wollebæk *et al.*, 2000) which represented about 26% of the population.

In 2004 voluntary clubs within the Norwegian Olympic Committee and Confederation of Sports had close to 1.65 million memberships. The voluntary sector has remained strong with membership increasing by approximately 114,000 from 2002 to 2004, an increase of about 7% (Statistics Norway, 2004). In addition, there were company clubs for employees with about 160,000 members (Statistics Norway, 2004). The latter can be assumed to be substantially voluntary clubs as well, even though they would receive some financial support from their employer. As noted in relation to the earlier data on membership these numbers do not correct for multiple club memberships, but even allowing for some double counting the membership rate is high by European standards.

Sport within the education system is less prominent in Norway than in the other three countries. Norway does have PE programmes at primary and secondary school levels, but very little outside the curriculum. During recent decades sport education has been offered in high schools and sport colleges. According to Statistics Norway, in 2004 there were close to 8,000 pupils (*ca.* 5% of the total), having specialised sport studies as part of their curriculum at high school level. In addition, there are a number of colleges offering studies in sport and outdoor life.

The amount of professional sport in Norway is so limited that it is probably more accurate to talk about a semi-professional sector. The most important professional sport is football where the teams in the upper league consist of full-time paid players. The size of the league, at 14 teams, is modest and the combined turnover was only 600 million Norwegian crowns or about £40 million in 2000 (Ohr and Solum, 2000). To a large extent Norwegian professionalism consists of exporting and importing players to and from foreign clubs or leagues. The English Premier League has for a long time received a significant number of Norwegian players. Similarly, some elite cyclists join foreign clubs as do handball players. Although the population of

Norway is too small and the economic base too narrow to develop an extensive professional sports system the significance of (semi)-professional sport is nonetheless increasing.

The pace of commercialisation of individual training seems to be as fast as in the other countries. Fitness training studios have become increasingly common with *Norges Treningssenter-forbund* having more than 140 fitness training studios and claiming to have about 300,000 members, corresponding to 6.5% of the population (NIF/KKD, 2003). For the adult population commercial studios have overtaken the voluntary club as a more important setting for physical activity. Perhaps of greater significance is the overlap between commercialisation and the trend towards individualisation of physical activity. Increasingly, the most important settings for physical activity are the informal arenas. In Norway the sports active population over 15 years of age report that they train alone more than four times more often than they train in a sports club (NIF/KKD, 2003).

There are large variations in ownership and operation of facilities across the country. About three-quarters of indoor multi-use facilities and swimming pools were owned by government (Lange, 2003a), and about 80% of indoor soccer and ice halls were owned by government (Lange, 2003b). As to outdoor facilities the sport organisations own approximately 70% of the flood-lit tracks and 50% of the football grounds (Sundbergutvalget, 2003). Facilities may be operated and maintained by local government, or they may be run by the sport clubs and organisations. In short, the role of local government is substantially that of a major facilitator while the operational and delivery functions of sport activity are mainly left to the voluntary sector.

To sum up, the Norwegian sport sector seems fairly similar to the German dual structure, insofar as the voluntary sector is clearly dominant. However, the rapidly increasing significance of people training on their own or in commercial training centres indicates that voluntary sport in Norway may face a greater challenge than Germany from the increasing individualisation and commercialisation of sport and recreational activity.

Cross-comparison of settings for sport and physical activity

Does the sport sector, in terms of national delivery structure and/or organised settings at an aggregate level, fit into the welfare regime classification outlined in Chapter 1? The empirical evidence so far points to a more nuanced picture, than does the simple model of welfare systems of Esping-Andersen (1990). It is true that the Canadian and English systems of delivery are different from those of Germany and Norway, but the major distinction is not market versus voluntary or state solutions. The main difference is that Canada and, more particularly, England have a much wider and diverse spectrum of settings for organised sport and physical activity than Germany and Norway where the voluntary sector has had a dominant role, even though it is increasingly challenged by the commercial fitness studios. Moreover, in England government has a more direct role in the organisation of sport than might have been expected. However, it should be emphasised that, previous observations notwithstanding, the main similarity is that in all the four countries the voluntary sector plays a significant role.

The simplest interpretation of this pattern may be that tradition plays an important part in shaping the structures of sport. In every country, the sport structures seem to change fairly slowly. Not only is the voluntary sector relatively stable, but the significance of other sectors, such as municipal provision, are also slow to change. However, this is not to say that the sector is static. The commercialisation of sport in terms of increased professionalism, expanding consumer sport equipment markets and the individualisation of leisure habits, for instance expressed by the 'bowling alone' metaphor (Putnam, 2000), seem gradually to be altering the sport and recreation structures and participation patterns across countries. However, the growth of the commercial sector does not imply that the other sectors are shrinking. It is rather a question of changes in activity shares and market growth being absorbed by the private sector, while the other traditional sectors broadly maintain their position or change only slowly.

Voluntary sport organisations and resources

The relative stability of sport structures may indicate that historical roots and institutional inertia are important in sports development. This seems also to be a correct observation as far as the voluntary sector is concerned. In all the four countries local voluntary units, sport clubs and the like organise and run sport activities while NSOs regulate their activities and organise competition, coaching and related activities within each specific sport at national and regional levels. Since the end of the nineteenth century these two types of organisations have had a central role in sports development. Even if the voluntary sector is of different size in the four countries it is still a core group of actors for organising and developing of sport activities.

Sport clubs

The local sport organisation, the club, league or similar, is the core unit for sport and recreation activities. Sport and recreation first and foremost takes place in the local community. A recently published survey identified 33,649 non-profit and voluntary organisations within the field of sport and recreation in Canada. Of these close to 24,000 were located in the neighbourhood, city, town or rural municipality Statistics Canada (2004a). A fairly large number operate also at regional and provincial levels, while there are only a relatively small number which are located at the national level. The English voluntary sector comprises the NGBs and their affiliated clubs, most of which are single sport non-profit community clubs. England has over 106,000 clubs with 8.2 million members giving a relatively low average membership of about 80. In 2004 there were 90,305 clubs registered by the state level German Sport Confederation (Deutscher Sportsbund, 2004). Having close to 23.6 million members, this gives an average club size of about 270, considerably higher than in England. A survey from 1992 showed that 35.2% of the clubs have 100 members or less, 34% have from 101 to 300 members and 5.5% have over 1,000 members. These large clubs accounted for almost 30% of total memberships. Most clubs, approximately two-thirds, offered only one sport discipline, reflecting a tendency identified by Heinemann and Schubert (1999) towards smaller, more specialised clubs with fewer members by comparison to the 1970s. In 2004 there were 7,633 voluntary clubs within the Norwegian Confederation of sport having approximately 1.65 million members. In addition, there were 4,542 clubs organised by employees with about 317,000 members (Statistics Norway, 2004). Most clubs are small: in 1998 54% of the clubs had fewer than 100 members and only 2.5% had 1,000 members or more. About one half of clubs offered only one sport (Enjolras and Seippel, 2001) and were part of a trend towards an increase in the number of specialist clubs (Skirstad, 2002).

As shown in Table 4.1, clubs and other local sport organisations are numerous in all countries. The density of clubs in relation to the size of the population is highest in England and Norway, lower in Germany and lowest in Canada.

Sport organisations: stability and change

The extent and nature of stability and change in the structure of sport organisations, their numbers and members/participants in different countries, tell us something about the dynamics of the sport sector.

Table 4.1   Local non-governmental and voluntary organisations within sport and recreation

Country	Approximate number of units	Approximate population (m)	Population per unit
Canada (2003)	24,000	30	1,250
England (2002)	106,000	50	470
Germany (2004)	90,000	80	900
Norway (2004)	7,600	4.5	600

Sources: Statistics Canada (2004a), Carter Report (2005), Deutscher Sportsbund (2004), Statistics Norway (2004).

Table 4.2 lists the five most popular sports in each country by club membership. The figures for England, Germany and Norway refer to recorded club memberships. Given the lack of equivalent data from Canada we have had to rely on self-reporting of club membership from a survey. The table seems to reflect sport traditions as well as upcoming sports in the various countries.

In all countries the top five sports account for over half of total memberships. In the first place we see that national sports particular to each country are present on the top five list in all countries: football, bowls and cricket in England; ice hockey in Canada; gymnastics in Germany and ski sports in Norway. Secondly, football, probably the most global sport of all is popular in all the countries. Golf, another sport increasing in global popularity, is also among the top five in three of the countries. Perhaps surprisingly, given its largely non-commercial status, the same is true for gymnastics, a traditional sport being modernised through the introduction of new disciplines.

The sports with the largest memberships are important in terms of resources and power and will often be among the richest as they usually generate interest from the media and commercial sponsors. As regards the structures of sport this table reinforces the importance of tradition, this time in relation to national sports. Ice hockey in Canada and ski sports in Norway for example, maintain a substantial stability in the national sport landscape. However, the picture is not static as new sports, in particular those becoming recognised as the most global, may gradually increase their popularity as football (soccer) has done in Canada and golf in Norway.

Table 4.2 The five most popular sports by club membership

	Top 5 sports	Share of total club membership (%)	Aggregate total for the top five sports (%)
Canada (Canadians aged 15 and older belonging to sport clubs/ community leagues, 1998)	Golf Ice hockey Baseball Swimming Football (soccer)	16.00 13.90 11.80 7.90 6.40	55.90
England (Members in sport clubs 2002)	Football Golf Gymnastics Bowls Cricket	30.50 10.80 10.10 7.20 5.40	64.00
Germany (Members in sport clubs 2004)	Football Gymnastics Tennis Shooting Track and field	25.10 20.30 7.10 6.10 3.50	62.10
Norway (Members in sport clubs 2003)	Football Ski Golf Handball Gymnastics	23.80 9.30 7.50 6.40 4.70	51.80

Sources: Sport Canada (1998), Carter Report (2005), Deutscher Sportbund (2004), Statistics Norway (2003).

As regards national sport federations the number and type vary between the four countries. The number is an indication of the diversity of a country's sport. Three of our countries have roughly the same number of NSOs recognised by central/ national level sport institutions. In Germany 55 sport federations are currently linked to the national umbrella organisation of sport, the German Sport Confederation, and in Norway the same number of sport organisations, 55, are linked to the Norwegian Olympic Committee and Confederation of Sports (NIF/NOC). In Canada there are 52 federations that are members of the Canadian Olympic Committee thus being either Olympic or Pan-American sports. There are also, in Canada, recognised organisations outside this group bringing the total number of NSOs close to 60. Most of these sport organisations are competing internationally, although there are also some special Canadian sports like ringette, where competition is overwhelmingly domestic.

In contrast to the other three countries in England there are some 100 and so recognised sports (Carter Report, 2005). However, under the Central Council of Physical Recreation (CCPR) umbrella there are close to 270 different national bodies many of which cover the same sport in different home countries. Of these approximately 170 are UK and English NGBs. However, it is not necessarily the case that there is a wider set of sport activities in England than in the other three countries. Indeed, having less of a winter sport tradition the opposite may well be the case. The larger number of NSOs in England suggests a larger plurality in the sport landscape indicating more specialised organisations. For example, there is a long tradition of gender-specific organisation, although a number of gender divided organisations, such as those for cricket, football, squash and hockey, have amalgamated since the early 1980s (White, 2003).

Pluralism at NSO level is also evident in Canada where, at the provincial level, there may be a number of different organisations not linked to NSOs recognised by the government. In the province of Alberta for example, more than 70 provincial sport organisations and about 30 recreation organisations are mentioned in the provincial government's records. Despite the comparatively low number of NSOs in Germany, sport clubs reported in a 1992 survey that they offered more than 240 different sport disciplines (Heinemann and Schubert, 1999) suggesting that new sports may be incorporated into the existing club structures and national organisations.

NSOs may be responsible for several different sports as is the case with gymnastics where new sports activities such as aerobics have developed and been incorporated within existing structures. The extent to which new sports are absorbed into an existing NSO or develop a separate organisation differs between countries and may be affected by the extent to which the grouping-related sports in one NSO was an established practice. Whether a sport discipline may be related to others in a common NSO, or not, vary among countries. For instance race walking has its own organisation in Norway, while in Canada it is included in Athletics Canada. In contrast, ski-jumping and cross-country skiing are both within the Norwegian Ski Federation, while they have separate organisations in Canada.

Sport is becoming more diverse in all the four countries. New sport activities, like blade sports, are emerging and older ones, like snowshoeing in Canada, may be experiencing a renaissance. In general, the number of new sport organisations is increasing over time as new sports are being created, established and institutionalised. Among the newcomers in Britain are the American Football Association formed in 1987 and the British Mountain Bike Federation of 1987 (Theodoraki, 1999). In Germany there are almost twice as many national sport federations today as in 1950. According to Klages (2002/2004) a differentiating process took place in the 1970s and 1980s with development of new sports within federations and also the establishment of new sport federations. New American sports arrived, like aerobics, baseball and American football and new clubs, leagues and associations were formed (Hardman and Naul, 2002). In Norway in the post-war period the number of federations in NIF/NOC has more than doubled, from 23 in 1946 through 33 in 1965 (Tønnesson, 1986) to 55 in 2004. Newer sport federations include kickboxing and snowboarding, American football, softball, baseball, triathlon, Frisbee and rugby.

Overall it seems that the pattern of NSOs is, to an extent, more diverse in Canada and England than in Germany and Norway, a fact that may be linked to the more pluralist political and social systems in these countries in general and, as will be discussed more fully below, a consequence of the stronger umbrella (confederation) structures in the latter mentioned countries resulting in new sports being more likely to be incorporated into existing sport organisations.

Perhaps most striking is the extent of change within the overall pattern of NSOs. However, the effect of the emergence of new sports and other sources of change on the structure of independent NSOs in each country is not clear-cut. On one hand, new and specialised organisations are being created. On the other hand, there are processes evident which lead to a simplification of structures for example, by the integration of disability sport into mainstream NSOs as is happening in Canada and Norway, or by the merger of former independent English organisations for women and men, or by linking fairly different types of sport in terms of skills into one common administrative structure as in Norway where bandy (a sport similar to football, but on ice), hockey (field hockey) and indoor bandy share a common organisation. Possibly, the consequences in the long term may be a more complex and pluralist picture in all countries at the NSO level with regard to the range of activities for which each NSO is responsible.

Resource inputs

Methodologically, to compare sectors across countries is always difficult because data are often collected differently and in

Table 4.3 Civil sector, recreation and culture

	Canada (2003)	UK (1995)	Germany (1995)	Norway (1997)
Civil sector – in total				
Expenditures as a proportion of gross domestic product	6.7	6.8	4.0	3.7
Civil society sector – employment as a proportion of economically active population	8.9	5.0	3.6	3.0
Volunteers as a proportion of economically active population	3.2	5.6	3.0	5.1
Recreation and culture				
Recreation and culture – volunteers as a proportion of total civil society sector	23	21	33	51
Recreation and culture – expenditure as a proportion of gross domestic product	0.7	1.0	0.4	0.7
Recreation and culture – employment as a proportion of economically active population	0.8	1.2	0.2	0.4
Recreation and culture – volunteers as a proportion of economically active population	0.7	1.2	1.0	2.6

Source: John Hopkins University (2006). The comparative non-profit sector project. www.jhu.edu.[2]

diverse settings. The John Hopkins University civil society project tries to overcome some of the problems by adopting a common methodology, which makes it possible to compare across countries. Unfortunately, the statistics published do not treat sport and recreation as a distinct sector, but combine it with culture. The figures presented in Table 4.3 must therefore be discussed in conjunction with other empirical evidence in order to identify the particularities of the sport and recreation sector. It should also be noted that the data are from different years.

The civil sector's position in the national economy in general, and the position of recreation and culture in particular, are presented in Table 4.3 above. We see that there are a number of significant differences between the countries. First, the civil sectors in the UK and Canada are more integrated into the formal economy as compared to Germany and Norway as indicated by the civil sector representing a larger share of GDP and employment in the former two countries than in the latter. This comparative pattern is more evident within the recreation and culture sector. Again regarding the UK, the sector is, to a larger degree, integrated in the formal economy, whereas the sector in Germany is least integrated. Norway and Canada are in between, but recreation and culture in Norway differs from Canada by being less reliant on salaried staff.

In all the four countries recreation and culture are the largest voluntary sector, particularly in Norway, where it comprises more than half the voluntary sector, and in Germany, where it accounts for one-third of all voluntary activity. In Canada and the UK the proportions range between one-quarter and one-fifth of total voluntary activity. The greater reliance on volunteer resources as opposed to employed people in Norway and Germany than in Canada and UK is clearly demonstrated by the last two lines of the table. The figures show that in the two former countries the volunteer share of aggregate (employed and volunteer) human resources is much higher than in the latter two.

To get a clearer idea of the specific situation of sport and recreation in each country, we will have to examine data specific to the sport and recreation sector of each country. Starting with Canada, sport and recreation organisations have a strong volunteer base, even if some organisations do also rely on employed resources Statistics Canada (2004a). It is estimated that 5.3 million people are volunteering in sport and recreation organisations representing more than one-quarter of all volunteering. Of the sport and recreation organisations 27% had paid staff. Bearing in mind that 90% of sport and recreation organisations are local and regional, while the rest are located at provincial and national levels, and assuming that most of the latter have salaried staff, it might be reasonable to suggest that about one-fifth of the clubs and other organisations at local/regional levels also employ salaried staff. Organisations in sport and recreation are estimated to employ about 131,000 staff (Statistics Canada, 2004a). On the basis of estimates of volunteer hours worked in sport and recreation organisations the contribution of paid staff can be roughly estimated as equal to half that of the volunteers.

In England more than 26% of all formal volunteering take place in sport and recreation organisations (Nichols, 2003). The figure for frequent volunteering in sport was estimated at 4% of the adult population in 2003 compared to 3% in the arts (Fox and Richards, 2004). For England it is estimated that close to 15% of the adult (aged 16+) population volunteered in sport in 2002. However, England, probably more than most countries, also uses employed people in voluntary sport organisations. It has a long tradition of employing people in work, such as sport development and coaching. These professions can be found both in the government sector, in local/regional governing bodies and in the club sector. Total employment in the English voluntary sport organisations was estimated at about 37,900 employees in 2000 (Cambridge Econometrics, 2003). Formal volunteers in sport and recreation within the UK sport organ- isation structures (clubs, events and competitions/leagues) was, in 1996, estimated to be equivalent of about 100,000 person years (Nichols, 2003).

In Germany most clubs were managed by volunteers in the early 1990s. Heinemann and Schubert (1999) estimated that vol- untary work accounted for 4–5 times the financial contribution of the members. They argue that salaried work is of less import- ance and estimated that, for the whole of Germany, there were approximately 6,000 employees, mainly part-time, working in sport clubs in administration, coaching or facility maintenance roles. However, according to Pitsch and Emrich (2000) close to half of all German clubs rely, to some extent, on paid work.

In Norway the sport sector is the largest volunteer sector with about 27% of all membership in voluntary organisations in 1998 (Wollebæk et al., 2000). Volunteer work is a very important resource in Norwegian sport. According to survey data in 2002 70% of sport clubs based their activity exclusively on voluntary work, and in another 19% of clubs from 90% to 99% of the work was undertaken by volunteers. Despite the significance of vol- untary work 24% of clubs reported that they had employed staff in the previous year. In total it is estimated that voluntary work contributes eight times that of the salaried staff to the delivery of club services (Enjolras et al., 2005).

To conclude, it is clear that volunteer-based recreation and cultural activities represent a significant part of the national economy in general and the civil sector in particular. The coun- tries differ though, within the recreation and culture sector, with Germany and Norway being more heavily reliant on vol- unteer resources than Canada and England who use relatively more salaried staff. Country-specific information for sport and recreation in particular seems to indicate that the differences

Table 4.4 Sources of income for culture and recreation (%)

	Canada (2003)	UK (1995)	Germany (1995)	Norway (1997)
Government	18	14	20	29
Philantrophy	19	2	13	13
Fees	63	84	66	58
	100	100	99	100

Source: John Hopkins University (2006). The comparative non-profit sector project. www.jhu.edu.[3]

reported for the recreation and culture sector are equally valid for the sport and recreation sub-sector. This pattern may be interpreted as part of an overall picture where the civil sector in Germany and Norway is less integrated into the formal economy than in Canada and England.

Revenue structures

The John Hopkins University civil society studies also contain data on revenue structures, but again with the limitation that recreation and culture are combined. It is therefore necessary to supplement the John Hopkins data with data that relate specifically to sport and recreation.

As indicated in Table 4.4 there are some sharp differences between the countries. The fee component includes membership dues, service charges, investment income, and income from the sale of goods and services. In UK the fee component of revenue is 84% which is significantly higher than in the other countries where the share is between 58% and 66%. In all countries, the recreation and culture sector receives a substantial share of its income from government: Norway ranks highest with 29% and UK lowest with 14% with Canada and Germany having 18% and 20%, respectively.

Data for all types of sport and recreation organisations (i.e. excluding cultural organisations) in Canada indicate a relatively mixed financing structure. Membership fees account for 25% of revenues and commercial activities are estimated to contribute 40%, most of it in charges for goods and services (Statistics Canada, 2004a). A local Canadian club may, for example, sell

Christmas cards and Christmas trees, and organise bingo to finance its activities. Government support accounts, on average, for 12% of revenues while gifts and donations account for a further 20%. Self-financing (e.g. membership and user fees and income-creating activities) thus accounts for about two-thirds of the sport and recreation sector's revenue budget.

Recent aggregate revenue estimates for England indicate an even stronger reliance on self-financing activities (Carter Report, 2005) than UK data for recreation and culture in the mid-1990s. Membership fees account for 37% and commercial activities for 53% of revenues for the sport sector as a whole, whereas government financing represent only 9%. The club bar is an established institution within English sport with the lion's share of commercial revenues being derived from the sale of food and beverages.

In Germany, data from the early 1990s indicated that self-financing accounts for about 80% of club income. Membership fees represent 55% of income and 25% is commercial income from selling goods and services to non-members as well as to members. Direct government support was estimated at 11% and donations at 7% (Heinemann and Schubert, 1999). In Norway, survey data from 2000 show that sport clubs generate 84% of their income with membership fees accounting for 29% and commercial activities for the remaining 55%. In Norway raffles, bingo and other income creating activities have strong traditions and accounted for close to half of the commercial income. Gifts and donations and direct revenue from government both contribute 7% (Enjolras and Seippel, 2001).

Not surprisingly, sports organisations operating at the national and provincial levels receive more substantial government support. Sport organisations at national and provincial/*länder* levels may get support to work on competitive/elite level sport, as well as for their co-ordinating functions towards local level units. One Alberta provincial sport organisation reported that it got 42% of its funding from government and another provincial level organisation reported that government funding accounted for 30% of its income while a NSO indicated it received 60% of its funding from federal government. A representative from Sport Canada observed that, in total, money from federal government to NSOs represented approximately one-third of their income. The Carter Report (2005) noted that government funding accounted for 30–50% of the income of English NGBs apart from the largest bodies that were mostly financed by sponsorships and the commercial activity. According to a representative from the German Ministry of Interior NSOs that receive support get between 40% and 70% of their total income from public funds. However, wealthy sport organisations like football and tennis do not receive any government funding. In Norway as well the sport organisations' dependency on public funds varies considerably. According to Enjolras (2004) almost one-third of the NSOs receive 70% or more of their funding from lottery money transferred by the national sport confederation. On the other hand, about one-third receives 30% or less from lottery, and are mainly financed by commercial income.

Summing up, the empirical evidence on the distribution of revenues seems to reflect country-specific differences. On average, voluntary sport organisations receive approximately 7–12% of their revenues direct from government, but are substantially self-financing with between two-thirds and 90% of their activity funded by membership fees and income generating activities.

Comparison of voluntary sport structures

The evidence presented indicates that there are differences as well as similarities between voluntary sport in different countries. First, even though it is difficult to make exact comparisons with regard to the size of the voluntary sport sector (club members/ sport club participants), it seems reasonable to suggest that the sector is considerably larger in relation to population size in Norway and Germany than in Canada and the UK. Despite the substantial contribution by volunteers in the UK the contribution is probably the smallest of the four countries when total population size is taken into account. Secondly, the Canadian and English sports sectors are more diverse than those in Germany and Norway with regard to the number of different sport and recreation organisations. However, it should be noted that in both Germany and Norway new organisations are being established as a consequence of the emergence of new sport activities. Third, in all countries sport and recreation is the largest voluntary sector, and it makes extensive use of voluntary resources. The Norwegian and German voluntary sectors seem to be dependent on voluntary resources to the greatest extent and voluntary sport seems less integrated into the formal wage-based economy than in Canada and England. Fourth, as to revenue structures in all countries, voluntary sport relies for the bulk of its funds on membership fees and the sale of goods and services. Government support accounts, very roughly, for approximately one-tenth of the clubs' income budget in all the four countries, although government support is more important for the revenue budget of national level sport organisations in all countries.

Basis for voluntary sport co-ordination and interests

The key question in this section concerns the extent to which there are significant differences in the ways that voluntary sport is organised and promotes its collective interests. As we shall see each country has its particularities. Three issues that may be useful to explore are: (i) the core principles and units of co-ordination of general sport interests, (ii) the locus of power of voluntary sport and (iii) voluntary sport legitimacy. The first issue deals with the overall structure for participation in the development and implementation of sport policy. The second issue is a complex one and our focus is limited to a discussion of the units/levels of the voluntary sport system where power is located in terms of resources and relationships. The third issue examines an important basis for interest group policy, namely the arguments that are put forward to the public to justify the importance of voluntary sport.

Canada

Canada, in area the second largest country in the world, has about 30 million inhabitants, distributed over a vast area. The geography and the fact that it is a federal state strongly impacted on the organisation of voluntary sport.

In Canada there is no single national sport body responsible for co-ordinating the multiplicity of sub-national voluntary sport organisations, nor is there a national organisation representing the interests of NSOs. Canada has though other types of national umbrella organisations with specific concerns, some with linkages to provincial levels (Hall, 2003). It may possibly be argued that the main mechanism for horizontal national co-ordination of the Canadian sport system is through different types of multi-sport functional organisations. First, there are national games organisations such as the National Olympic Committee, Canada Games, the Commonwealth Games Organisation of Canada, the Paralympic Association of Canada, the Artic Winter Games International Committee (based in Canada, but also involving people from other countries). Looking at the overall structures, in Canada and UK, the Olympic Committee is a unit generally independent from other organisations within the sport system although in Canada the Olympic Committee is also responsible for Pan-American sports. Secondly, there are multi-sport/service organisations (MSOs) which include the Coaching Association, and the Aboriginal Sport Circle. The national sports federations like Athletics Canada and Ski Canada operate in parallel to the MSOs rather than being integrated within them.

In general, the sport system consists of a multiplicity of organisations each responsible for different functions and crossing different jurisdictional boundaries, but with weak co-ordinating mechanisms for voluntary sport as a whole. An exception is the Olympic Committee which has significant financial resources and some co-ordinating powers with regard to Olympic and Pan-American sports. Another modest exception is the Calgary Olympic Development Association (CODA) which supports winter sports with legacy funds from the 1988 Olympic Games.

The national level sport organisations are, to a large extent, focussed on high performance although they may be concerned with other tasks as well, encouraged by government funding, such as sport for people with disabilities and for women. Recently, sport organisations have been encouraged by modest amounts of 'pump-priming' funding from government to direct their efforts at the participation side (see Chapter 7 on *sport for all*), but that is not where their main focus is. As expressed by one interviewee: '*The difficulty is that the NSOs and the multi-sport federations want to develop athletes to enter them in national and international competitions. They are interested in grassroot development only as a form of recruitment and development*'. Most NSOs are volunteer based and depend on resources from national government and MSOs like the Olympic committee, and thus their focus is maintained on international excellence.

Canada is a federal state and recreation and culture are under provincial jurisdiction. The NSOs have units at the provincial level which receive support from the provincial government. Most of the major Canadian sport organisations depend on the provincial club structure to establish a pathway for coaching and competition to attain high performance levels (Green and Houlihan, 2005). For probably most of them, like Athletics Canada, it is the provincial organisations that have the strongest links to clubs and individual members. The relationship and division of labour between the NSO and the provincial organisations within a sport is not necessarily clearly defined. According to one interviewee most sport organisations have not been able to define these responsibilities precisely to create a clear elite development pathway.

Provincial level organisations may work at all levels of the sport development pyramid, from grassroots and recreation activities up to high performance. Referring to two provincial sport organisations in Alberta, athletics and swimming, it seems that they distinguish fairly clearly between talent development and competitive sport and other activities. Both organisations have a fairly clear focus at the competitive end, even though they also have broader activities like running participation programmes. The organisations distinguish clearly between the full members and the people that they reach with broader offers of sport and recreation activity. For instance, Swimming Alberta reports that it has about 9,000 members, whereas more than four times that number participates in its summer swimming programme. Athletics Canada nationally has about 10,000 members, but if children participating in Athletics Canada-organised activities were included the likely number would reach 250,000.

The impression is thus that many sport organisations, even at provincial level, are largely competitively and talent development oriented. However, there is some variation with, for example, a team sport like football having a fairly broad base of participation and being very popular among children. Similarly, there are also a number of provincial organisations/programmes engaged in recreation and heavily involved at the low end of the performance pyramid, such as KidSport Alberta and Alberta 55 Plus. In addition, school sport competitions which are organised at different age and ability levels operate in parallel to, but distinct from, those activities within the sport voluntary sector.

Provincial sport organisations largely run their activities independently of the national organisation, except for their involvement in elite development programmes. For example, coaching programmes are mainly organised at the provincial/ regional and local levels with support from public, private and voluntary sources. This pattern of voluntary organisation from the national level and downward to the local level indicates a diverse landscape with overlapping responsibilities, a geographical differentiation along federal structures, and a limited degree of co-ordination (see Figure 4.2).

To compensate for the lack of a co-ordinated formal voice for voluntary sport a group of individual sport leaders recently formed an informal network called 'Sport Matters Group' as an advocacy group acting on behalf of sport. It has developed a broad network of contacts within the Canadian sport sector and refers to itself as a voluntary group of national and provincial sport leaders. It involves over 90 organisations and sport leaders actively involved in public policy issues regarding sport and physical activity.

At provincial levels the patterns of organisation and co-ordination are more varied. In some provinces, like in British Colombia, voluntary sport has a longer history and is better organised than in provinces, such as Alberta. In British Columbia a voluntary umbrella service and advocacy organisation of sport has existed for four decades whereas in Alberta an advocacy organisation for sport was revived as recently as 2004. This

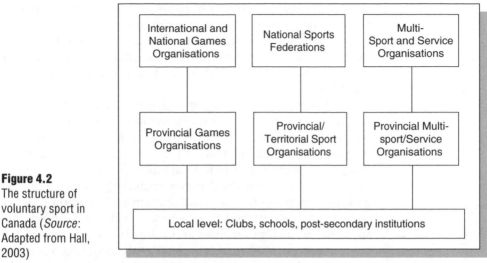

Figure 4.2
The structure of voluntary sport in Canada (*Source*: Adapted from Hall, 2003)

organisation existed 15 years previously as a lobby group, but was incorporated into government as a 'sport council'. A similar need to establish a voice for sport at the local level resulted in the establishment of Edmonton City Sport Council some years ago. A stronger advocacy role is fulfilled by Alberta Recreation and Parks Association, a provincial unit of a long established national organisation. It defines itself as a voluntary body even if it has many municipal members in addition to individuals being concerned with development and recreation in Alberta.

To sum up, the main organisational principle of Canadian voluntary sport appears to be structural differentiation. The voluntary sport sector is structured along several dimensions including function and geography. First, there is considerable diversity in terms of the many national and provincial organisations concerned with sport and recreation. Secondly, provincial organisations seem to operate relatively independent of the national units to which they are affiliated. Third, except for the Olympic Committee, there are no strong overarching structures co-ordinating all activities of voluntary sport, there are only relatively loosely linked advocacy bodies.

As a consequence of this diverse system, it is not possible to talk of one national locus for power of voluntary sport. Possibly, it may be said that there are differentiated networks of influence, represented by voluntary network organisations of different kinds. The sport community does take lobbying initiatives and this occurs within different arenas. The Olympic Committee recently engaged in lobbying of the federal government primarily because it wanted better co-ordination of the resources from different funding partners to enhance elite athlete development. The Committee also campaigned, but not quite so forcefully, for an increase in funding for mass sport arguing that mass participation in sport was important whether or not it had the potential to benefit elite sport.

The 'Sport Matters' group is active in lobbying. In a recent Pre-Budget Consultation Brief (Sport Matters Group, 2006) to the Minister of Finance the group argued for increased federal support to sport and recreation broadly defined. It argued for (i) an increase of long-term federal funding of 1% of total health care spending, (ii) for fiscal policy, including tax policy measures, to be used to increase participation and to promote sport and physical activity and (iii) for long-term federal funding for sport and recreation facilities and infrastructure. It argued for 'the achievement of broader societal goals including a healthy economy and a healthy population', and it claimed that 'arguably more significant is the contribution that sport makes to defining our national character and to generating national pride'. As far as the broader social objective is concerned, a number of issues are mentioned including obesity, chronic diseases, crime, and linguistic, religious and cultural barriers. The recently established Sport Alberta, at provincial level, adopts a broad approach for sports advocacy stressing excellence as well as participation.

This lack of overall co-ordination in voluntary sport organisations leads to a relatively strong role for government units, provincially as well as nationally. It is government units like Sport Canada at national level and at provincial government organisations like Alberta Sport, Recreation, Parks & Wildlife Foundation that take the lead in co-ordination of sport. Governments have thus tended to lead processes related to development of overall sport policies.

England

It is not easy to make an 'understandable' map of how voluntary sport is organised in England. At the national level there are three types of core actors: (i) The NSOs and the NGBs, (ii) Central Council of Physical Recreation (CCPR), and (iii) the British Olympic Association (BOA). At sub-national levels there are Regional Federations of Sport, local voluntary organisations, and of course local sport clubs.

In many sports each home country has a NGB of their own responsible for their sport although in some sports the organisation is at UK level. The NGBs are concerned with competitive sport at international and national levels, but they are also concerned with grassroots sport. An example of this broad approach is the national ice-hockey organisation which organises a national team, a professional league and amateur leagues for men, women and youth. Another example is of course the Football Association, the largest organisation of them all with 1 million members and which has an elaborate infrastructure at regional, county and local/district levels. Different NSOs may be organised with different geographical boundaries that do not necessarily match the official government regional structure. English NSOs are probably much more integrated in relation to their geographical sub-units and clubs and have generally greater responsibility for and influence over the whole sports continuum than do their Canadian counterparts.

The main voluntary-based, integrating unit of sport in England is the CCPR which is an umbrella organisation covering all the UK. The membership associations are NGBs or representative bodies with a supportive role in sport and recreation. The member organisations are very diverse and distributed across six different divisions: (i) the Games & Sports Division, (ii) Division of Interested Organisations, (iii) Major Spectator Sports Division, (iv) Movement & Dance Division, (v) Outdoor Pursuits Division and (vi) Water Recreation Division. There are also regional federations of sport which comprise the regional and county governing bodies and any district and local sports councils within the region.

The CCPR was a key organisation in the 'successful application of pressure of the sport lobby' for government involvement in sport from the 1960s. According to Houlihan and White (2002, p. 18) 'By the early 1960s the CCPR, partly funded by a government grant, had established itself as the primary advocate on behalf of sport'. The CCPR's principal task 'is the co-ordination and representation of the members interest within the relevant national and regional sports policy forum' (Digel, Burk and Sloboda, 2003), that is, they act as an interest group mainly on *sport for all* questions. Having as members a very broad range of organisations including elite-oriented governing bodies and spectator sports, it covers *sport for all* in its widest sense though, meaning all kind of sport and recreation. The organisation has, however, nothing to do with organising and running the actual sporting activity. It is an advocacy organisation without direct operational functions and much of the advocacy work of the Council is cross-divisional.

The role of the CCPR is directed at general issues such as sport funding, and the legal and business environment. Tax alleviation for income-creating activities is one area where it claims to have had success. In the 'Challenge for the next Government' (CCPR, 2004), launched in November 2004 the CCPR called for a doubling of Exchequer funding for sports and recreation. In a document titled the Red Book (CCPR, 2005) sent out in March 2005, the benefits of sport for society were broadly outlined. Addressing different ministries of Government the organisation promoted many advantages of sport including winning medals, improving school attainment, tackling obesity and osteoporosis, and tackling crime.

The BOA is the major non-government cross-discipline organisation with funding and operational influence across sport disciplines, and it is one of the few Olympic Committees that does not receive significant finance from government. The BOA, of course, is particularly concerned with Olympic sports and their medal-winning potential and would have direct access to government on many issues.

To conclude, there is a certain degree of co-ordination of sport in England. The main principle seems to be a dual division of labour between *sport for all*, broadly defined, and elite sport with these responsibilities divided between two main actors: the CCPR and the BOA. The CCPR is a lobbying umbrella organisation formally representing most of sport organisations in England and UK. Even if its powers are limited by its broad and diversified membership base, it has a solid historic claim to be 'the voice of sport' in the UK. The BOA, being financially independent of the government, has influence regarding elite sport especially since the award of the 2012 Olympic Games to London.

As was the case with Canada it is difficult to talk about a national and common locus of power for voluntary sport: the CCPR and the BOA are *dual loci of influence*, though. In terms of broad operational co-ordination of sport activity and funding, these two organisations are not core actors as most responsibilities and economic resources rest firmly at the government level. However, as the analysis in *Game Plan* (DCMS/Strategy Unit, 2002) makes clear the structure of sport is complex in England. Key organisations involved in sport are a mixture of quasi- and sub-government organisations like Sport England, UK Sport, Regional Sport Boards, Local Authorities, Higher Education Institutions, etc. on the one hand and voluntary/private sector bodies, like NGBs, regional, county and local level NGBs, voluntary and commercial clubs, etc. on the other. It can be argued though that power lies substantially in the hands of government institutions due to their control over funding through agencies, such as Sport England for mass participation sport and UK Sport for high performance and, particularly, Olympic sports.

Germany

The basic structure of the sector was shaped by the organisation of sport after the Second World War. In 1950, an umbrella organisation for sport in West Germany was established, the German Sports Confederation (*Deutscher Sportbund*). Before the war there had been different pillars of sport, for example, for Jews, Christians and workers. This new sport organisation was a unitary organisation covering all groups and aspects of amateur sport with the exception of the National Olympic Committee which worked independently of the German Sport Confederation. However, in May 2006, the Olympic Committee and the German Sport Confederation merged into one organisation, the *Deutscher Olympischer Sportbund* (Figure 4.3).

The following description is based on the organisational structures before this merger, and does not investigate the motives for the amalgamation.[4]

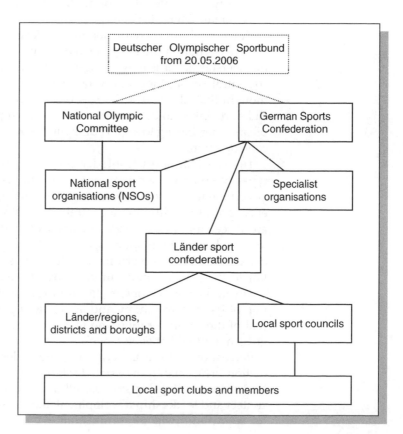

Figure 4.3
The organisation of sport in Germany

Voluntary sport as it is constructed under the German Sport Confederation is an integrated system with two main pillars. First, there are 55 national sport federations with particular responsibility for elite level and, to varying degrees, responsibility for sport participation. Second, there are 16 regional sports associations attached to the different states (*länder*). Both sets of organisations have units at lower geographical levels and these lower level units may be in contact with the government units at their own level. Of particular importance are the local sports councils which co-ordinate sport interests within a community / district or similar.

In addition to the two main pillars, there are other federations with particular responsibilities for organising sport for specific groups such as university students, police, postal workers, YMCA members, Catholics, and Jews, or for specific sports interests such as akidio and motor-sport. Moreover, there are six different organisations for education and science like the Association for Physical Education Teachers and German Association for Sport Science. Finally, there are two promotional organisations, the Foundation for Safety on Skiing and the German Olympic Society.

However, the clubs with their individual members are the basic units of German sport and given the number of clubs and the high membership level it may be argued that German sport is, in a structural sense, thoroughly organised. That does not mean, though, that all sport activity is co-ordinated from above. The clubs are linked to the superstructure by being members of both pillars. They belong to a sport discipline as well as to a *länder* level confederation.

The German Sport Confederation has responsibility for all types of sport in Germany and it maintains contact with the government at federal (*Bund*) level, in particular in the area of elite sport. In addition to a central administrative section there are three operational departments within the Confederation responsible for elite sport, *sport for all* and youth sport. Each department has a governing structure of its own, but they are linked by a board and administrative leadership structure at the overall level. As for German youth sport, it has an organisation of its own which, by and large, has a parallel structure to that of the Confederation and to that found within the federal government and at *länder* level.

Recreation, culture and education are under the länders' jurisdiction. The *land* sport confederations have correspondingly lead responsibility for *sport for all* in a broad sense, for youth contact and leadership development, the physical infrastructure for sport, and general administrative issues, and not least for contact and partnership with the *land* level governments. The *Länder* Confederations cover all forms of sport within their area, *sport for all*, youth sport, competitive sport and, in co-operation with the German Sport Confederation and the NSOs, also for elite sport/talent development. They are regional umbrella organisations, some of which have extensive resources because the main responsibility for sport participation/*sport for all* is located at the *land* level.

The NSOs have the main responsibilities within their sport and, as the membership numbers indicate, they have a broad membership base in their affiliated clubs. The balance between elite sport and mass sport at the national level differs between the federations. For instance, the national gymnastic organisation reports that it is more mass oriented than elite oriented while the table tennis organisation states that its main focus is the elite level, but that it is also concerned with recruitment and participation issues. The national sport federations have regional sub-units spread among the *länder*, but they do not always map on to the official structures. There are linkages between the national organisation and the regional/*land*-level organisations not only in terms of democratic and governing relations, but also in terms of activities and programmes. These sub-units may get support from the *länder* level sport confederations.

A number of interviewees observed that the German structure of sport was complex; 'Even the Germans have problems to understand it' was one typical comment. The main principles of co-ordination are a unified system, based on subsidiarity. These principles are clearly demonstrated as far as structures are concerned, and are even more pronounced now that the Olympic Committee has also joined the unified system. *Einheit in der Vielfalt*, in English 'Unity in Diversity', is the vision for German sport agreed at the end of 2000 by the convention of the DSB.

In line with its historic tradition of empowerment of people, social integration and solidarity are identified as the basis for sport alongside the narrower concerns of *sport for all* and high performance sport. These values were endorsed in the subsequent policy statement, *Sportpolitische Konzeption des Deutschen Sportbundes*, of 2003 where the significance of sport was linked to a number of social issues, such as the development of social capital and citizenship, health improvement, meeting the social and development needs of different target groups including children, older people and families, which moved beyond those linked to sport development in its narrow sense.

It can be argued that there is a dual locus of power in German sport – one at the federal level and the other at the level of the *länder*. First, with regard to elite sport, the power was divided between the DSB central unit and the Olympic Committee. It may be assumed that in the future power will be concentrated at the core of the new confederation, the *Deutscher Olympischer Sportbund*. Secondly, with regard to *sport for all*, the picture is more complex. The *sport for all* division of former DSB has a major responsibility to promote the idea of *sport for all* as will be discussed in Chapter 7. However, most resources (personnel) and funding power (lottery money) are at the *länder* level with the *länder* confederations whose major responsibility is for mass participation although they do have some concern with talent identification and elite sport development at *länder* level. The second location of power within the voluntary sport system can thus be claimed to be placed at the *länder* sport confederations. As to the relationship of the sport sector to different levels of government there are in fact matching loci of power on the government side, represented by the Ministry of Interior for elite sport, and by *land* governments for sport and recreation in its wider sense.

Norway

The organisation of Norwegian sport has a number of similarities to the post-war West German model. It is unitary at the overall national level, and it comprises two pillars with area-based regional and local organisations on the one hand and the NSOs on the other (see Figure 4.4).

The larger federations among the 55 national sport federations have sub-units at county level or at regional level. The national confederation (NIF/NOC) comprises three main service departments: for top sport; children, youth and mass sport; and for social issues and relations with county level organisations. NIF/NOC retains lead responsibility for contact with the national government.

The overall vision of the united sport organisation is summarised in its sport policy document (NIF/NOC, 2003) for the period 2003–2007 where the promotion of *sport for all* is declared as the overall mission. A particular vision is expressed for children and youth incorporating the values of inclusion, pleasure and ability in line with personal wants. The concrete objectives stated in the policy document are to get more youth into sport, to increase the number of people actively involved in sport clubs, to strengthen voluntary efforts in sport clubs and to improve top level results. A new sport policy document is planned, for which the Sports Board has given preliminary priority to health challenges, enhancing quality in children and youth sport,

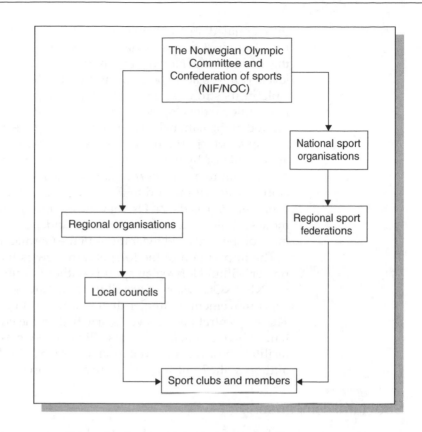

Figure 4.4
The structure of
Norwegian sport

financing of sport, and a stronger focus on promoting physical activity and the associated infrastructure.

The NSOs are concerned with regulation and facilitation of activity within their sports, coaching, sport education, sport policy and elite sport. They have a broad membership base at the club level and are concerned with both mass and elite sport. Many of the them have sub-units at county or a higher aggregate regional level. County level organisations have responsibility for common *sport for all* issues such as organisation (club) development, competence development, local sport policy and local government contact. In comparison to the German *länder* the county level organisations operate with very modest resources. In most municipalities there are local sport councils where the local sport clubs are represented.

The main co-ordinating principle of Norwegian sport is one of unity and geographical differentiation. The system is similar, but not identical to the German system. It is similar in having one co-ordinating unit at the national level, in principle covering all forms of sport: it is different in terms of the way that geographical sub-structures are handled where a geographically differentiated structure with several tiers may be practical in many national voluntary organisations. It is debatable whether the overarching Norwegian sport structures at sub-national levels can be said to be characterised by the subsidiarity principle in its stronger sense. To a large degree policy measures like strategic developments and funding principles are firmly located at the national level. For example, government funding for top sport, sport federations and regional sport associations are negotiated by the central sport confederation. Even though Norwegian regional sport organisations have the same democratic rights with regard to the governing of the national sport confederation as the NSOs, they are operating on a much more modest scale in terms of resources and power compared to most of the *land* level federations in the German *länder*.

The implication of the foregoing review is that the locus of power within Norwegian sport is without doubt found within the NIF/NOC system. Overall the structure of the Norwegian sport movement is simpler than that found in other countries. This concentration of power is matched by the government system, where the major responsibility for policies, funding and facilitation of mass as well as elite sport is also located in one authority, the Ministry of Culture and Church Affairs.

Structural comparisons

In Table 4.5 we sum up the main characteristics of the organisation of sport in the four countries.

We see that despite some similarities the co-ordinating systems of sport are substantially different. The main differences

Table 4.5 Summary of the organisation of voluntary sport organisations and the role of government

Characteristics	Canada	England	Germany	Norway
Co-ordinating principles of voluntary sport	Functional and geographical differentiation	Dual division of labour between top sport and *sport for all*	United system	United system
Locus of influence within voluntary sport	Differentiated networks of influence	Dual institutions of influence	Dual levels of influence	One centre of influence

concern the character of the formal co-ordinating structures within the voluntary sport sector. The countries could possibly be ranked as follows along the dimension unity versus diversity of voluntary power: (i) Norway, (ii) Germany, (iii) England and (iv) Canada. Further examination of the distribution of power within the sports sector is provided in the following chapter which explores policy structures and values.

Summary discussion

The primary focus of this chapter has been to provide an analysis and comparison of the structures of sports organisations and the organisation of sport activities. However, it is readily acknowledged that an understanding of the dynamics of sport policy requires that the analysis of the structure and operation of sports organisations is complemented by an analysis of public policy for sport and the role of public sector organisations. The analysis of public policy and the role of the public sector will be undertaken in the subsequent chapters and consequently the data and comparisons presented here cover only some of the theoretical perspectives and dimensions discussed in previous chapters.

One point of departure for our comparative study has been expectations based on the Esping-Andersen typology of welfare regimes (see Chapter 1). In liberal welfare regimes like Canada and England we should expect commercial interests to play a central role and government involvement to be relatively limited. In a conservative welfare regime, like that found in Germany, one would expect voluntary associations to dominate, and finally the state should play a major role in a social democratic regime such as Norway. However, the picture we have painted of sport clearly indicates that we have to modify these general expectations.

As we have pointed out earlier in Chapter 3 developments in the sport sector should be related to the deeply rooted driving forces that permeate domestic processes, that is globalisation, commercialisation, politicisation and governmentalisation. As we have seen in the case of England government plays a more central role in the organisation of sport activities than we would expect in a liberal welfare regime. In Norway, by contrast, the organisation of sport activities is left substantially to voluntary sport organisations. The Norwegian government has an important role, but perhaps a role that is somewhat different from what one would expect in a social democratic welfare regime as government is not directly involved with the organisation of activities. In Norway, as in Germany, government is more of a facilitator than a service deliverer and thus plays an important role as a provider of funding. With regard to commercialisation of sport, we do see such tendencies, but in all the four countries, including Canada, voluntary/not-for-profit associations still play a major role even though they are challenged by the professionalisation of some sports and the expanding commercial sector, especially fitness centres for individual training.

The structure of sports organisations may be related to variations in state structures as discussed in Chapter 2. We have selected two unitary and two federal states for our study. In general, the unitary UK/England and federal Germany were considered to be relatively centralised while federal Canada and unitary Norway in particular were considered to be more decentralised. To some degree sport organisations reflect these characteristics. Sport organisations on the provincial/*länder* level in Canada and Germany play a stronger role than meso/county level organisations in England and Norway. However, we find unified sport organisations in both the federal Germany and in unitary Norway. In contrast we find rather fragmented sport organisations not only in the federal case of Canada, but also in the unitary case of UK/England.

These findings seem to be more in line with our expectations with regard to types of government system and concentrations of public and private power as discussed in Chapter 2. We expected power relations in Norway and Germany to be characterised by relatively high degrees of concentration of power (and corporatism), while Canada and England were expected to be more pluralist with higher degrees of dispersion of power. No doubt, sport in Canada and England *is* more pluralist/fragmented than sport in Germany and Norway. We have, however, seen that the unitary sport sectors in the latter countries have become more heterogeneous as new sports have developed. Sports organisations have become more specialised and supplemented by commercial or semi-commercial actors outside the traditional 'voluntary sport movement'. In other words, Germany and Norway seem to be moving in a more pluralist direction, a move that may be related to pressures arising from trends in globalisation.

Finally, we have noted some expressions of the expected tendency towards generalisation of the interests of sport. Sport in Canada and England seems to be somewhat more competitive and elite oriented than in Germany and Norway, but in all countries the importance of *sport for all* and possible effects with regard to health, social inclusion etc. are emphasised. References to more general societal concerns – and not only to the intrinsic value and self-interest of sport – seem to broaden the appeal and thus to enhance government support for sport.

Notes

1 The statistics are published at http://www.dssv.de/index1. php?hm=J&m=1 Ekcdaten 2005 – die offiziellen Daten über den deutschen Fitnessmarkt im Jahr 2005

2 The data is presented at the web-site (http://www.jhu.edu/ %7Ecnp/country.html), July 1st 2006, under the heading 'Findings by Country', in a table named Workforce, expenditures and revenue data.

3 See preceding footnote.

4 Our study is based on data collected before the merger. However, the lower level organisations were not directly affected by the merger.

CHAPTER 5

Sport policy: structures and values

Introduction

The review in Chapter 3 indicated that increased politicisation and governmentalisation of sport were prominent features in the recent history of all four countries, although the depth and pace of these forces differed. In this chapter we will examine these developments more thoroughly, and while not neglecting politicisation, greater emphasis will be given to governmentalisation, that is the government's involvement in sport and the 'use' of sport by the government to promote and further its objectives rather than the use of sport by politicians, political parties or interest groups to promote their objectives (see Munk and Lind, 2004; Bergsgard, 2005). Although differences in party politics regarding sport will be touched upon, it is the system that is developed to promote and implement these governmental objectives that is the object of our study. We will begin with a brief outline of the political system of the four countries and the location of sport policy and politics within this system, before exploring the government's relations with the sport sector, and the objectives and priorities that are connected to the public's involvement in sport.

The main question we raise in this chapter is why and how are the public authorities involved in sport? Especially in answering the 'how' question, we will make use of some of the analytical dimensions identified in Chapter 2. To describe the location of the sport policy and politics field within the political system, we will focus on the first two analytic dimensions: the state structure and executive-legislative relations. These two dimensions imply an emphasis on an analysis of the distribution of function (and power) between the different levels of government and between the elected politicians (i.e. the legislature) and the administration (i.e. the executive). In this section of the chapter where we discuss the government's relations with the sports sectors, we will touch upon the corporatism versus lobbyism dimension and the degree of segmentation in the field of sport policy. These discussions will, however, be more elaborated in the concluding chapter. In Chapter 3 we identified the more deep-rooted values and ideology connected to the development of sport in each country and the motives for public involvement. While sensitive to the importance of covert and informal policy objectives, we will, in this chapter, take as our starting point for analysis the manifest and formal objectives and priorities that are presented in government reports, especially the relative priority given to high-performance sport and mass sport. This discussion relates to the dimension concerned with the generalisation of interest.

Government responsibilities for sport

In this section the focus is on the distribution of responsibility for sport across different levels of government in each country and how the sport policy process has adapted to that division of power.

Canada

Government structure and sport policy • • •

As pointed out in Chapter 2, Canada is a federal and decentralised country. Substantial governmental power is located at regional (provinces/territories) and local level. Over 90% of the total public funding of sport that was £2.12 billion (CAN$4.5 billion) in 2004/2005, is spent at the regional/local level (Carter Report, 2005, Appendix 2). Further, the Canadian political culture is strongly influenced by the liberal Anglo-American tradition that emphasises limited state intervention. 'Canada's style of governance can best be described as a liberal democracy, within a federalist system of power sharing,' writes Macintosh (1996, p. 39). The consequence for sport policy is that the Canadian federal state has traditionally shown little interest in sport, and that sport services and general policy have primarily been a provincial/local concern. However, from the 1960s, as in most other Western countries, there was an increase in public sector and especially federal government involvement in sport. In 1961 the Fitness and Amateur Sport Act was passed by the Canadian Parliament (Horna, 1989) and the Fitness and Amateur Sport Directorate (at first an advisory council) was created. In 1972 two separate divisions within the Directorate, Recreation Canada and Sport Canada, were established. The background for increased public involvement in sport was a general concern with the level of physical fitness in Canada. Another, and maybe a more important factor, was the increased focus on international success, and the national unity this success was expected to create. In the 1970s federal funding of the national sports organisations (NSOs) by Sport Canada increased, especially targeted to strengthen elite performance. Macintosh (1996, p. 53) writes: 'The NSOs flourished: they grew in size and effectiveness, but at the same time their traditional autonomy from government was gradually eroded because of the increased financial presence of the federal government.' By the mid-1980s some NSOs were receiving as much as 90% of their funding from the federal government.

However, as in England, the conservative/liberal climate of the 1980s affected sport, and the federal government reduced the level of funding allocated to the NSOs. Further, the focus on elite sport suffered a major setback at the end of the 1980s due to the Ben Johnson doping scandal at the Seoul Olympic Games.[1] The subsequent period has been characterised as unstable regarding the governments' relation to, and funding of, NSOs. There were cut-backs in the public funding of elite performance as part of the general cut-backs in government spending. However, although funding of NSOs had been cut severely, Sport Canada still covers, on average, one-third of the operational budget of NSOs.

The location of responsibilities for sport policy in Canada is summarised in Table 5.1. These responsibilities have shifted

Table 5.1   Levels of government, location of sport policy and main tasks in Canada

Level of government	Location of sport policy	Main tasks
National level	Department of Heritage/ Minister of Sport	Preparation of general policy guidelines, writing strategic plans on government sport policy. Contact with the Members of Parliament, presenting the budget for approval.
	Sport Canada	General policy guidelines, writing strategic plans on governments sport policy. Contact with, and providing support for, the sport sector, especially the NSOs. Support for High-Performance Sport Centres. Hosting strategy for major events. Lobby for sport within government.
	Canadian Parliament Standing Committee on Heritage	Budget review and approval. A small number of initiatives in the sport policy area.
Regional level	Provinces/territories • Departments • Arm's-length agencies (councils/foundations/ federations)	Responsibility for sport and recreation in the province. Supporting the regional sporting organisation. Supporting elite sport in the provinces. Co-supporting facilities with the municipalities. Promoting and supporting sport inside the school and university system.
Local level	Municipalities	Building and maintaining sport facilities. Supporting sport clubs and sport in the education system.

between different departments at the federal level, and also between the different levels of government in Canada. At the federal level sport is currently (2006) located within the Department of Canadian Heritage, and has its own Minister of State of Sport (and of Western Economic Diversification). The appointment of, first a secretary of state, then a minister of state for sport, has increased the focus on sport policy at the federal level in recent years. However, the recreational pillar in Canadian sport and physical activity policy is the responsibility of another department. Further, the National Recreation Statement from 1987 stated that the provinces have primacy in the area of recreation, which includes sport, and also have responsibility for sport in schools. Still, the federal government has the capacity to influence provincial policy especially through the use of its funding capacity. In the words of one official from Sport Canada, 'The (...) challenge that Sport Canada faces in increasing people's participation in sport, is that we do not actually offer anything. We have no infrastructure, we have no delivery system associated with the Federal Government. So for anything we do we have to use our funding powers ... So in that regard you are somewhat limited as to what you can do'.

In relation to elite sport the distribution of responsibility and power between levels of governmental is quite blurred as both levels are involved with research, team programmes, programmes for coaches, and games and championships. However, understandably, the federal level has responsibility for participation in international championships although the interface between schools, colleges and universities, and the high-performance talent development system is primarily at the provincial level.

In summary, the Canadian sport policy sector is quite dispersed when it comes to public and, as we have seen in the previous chapter, private power. In fact, one of our interviewees from Sport Canada emphasised that until comparatively recently one could not really talk of a Canadian sport system at all, since the coordination and cooperation between the levels and the agency were almost non-existent. However, he went on to argue that the situation had changed, with increased cooperation between the levels over the last 10 years. Another Sport Canada official pointed to 'the lack of leadership that has characterized Canada over the several years'. In keeping with the liberal tradition the government has been reluctant to accept leadership in sport policy with the consequence that a vacuum has developed. While other actors, like the Canadian Olympic Committee and some of the Canadian high-performance sport centres, have tried to fill that vacuum, 'nobody has the authority to provide the leadership, not even us, frankly', according to this Sport Canada interviewee. However, as mentioned earlier, Sport Canada does have 'spending power'. The federal government is the largest single provider of funding for sports with Sport Canada contributing around $Can35 million directly to national sport organisations, and around $Can90 million either to multi-sport organisations or directly to athletes through athlete assistance programme. Sport Canada's primary focus is competitive sport, both at the international level and at the grassroots level. Traditionally they have funded large parts of the elite sport system organised by the NSOs.

Another important element in the state sport system is the nine Canadian sport centres for high-performance sport which are mostly located at universities and are a mix of both multi-sport and single-sport-orientated centres. According to one Sport Canada interviewee, the centres have 'made a big contribution already. But the limitation [...] is that although they receive a lot of funding from us and we can provide some direction, they basically are independent in terms of decision-making, so that they select the sport that they want to work with and provide services based on negotiations with that sport'. Their independence is a function of their structure where, typically, the Centres' Boards of Directors will comprise a balanced representation from the three funding partners, the federal government (Sport Canada), the Canadian Olympic Committee and the Coaching Association of Canada.

A further revealing aspect of the sports system is the hosting of sport events strategy which is 'not a very good one', according to one Sport Canada official, because most hosting initiatives came from local actors (private and public) with little early federal involvement. However, if hosting bids are to be successful they would need, at some stage, to approach the Federal government to obtain funding. While in earlier years the federal government occasionally felt it had been trapped into providing financial support for city or provincial bids, this is no longer the case. According to a Sport Canada official, 'Our new strategy is saying, if you do not have our approval before you go for the bid, even if you get the bid, forget it. You do not get our money.' In addition, the official emphasised that it was important to develop a systematic national plan for hosting major sports events which would provide objectives concerning the number, type and location of events.

Recreational sport policy is the responsibility of the ten provinces and three territories in Canada with policy delivery relying heavily on provincial organisations such as Swim Alberta and Athletic Alberta as well as on bodies located at the community level such as schools, universities and the municipalities. In

Alberta, for example, sport and recreation is part of a huge department called Community Development (CD) that also includes libraries, arts and culture. In the department there is a Sport and Recreation branch with a director and inside this branch there is a sport sector, recreation sector and provincial games sector. In addition, there is an Alberta Sport, Recreation, Park and Wildlife Foundation that runs the programmes financed by lottery money. The board of the Foundation is voluntary although the Chairman is appointed by the Minister of CD, while the Director of Sport and Recreation is the General Manager of the Foundation. The staff are, however, government employees. With the economic cutbacks in the province in the 1990s the Foundation was brought in as more or less a part of the department. According to an Alberta official, 'Government has more and more started to use lottery revenues as general revenues. It is not as distinct any more. The government manages it all'. In Alberta around 75 sports-related organisations and programmes are funded through the Foundation including programmes that focus on high-performance sport where Alberta competes as a province. This arrangement is unusual compared to the other provinces, where the agencies that receive lottery money are less tied to the government. For example, in British Colombia they have transferred nearly all responsibility for distributing lottery money within the sport sector to a sport federation called Sport BC. It is important to note that the level of support given to recreational sport, but also to competitive sport and/or elite sport, varies considerably between provinces. According to an interviewee from the Canadian Olympic Committee, the province of Quebec is the most successful in sport, with an 'ideal structure' and an investment of $Can35 million a year in its sport system. Further, because Vancouver will host the 2010 winter Olympics, British Columbia has indicated that it will increase its level of investment, and has created an agency to distribute provincial funds to support its preferred programmes which are mainly directed towards elite sport development.

The jurisdictional tensions between levels of government and the substantial complexity of the sport system have prompted attempts, largely by the federal government, to achieve greater coherence. As one Sport Canada official explained:

I think the major change is more integration between the federal government and the provincial/territorial government in terms of acting in every area of sport. Whereas before we said: OK the federal government is mostly high performance, provincial government youth participation/ development.... But now we are all working together to increase sport participation. So sport participation is not just now the responsibility of the provincial … the territory, the federal level will also participate … and for excellence, the same thing.

A Canadian sport policy researcher also saw this aspiration 'as good news', noting that there was currently 'an awful lot of overlap and confusion'. However, he was not optimistic regarding the possibility of enhanced cooperation between the federal and provincial level: 'I am not very encouraged. I wish them well and hope that they do that [cooperate well]. But there are strong structural pressures against that.'

Executive-legislative relations and sport • • •

There is no separate standing committee for sport in the Canadian Parliament. Sport is mainly dealt within the Standing Committee on Heritage, which has taken some initiatives in the sport area and also scrutinises the sport budget. While there is an informal 'caucus' of parliamentarians who are interested in sport, it would be fair to conclude that Parliament does not play a significant role in the shaping of sport policy in Canada. As in other policy areas, the Parliament of Canada is more an arena for debate that an arena for policy-making. Sport Canada has little direct contact with the Parliament as contact with the administration is mediated by ministers. According to one Sport Canada official, 'in terms of Parliament I would say that there is no involvement in our work, other than when there are political issues', such as the lack of representation in the national team from French-speaking areas. Although the Sport Canada official added that 'every department and every unit within each department has to have its budget approved by the Parliament. So in that sense Parliament does decide what we do and what we do not', it would be accurate to argue that Parliament plays thus a minor role in sport policy by comparison to the central administration.

The role of Sport Canada indicates a degree of concentration of responsibility for sport inside the dispersed Canadian political system. The fact that Sport Canada has recently become active in a broader area of Canadian sport policy, and not just excellence is perhaps an indication of a trend towards greater concentration of responsibility within the administration and of integration between levels of government and between the government and the sport sector. However, the mutual suspicion between provinces and the federal government provides a substantial impediment to extensive administrative centralisation.

England

Government structure and sport policy • • •

In Chapter 2 we identified the UK as a liberal welfare regime. This implied that the state plays a limited role in welfare provision leaving a substantial part to the market and voluntary sectors. This liberal tradition has been strongly apparent in British sport policy. Before the Second World War the sports sector in Britain was dominated by voluntary organisations with the local authorities providing modest basic facilities. According to Holt (1992, p. 344) 'The small-state tradition of the Victorians was strong and resilient' and 'The ideology of amateurism discouraged the notion that sport was an appropriate sphere of state activity.' Today, however, government is deeply involved with sport. Table 5.2 shows the present distribution of government responsibilities with regard to sport in England/UK.

Milestones in the 'growing control by the state of sport', as Allison puts it (2001, p. 55), was the establishment of the Wolfenden Committee of Inquiry into British Sport in 1960 and the appointment of Dennis Howell as Minister of Sport in 1964. Further, in 1965 the Sport Council was established as an advisory board for the government which became an executive agency for policy implementation at a national level from 1972 (Houlihan, 1996; Houlihan and White, 2002). Later three further sports councils were established for Wales, Scotland and Northern Ireland providing a complex political/administrative structure for sport

Table 5.2 Levels of government, location of sport policy and main tasks in England

Level of government	Locations of sport policy	Main tasks
National level	Department of Culture, Media and Sport, DCMS (Sport and Recreation Division)	Providing general policy guidelines and producing strategic plans for sport. Supporting (with the Exchequer funding) UK Sport and Sport England, and providing their general policy direction. Coordinating sport policy initiatives across government and between the four home countries. Managing international relations and coordinating bids for major events.

Table 5.2 (*Continued*)

Level of government	Locations of sport policy	Main tasks
	UK Sport	Supporting elite sport at a UK level (both the athletes and the NGBs) and managing bids to host major events. Administering the UK anti-doping programme. Representing sport in international government forums. Supporting the modernisation of NGBs in England.
	Sport England	Supporting grassroots sport in England. Contributing to the development and maintenance of the sport infrastructure in England.
	The House of Commons Culture, Media and Sport Select Committee (CMSC)	Examining the administration, expenditure and policy of the DCMS and Sport England. Providing a critical commentary on the policy of the DCMS. Assisting the House in debates and law-making. Setting (to a limited degree) its own agenda regarding sport policy.
Regional level	Sport England Regional Offices	Strategic planning for the development of sport in the region. Coordinating the application for money for Sport England from the region, and allocating the money downwards. Coordinating sports initiatives and strategies among the other agencies at regional/county level as Regional Sports Boards, Regional Cultural Consortia and Regional Development Agencies.
Local level	County Council	Developing sport including a contribution to talent identification, through the education of coaches, employment of sport development officers and the provision of support and advice to clubs.
	Unitary City Council/District Council	Building, financing and running public sport facilities. Supporting community regeneration and social inclusion through sport.

in the UK. In 1997 the sports council structure for the UK and England was changed, and a new sport council, UK Sport, with responsibility for elite sport in UK was established, while the English Sport Council was renamed Sport England, and was set alongside the other three home sports councils.

In 1974 the Department of Environment was given responsibility for sport, and in 1975 the first White Paper for sport, *Sport and Recreation*, (Department of the Environment 1975) was published emphasising sport for all and the welfare role of sport. After a short period of a year when the Department of Education and Science had oversight of sport, responsibility was transferred in 1992 to the newly established Department of National Heritage with the aim of creating synergy between tourism, the arts and sport. In 1997, following the Labour election victory, the Department of Culture, Media and Sports (DCMS) was established and sport policy was included within the Department's remit. Although the DCMS and the Sport Directorate within it have lead responsibility for sport policy, other major departments have substantial influence over policy. Of particular importance are the Department for Communities and Local Government, due to its supervision of local authorities and influence over their spending, and the Department for Education and Skills (DfES), which has considerable influence over both curriculum physical education and out of school hours/extra-curricular sport.

In 1991 Collins summed up the complexity of the UK sport policy sector by arguing that it 'is managed through a hybrid and fragmented public–private and voluntary system with a quasi-non-governmental body, the Sports Council, as leader and coordinator' (1991, p. 261). Eleven years later, *Game Plan* concluded that '[t]he structure for administering and delivering sport in the UK is extremely complex' (DCMS/Strategy Unit, 2002, p. 38). One of the reasons for this complex structure is that sport is a devolved responsibility in UK, with each of the four home countries – England, Wales, Scotland and Northern Ireland – being responsible for sport within their borders, while the responsibility for much of the elite sport, especially Olympic sport, where they compete as UK, is located in London with UK Sport.

The 1990s was a transformative period for the government's role in sport policy. For much of the decade the sports councils were criticised for spending too much money on central administration and not enough on front-line services. These criticisms were being voiced at a time when local government budgets were under considerable pressure due to central government cutbacks and sports services were especially vulnerable due to their non-statutory status.

Collins (1991) noted a weakening of the independence of the non-department public bodies, a view shared by Allison 10 years later when he argued that Sport England had 'transformed itself, unseen, from a "ginger group" pressing the interests of sport in government to an agency used by government to control sport' (2001, p. 55). According to Houlihan (1996, p. 376) the sports councils have always enjoyed conditional autonomy dependent, to a substantial extent, on their willingness to operate within government policy guidelines. This is an assessment reinforced by the Central Council for Physical Recreation (CCPR), the umbrella organisation for most of the NSOs in the UK, which claims that the independence of the sports councils is notional.[2] Furthermore, several interviewees endorsed this perception of the independence of Sport England. One Sport England official suggested that over 'the last few years the government has said we will invest in you [Sport England] to achieve government objectives, not [Sport England's] Charter objectives', and concluded that the arm's-length principle 'is not a principle that exists anymore'. Another official from Sport England noted that earlier, in the 1980s, the Council was 'more concerned with being at arm's-length', and defending 'its relationship with the government as being independent', but now this position was articulated less frequently. The acceptance of a redefinition of the role of Sport England and its relationship to the minister and DCMS indicates a significant shift in the locus of power in English (and to a substantial extent UK) sport policy – from agencies and to the Minister for Sport and senior civil servants. This development also influences the relationship between lobbyism and corporatism. Sport England (and especially its predecessors, the GB Sports Council and the English Sports Council) has in the past often functioned as an advocate for the sports organisations within government. Recent developments indicate a significant weakening of that role.

Sport England's mission is 'to foster a healthier, more successful nation through increased investment in sport and active recreation'.[3] Sport England is responsible for mass sport and for developing and maintaining the infrastructure of sport, primarily through grant-in-aid from the Exchequer. It is also responsible for distributing National Lottery funds to sport in England through the Sport England Lottery Fund. In 2001–2002 the total of grants from Sport England, both from the Lottery and Exchequer, were £307 million. Among the recipients were local authorities (31%), National Governing Bodies, NGBs (22%), voluntary clubs (12%), schools (11%) and national centres (11%) (DCMS/Strategy Unit, 2002; Figure 7.6). UK Sport is responsible for issues that need to be handled at a UK level and particularly elite sport. Its key objectives are to:[4]

- Support sports of UK significance to achieve success on the international stage.
- Increase the influence of the UK in international sport.
- Administer an anti-doping programme designed to protect athletes' right to participate in drug free sport.

UK Sport runs the World Class Performance Programme to support talented athletes in Olympic/Paralympics sports and their governing bodies, and the World Class Events Programme with investment in organisations bidding for, and staging, major international sports events. Both programmes are financed by the UK Sport Lottery Fund. UK Sport has, since July 1999, distributed nearly £25 million per annum in grants to athletes and governing bodies.

The main function of regional level governmental and quasi-governmental organisations has been to implement national sport policy and to act as a conduit for grassroots feedback, that is, to manage the interface between delivery and policy, as an official from a Sport England regional office put it. The delivery structure for sport is by and large at the local level, that is, within the local authorities, the voluntary clubs and schools. The political institutions at regional level – Sport England regional offices with the Regional Sports Boards, Regional Government offices and Regional Development Agencies – have only limited political powers. There are, however, some signs of changes, with the Sport England regional offices being given increased autonomy from the headquarters in London. In addition, the establishment of Regional Sports Boards, separate from the regional Sport England offices and with power over the distribution of significant amounts of sports lottery funding, has added to the importance of the regional level.

The East Midlands may illustrate the role of the regional level in English sport policy. The East Midlands is, in many ways, typical of the English regions, as it is close to the English average for unemployment, deprivation and education standards, although above average in terms of per capita GDP (gross domestic product). As regards sport, the East Midlands is important both in terms of activity (100,000 active volunteers and 10,000 clubs), economy (fastest growing cultural economy) and administration (10 NGBs have their headquarters in the East Midlands and there are National Centres for 13 sports).

The following public regional bodies are or can be important factors in sports development: Sport England East Midland office (SEEM), Government Office for the East Midlands, the East Midland Development Agency, the Regional Public Health team and East Midland Regional Assembly. The East Midland Regional Sports Board has a chair appointed by the Minister and a membership selected after application, designed to represent the sport sector, politics and relevant public bodies. The role of the Board is to support the implementation of the Regional Strategy for Sport produced by SEEM (which reflects the national sport policy framework) and to make decisions concerning the distribution of lottery money and investment priorities. The Board is also supported by a Regional Sports Partnership consisting of the County Sports Partnership manager, regional representative for NGBs and members of SEEM's development team. The establishment of the Board is a part of the regionalisation mentioned above, however, it is debatable how much power is, in reality, devolved to the regional level, since the strategy and thereby grants and investment distribution are tightly constrained by national objectives.

The responsibility for sport at local level in UK is as complex as at the central level (Houlihan, 1996). A substantial proportion of the major and medium-sized cities (about 0.25 million plus population) are covered by unitary authorities, while outside the major cities the most common arrangement is a two-tier system of County Councils and lower-tier District Councils (Houlihan, 1996, p. 376). During the 1970s there were two important trends, first considerable investment by local government in building sports facilities, often with additional financial support from the Sports Council, and second the establishment of distinct leisure service departments. Local government expenditure on sport and leisure services held steady at around 5% of the total budget from the 1970s to the mid-1990s (Houlihan, 1996), but since then has come under substantial pressure which has only been partly compensated for by the availability of lottery funding. Moreover, budgetary pressure has been accompanied by a retreat from separate leisure services departments to the integration of sport and leisure services into larger cultural services departments. This process of integration has arguably intensified the pressure on the sports and leisure budget due to the need to compete with a series of well-established services which often have a more secure statutory foundation.

Despite evidence of considerable pressure on Local Authority sports budgets since the mid-1990s, local authorities still account for around 80% of the public expenditure on sport (Houlihan and White 2002, Table 7.4). In *Game Plan* (DCMS/Strategy Unit, 2002, p. 32) the breakdown of total public expenditure on sport was reported as: 2% from the DCMS, 11% from the Lottery and

87% from the local government. The Carter Report (2005, p. 47) provides a slightly different breakdown, attributing 67% to local government, 22% to the national lottery and 11% to central government. Despite the variation between the three publications,[5] they confirm the substantial contribution of local government.

Executive-legislative relations and sport • • •

In Chapter 2 the political significance of the legislatures in the four countries was discussed. The UK Parliament was categorised as an 'arena', implying that the Parliament merely discussed the government's policy rather than made policy. The UK Parliament's role can be said to be mostly reactive, insofar as it examines the government's policy, and discusses bills proposed by the government but rarely challenges the dominance of the executive. In The House of Commons, the elected chamber in the Parliament, matters of sport are discussed and debated in the Culture, Media and Sport Select Committee (CMSC). The Committee's remit is '[t]o examine the expenditure, administration and policy of the relevant government department and its associated public bodies' (CMSC, 2003, p. 5) and it has four overarching objectives: to examine and comment on the policy of the Department; to examine the expenditure of the DCMS; to examine the administration of the Department and to assist the House in debate and decision. In the session 2002–2003 four of the thirteen enquiries in the CMSC that were ongoing or started in 2002 were sports related and concerned the preparations for the Manchester 2002 Commonwealth Games, the London bid for the 2012 Olympics, progress with the Wembley national stadium project, and the issue of swimming facilities.

As can be seen the Committee tends to focus on issues that involve substantial sums of public money particularly major capital projects. Further, the first three enquiries were examples of the reactive nature of the Committee as each issue was subject to intense media debate while the fourth enquiry, into swimming facilities, was an issue identified by the Committee and its advisors. The work of the Committee tends to fall into one of two categories: first, and by far the most significant, oversight and scrutiny of the work of the DCMS, and second, attempts to influence the agenda of the Department. In summary, the Committee is essentially reactive in its way of working, which is normal practice for House of Commons select committees.

The DCMS is not obliged to take into account the comments or suggestions that the Committee makes. However, as an informant from the Department stated: while 'There is no obligation to follow the recommendation from the Committee, what is said is taken into account. The Committee's suggestions and recommendations are all fed into the general evolution of policy.' This indicates that the power of the Committee is to contribute to the public discourse on sport policy, to raise issues, to present another view, to help set the agenda for policy debate. The role of the Select Committee notwithstanding, the power to make budgets and set the strategic direction for policy lies firmly in the hands of the executive in the form of DCMS.

As discussed in Chapter 2 the political system in England is characterised by economic liberalism and by a pluralistic distribution of power across the public, voluntary and commercial private sectors. However, England is seen as part of a centralised unitary state where the locus of power and decision-making are at the central level. Houlihan and White (2002, p. 229) illustrate this concentration of power with reference to the National Lottery which because it was 'new' money, that is, its use was not constrained by historical commitments and thereby could be used more freely to carry out new policy initiatives, gave the central government considerable leverage over policy at sub-national level due to its control of the lottery distribution bodies. Moreover, according to Minton and Roberts (1989; see also Houlihan, 1997) even before the National Lottery was introduced, the Sports Councils used their funding capacity to steer local authority sports policy. Thus although most of the public expenditure is at a local level, Houlihan and White (2002, pp. 218ff) argue that local authorities have become progressively marginal in the development of sport. Since the mid-1980s sport has increasingly become a core agenda item for central government, and there has been an growing allocation of funds from the National Lottery to elite sport and an increase in specialist and centralised sports organisations. Houlihan claims further that since the mid-1980s school/youth sport and elite sport have emerged as policy priorities for funding at the expense of community sport/ *sport for all*, which is seen as primarily the responsibility of local authorities. At first sight our expectation regarding the locus of decision-making in England stated in Chapter 2 seems to be confirmed as the policy process is clearly dominated by the central government.

Germany

Government structure and sport policy • • •

The centralised and unitary nation-state has historically weak roots in Germany which has traditionally been divided into numerous state-like areas called *länder*. The number and the size of the *länder* has changed throughout history and today the country is divided into 16 *länder*, ten of which are from the former West Germany, five from the former East Germany, plus the unified Berlin. The *länder* are linked together in a federal structure with a central governing structure at national (*bundes*) level. Over time, the relationship between the national and the *land* (state) level have developed into a complex structure of laws, constitutional practices and procedural regulations.

The federal level has exclusive power in domains such as foreign affairs and defence, national citizenship and management, but tasks which are not specifically mentioned in the law as national concerns are, according to the constitution, the responsibilities of the *länder*. However, the development of the German state has differed from a literal interpretation of the constitution. The authority of the national level has increased, with the federal government being involved, and having the main legislative power, in many policy areas outside the terms of the constitution.

The present distribution of sport policy responsibilities between the different levels of government in Germany is shown in Table 5.3.

Table 5.3 Levels of government, location of sport policy and main tasks in Germany

Level of government	Political system	Location of sport policy	Main tasks
National level	*Der Bund* (Federal Authorities)	*Bundesministerium des Innern*, BMI (Ministry of Interior)	Supporting international elite sport. Dealing with sport science, anti-doping policy, etc. Coordinating national public policy towards sport. Preparing the *Sportberichte* (Sport Report) for the *Bundestag* every fourth year.
	Bundestag (Parliament)	*Sportausschuss* (Standing Committee for Sport)	Making recommendations on the federal budget. Discussing and passing laws regarding

Table 5.3 (*Continued*)

Level of government	Political system	Location of sport policy	Main tasks
			sport (although law in the area of sport is rare). Discussing the Sport Report from the Ministry of Interior.
Regional level	*Länder* Government Parliament	Sport seen as a part of culture, but located in a variety of ministries, often together with health or interior affairs. Some *länder* have a specific sport law. Some *länder* have a specific sport committee in the parliament.	Promote sport, especially recreational sport but also elite sport, through constructing facilities (often as support to the municipalities), support the LSB and the specialised federations at *länder* level, provide salaries for coaches and other staff. Support for school sport (e.g. by paying salaries of physical education teachers).
Local level	*Regieringsbezirke* (Districts) *Landkreise* (323)/ *Kreisfreie Städte* (116) (Boroughs) *Gemeindre/Städte* (13.837) (Communities)	Sport located in various departments, in bigger cities as a separate department, in smaller communities often together with culture and youth affairs.	Planning, building and supporting sport facilities for sports clubs and participants.

From about 1970 onwards sport policy became an increasingly significant national concern (Eulering, 2000). However, according to the German constitution, the main responsibility for sport is at the level of the *länder* (Article 30): 'Only if the matter exceeds the concerns of a single *länder* does the matter then lie with the federation,' according to Heinemann (1996, p. 171). This implies that elite athletes and federations that represent

Germany at the international stage are mainly a federal responsibility. However, Germany has no ministry of sport, perhaps a consequence of the strong post-war concern to re-establish sport as part of civil society (see Chapter 3; Heinemann, 1996). This does not mean that there are no structures for sport at federal level. The Ministry of Interior has responsibility to support elite sport development, to coordinate sport with the government and to liaise within sport organisations, the *länder*, and the Conference of the Ministers of Sport from the *länder*.

In Chapter 2 we suggested that responsibility for German sport policy-making was dispersed. As mentioned above, the constitution, which limits the power of the federal government and protects the role of the *länder*, is important in maintaining the dispersal of power as is the strong social and political commitment to autonomous sports organisation. Even acknowledging the influence of the federal Ministry of Interior on sport and especially elite sport at national level, it is accurate to conclude that sport policy-making is spread not only between the levels of government, but also across other policy domains such as culture, defence, family, economic development and health.

Länder are important both individually and collectively. An annual conference of the *länder's* sport ministers is an important arena for the discussions of sport policy. The agenda of the conference is prepared by the 'sport referents', the administrative leaders of sport of the different *länder*, who meet four times a year in a series of permanent and non-permanent working groups. Although the primary purpose of the conference is to allow the *länder* to discuss sport policy the Ministry of Interior, The German Sports Confederation (*Deutscher Sportbund*, DSB),[6] and the *land* sports confederation (*Landessportbund*, LSB) in the *länder* that hosts the conference are invited. Specialised sport federations are not normally invited unless there is some specific event, like the 2006 World Cup in football, in which case the relevant federation would be present. The annual conference is the closest one comes to a general assembly of German sport. According to the DSB interviewee the conference is 'the only real coordinating body where you have all elements involved'. The conference is concerned with policy coordination amongst the *länder* and policy issues on the national and international stage.

A review of the 28 conferences between 1977 and 2003 indicated that the most frequently discussed topics were: doping in sport, the relationship of *länder* to the federal government and the European Union (EU), sport and health, the 2006 World Cup preparation, elite sport and sport facilities. However, as one interviewee at *land* level pointed out while '[t]his conference discusses a whole range of issues. ... [i]t would be an overstatement to say that this is the place where national sport policy is made'. The power of the conference is limited by the lack of legal power and by the necessity to work by consensus. It is fair to say that the Sports Ministers' conference plays mainly a reactive role responding to the policy initiatives of other actors rather than a policy leadership role. However, even when it does take a more policy-making role implementation still takes place in each of the 16 *länder* often resulting in very different policy at 'street level'. Because of their dominance of the implementation process the *länder* have a strong claim to be the most important public actor in the area of sport policy and politics in Germany.

The *länder* support sport through the provision of financial support to communities for the construction of sport and leisure sites, the payment of salaries of trainers and coaches, funding the sports organisations at *land* level, meeting the running costs of the associations of youth education, the education and training of sports teachers and funding of sport research at universities. The priority of the *länder* is the promotion of recreational sports inside and outwith sport organisations, although they also support elite sport (Engelhardt and Heinemann, 2003).

Nordrhein-Westfalen (NRW) illustrates the significance of sport and the common administrative arrangements for sport within the *länder*. NRW is typical in locating sport within the Ministry of Urbanism, Inhabitation, Culture and Sport. The sport budget in 2003 was over €100 million and covered support to clubs, sports organisations and the development of facilities. Around 30% of this total came from the 'Lottery 77' and was transferred to the land sport confederation (*Landessportbund Nordrhein-Westfalen*, LSB) which distributed the money to the specialised federations (the '*spitzenverbände*' at land level) and to the local clubs. *Land* federations and clubs also received some public money from the government, mostly to fund specific programmes and activities.

The second main channel for public support for sport is through the municipalities. After a change in the financial system the municipalities now receive around €3.5 per inhabitant, around €60 million in total, to develop the sport infrastructure. There also seems to be a tendency for a greater percentage of *land* government money for sport to be transferred directly to the municipalities. In NRW there is also a foundation established by the government, but outside the public budget, that supports the elite sport system. The foundation received nearly €7 million from the lottery in 2004.

Contact between the government and the sport sector in NRW is largely through the LSB as there is no direct contact with the specialised federations in NRW, unlike at federal level. The head of the sport department is a co-opted member of the executive board of LSB and there is a close and almost daily contact between the executive and LSB. While there is no distinct sport law in NRW, there is a separate sports committee in the *land* parliament that deals with sports matters. Although there are occasional disagreements over the allocation of funds to elite sport, youth sport and talent development there is a general consensus on sport in the *land* parliament.

In specific areas there is collaboration between the different governmental levels. The federal level and NRW currently cooperate to fund a training and sport management academy, while NRW, the federal government and municipalities jointly fund three Olympic training centres.

The principle of subsidiarity is important to an understanding of the division of labour between the different levels in Germany. Subsidiarity requires that tasks be placed at the lowest possible level where they can be implemented effectively. The underpinning assumption is that the responsibility for services should, as far as possible, be located locally and as close to the user as possible. Consequently municipalities have substantial responsibility for core delivery functions in sport as indeed in many other services.

At the municipal level support is mainly directed towards mass sport and recreation and administrative responsibility is often located within a youth or education and culture department. A primary responsibility of the municipalities is the construction, maintenance and subsidy of sports facilities and the fulfilment of these responsibilities often requires close cooperation with the land government, voluntary sports organisations and, occasionally, with the commercial sector.

In Germany sport is supported financially by the public authorities both indirectly and directly. Indirectly, sport is subsidised though the tax abatement for non-profit clubs and federations, and also by the remission of income tax from donations to sports clubs. Further, sports clubs obtain the use of public sector facilities either free or at a very low cost. A more direct form of financial support is the grants to the sports organisations, especially at the *land* level from the lottery, from various departmental *länder* budgets and from the federal budget. As an informant from DSB pointed out: '[T]he main focus is the lottery ... [it is] the responsibility of the states [*länder*] although in 16 states you have different rules and regulations.' In some *länder*, Brandenburg for example, over 50% of the funding for sport between 1995 and 2005 came from the national level lottery. There is also a lottery '*GlücksSpirale*' at the federal level which was established to help fund the 1972 Olympics in Munich and the World Championships in football in 1974, but continued after these events. In 1998 45.5 million DM (around €26 million) was distributed to sport from the lottery, 30% to the DSB, 5% to the NOC (National Olympic Committee), 25% to *Deutsche Sportshilfe* and 40% to the LSBs.

In total, the federal government granted more than €0.25 billion in support of sport. The Ministry of Interior is the main contributor with about €200 million which is around 80% of the total federal allocation. Federal funding of sport, especially from the Ministry of Interior, has steadily increased over the last 20 years. In the mid-1980s support from the federal level to the sport sector was around €120 million (Heinemann, 1996, p. 182). During the same period support from the *länder* to sport totalled around €1.4 billion, and from the municipalities €2 billion. In summary, 3% of total public expenditure on sport came from the federal level, 40% from the *land* level and 57% from the local level. Over 15 years later the international comparison in the Carter Report gives the following distribution for Germany (2002): 3.3% from federal government, 17.1% from the *länder* governments and 79.6 % from the local government (2005, Appendix 2). Acknowledging the difficulty of obtaining accurate figures it is clear that, as in England, the local level is by far the most important for the provision of facilities and the delivery of sport services.

Executive-legislative relations and sport • • •

Even if there is no separate ministry of sport, there is a Standing Sport Committee (*Sportausschuss*) in the national parliament, the *Bundestag*. The Committee was created at the time of the Munich Olympic Games in 1972 and its role is, like other committees in the German Parliament, to discuss laws assigned to it. The area of sport is, however, an area with few legal instruments except, for instance, in the area of doping. However, the Committee also reviews the budget for sport and gives its recommendations to Parliament although it is the Committee of Finance that has final responsibility for the size of the budget and service priorities. At federal level there have been no politically significant controversies concerning sport in recent years as it is generally seen as an important social good and a personal development factor of great value. In the parliamentary Sport Committee there is nearly always consensus and has been refereed to, by Mr. von Richthofen, President of DSB, as a sport fraction to signify that it works across the political parties (*Deutscher Bundestag*, 2003, p. 9). As a representative from DSB explained, 'It is an agreement across the parties that we are autonomous, we are not subjected to instructions.' However, the relationship between the federal government and the Committee is not extensive as sport organisations tend to address questions on finance direct to the executive rather than working through the legislature. Consequently the government, in collaboration with sport organisations, develops policy principles for discussion in the Parliament and every fourth year the Ministry of Interior presents a report (*der Sportbericht*) on sport and sport policy to the Parliament, which is discussed in the Committee. In summary, it is the executive that sets the agenda for policy debate and the legislature plays a relatively minor role.

Similar to the federal level, there seems to be a general agreement on sport policy objectives at the *land* level whichever party was in power. Interviewees at the *land* level agreed, arguing that irrespective of the party in office *land* governments 'find the same line of policy'. A high level of consensus is also evident at the municipal level. One local interviewee said that one could talk about a type of 'sports fraction' which cuts across the different parties in the municipal council. Consequently, it is clear that there are very few differences between the political parties regarding sport policy in Germany. While the degree of consensus should not be exaggerated as agreement on the goals may not always imply consensus on the means, the overall conclusion must be that party ideology has relatively little impact in the area of sport policy at the sub-national level. It is also clear that, as at the federal level, the executive dominates the policy process leaving only a marginal role for the legislature, an observation reinforced by the fact that the majority of the *länder* have no distinct sport law.

In Chapter 2 we categorised Germany as a centralised federal state, but the extent of centralisation was open to debate. In relation to sport policy our expectation was that the policy area would be dominated by the *länder*, which indeed is the case. Sport policy at the *land* level is comprehensive, covering not only recreational sport but also elite sport. The significance of *länder* (and municipalities) notwithstanding there is evidence that the federal level is increasing its authority and involvement across a widening range of domains, passing laws that the *länder* are delegated to implement. Such tendencies are clearly evident in sport where the federal level has increased its involvement beyond elite sport and increasingly sees sport as a part of wider societal/welfare policy. The federal government contributes for instance to mass sport through the '*Goldenen Plan Ost*,' that is an initiative to modernise and rebuild sport facilities in the former east and which will be discussed in more detail in Chapter 7.

Norway

Government structure and sport policy • • •

In the post-war period Norwegian politics were distinctive for the dominance of the Labour Party. The Labour Party's socialist planning regime, also named the social functionalist project (see Chapter 3), highlighted the expert's role in shaping and implementing policy at the expense of the elected politicians (Slagstad, 1998; Nordby, 2000). It has been claimed, as we discussed in Chapter 2, that the locus of the political decision-making process was embedded in the government's corporate relations with different interest organisations, and not in the Parliament (Rokkan, 1966). However, several political scientists have pointed out that Parliament has steadily increased its power at the expense of the government over the last 30 years (Olsen, 1983; Rommetvedt, 2002a, 2003). Table 5.4 summarises the distribution of sport functions between different levels of the Norwegian political system.

In relation to sport policy it is fair to say that power, to a large degree, was concentrated in the hands of the executive. When the Money Game Act was adopted and the National Gaming Corporation (*Norsk Tipping*) was established in 1946, it was decided that the gaming profits earmarked for sport should not be included in the fiscal budget of the State.[7] Consequently decisions regarding financial allocations to sport organisations were made at Ministerial level and not by the Norwegian Parliament. In the Ministry it was the Office for Youth and Sport that had the responsibility of allocating the gaming money. However, this allocation did not take place without rather noisy debate between the Office and the sports organisations. Consequently a governmental Sport Council (*Statens Idrettsråd*) was established, as an intermediate body between the two parties. The members of the Council represented the Norwegian Confederation of Sports (NIF) and the Ministry of Education and Church Affairs which was then responsible for sport policy. The Council was typical of the many corporatist bodies that were established in Norway at that time (Goksøyr *et al.*, 1996).

Up to 2002, nearly 20 billion NOK (*Norwegian Kroner*) had been allocated from gaming profits to sport, and in recent years the annual average allocation has been 1.2 billion NOK. The gaming/lottery profits are the primary source of finance for NIF/NOC. Since the 1990s, between 80% and 90% of NIF's income has come as revenue support from gaming profits (Enjolras, 2004; Bergsgard, 2005). Gaming profit also accounts for a substantial proportion of the total budgets of some national sport federations. Although the average contribution

Table 5.4 Levels of government, location of sport policy and main tasks in Norway

Level of government	Location of sport policy	Main tasks
National level	Ministry of Culture and Church Affairs: Department of Sport Policy	Allocating lottery money to sport (NIF/facilities/specific purposes). Dealing with general facility policy questions, and setting out guidelines for the financial support of sport facilities. Writing government documents on sport/preparing proposals (bills) and reports (white papers) on sport for Parliament. Implementing the government's policy on anti-doping, inclusion of marginal groups in sport, international sports cooperation, etc. Undertaking research and development on sport.
	Parliament: The Standing Committee on Family, Cultural Affairs and Government Administration	Preparing recommendations on proposals (bills) and reports (white papers) on sport submitted by the government that form the basis for debate and voting in the *Storting* (Parliament). MPs present private members proposals and bills on sport.
Regional level	The Counties: Sport located in various departments such as Culture, Regional Development	Planning for, and distributing of, governmental lottery money for facilities in the municipalities. Supporting regional sports organisations.
Local level	The Municipalities: great variation regarding the location of sport, both administratively and politically	Implementing national sport policies through municipal planning decisions and preparing applications for lottery money for facilities to be submitted to the counties. Owner/part owner of sport facilities. Capital support for facilities. Supporting running costs in sports clubs.

is approximately 20% of the income, for one-third of the national sport federations gaming profit accounts for as much as 70% (Enjolras, 2004). The central government is also a significant contributor to the development of sport facilities across the country with around 20% of capital support coming from the lottery money which is often used to leverage in additional funding from local authorities, the sport clubs themselves, or commercial interests (Langkaas (ed.), 1997).

In the period from 1950 to 1982 sport policy was the responsibility of the Office for Youth and Sport under the Ministry of Education and Church Affairs. Arguably, the power to develop a comprehensive sport policy comprising voluntary sport organisations and their activities as well as sport in education and physical activities for the young people was more concentrated in this period than later. Today sport in education and youth activities are part of the responsibilities of the Ministry of Education and Research and the Ministry of Children and Family Affairs. However, if we exclude sport in education, the main responsibility for public sport policy is now concentrated in the hands of the Ministry of Culture and Church Affairs, more correctly in the Department of Sport Policy within the Ministry.

Although it is clear that the central government plays an important role in sport policy it should be noted that most Ministers of Cultural Affairs have shown little interest in sport policy and consequently the sport bureaucrats in the Ministry, in collaboration with NIF/NOC, have played a dominant role. In fact, it has been argued that some of the leading bureaucrats of the sports department of the Ministry have functioned as virtual Ministers of Sport partly due to the political leaders' lack of interest and knowledge, and partly due to the strong personality of some of the leaders of the sports department (Tønnesson, 1986; Goksøyr et al., 1996; Bergsgard, 2005). In summary, national sport policy is dominated by the Department of Sport Policy within the Ministry of Cultural Affairs and, with some important exceptions, Parliament plays a minor role.

The above discussion was focused on the national level but in the Norwegian political system there are two other governmental levels, the counties (*fylker*) and the municipalities. In Chapter 2 Norway was categorised as a unitary decentralised state. On the one hand Norway is unitary insofar as all the legislative activity is at national level as in the framing of the taxation system and the establishments of regularity frameworks. The county level has no legislative authority and has much less political power than the *länder* in Germany and the provinces in Canada and, consequently, are more similar to counties in England. Moreover, there has been a reduction in tasks of the counties in recent years, further reducing their political significance. On the other hand the Norwegian political system is decentralised insofar as there are areas of policy where the decisions regarding priorities are left in the hands of local authorities along with the implementation of national political decisions.

While counties are rather marginal to the sport policy process and to the delivery of sport services the same is not true of the municipalities. The municipalities support sport with around 1.5 billion NOK, both as capital support for building facilities and as revenue support to cover the running expenses of sport clubs (Opedal and Rommetvedt, 2006). The municipalities also own around one-half of the sport facilities, and are the dominating actor when it comes to building and operating bigger and more expensive facilities (Langkaas (ed.), 1997; *Sundbergutvalget*, 2003). Municipal financial support accounts for around 55% of the total public support to sport. This distribution is contrary to that found in the public sector in general where the central government turnover accounts, on average, for two-thirds of the total public expenditure (Statistics Norway, 2003: table 574). There is a great variation at the local level regarding the structure of the political system and sport's administrative location within it (*cf.* Berg and Rommetvedt, 2002a, b). Gradually most municipalities have abandoned the highly sectorised form of organisation, and local sport policy has become a part of the responsibilities of broader cross sectoral political and administrative units comprising policy areas like education or environment or business development.

Executive-legislative relations and sport • • •

Norway is a constitutional monarchy but the Norwegian political system is rooted in the principles of parliamentarianism. The government needs support, or at least acceptance, from the majority in the Parliament. From 1985 to 2005 all Norwegian governments were minority governments, either single party or coalition governments. In the 1980s and 1990s the legisla-ture seemed to strengthen its position *vis-à-vis* the executive (Rommetvedt, 2002a, 2003). However, there were other important trends evident during this period, such as economic liberalisation that started around 1980 and implied a more significant role for the market, and internationalisation/globalisation which resulted in the transfer of some power from the *Storting* (Parliament) to international regulatory organisations (Østerud *et al.*, 2003). Consequently the developments regarding the power of the Norwegian Parliament have been described by Nordby (2000, p. 22) as a 'democratic twofold movement: increased power in relation to the executive authorities, reduced power in relation to the market and the international society' (authors' translation).

As regards sport policy and politics, public power at national level has mainly rested in the hands of the executive in Norway.

The power of the government to allocate gaming/lottery money has given the executive considerable influence over sport policy. However, the formula that determines distribution between the different beneficiaries of gaming/lottery money (art, science and sport) is set out in the Money Game Act. Any alteration of the distribution formula is thus in the hands of the legislative assembly, the *Storting*. However, the Money Game Act provides only very general guidelines for the use of lottery money for sport and apart from the Money Game Act there are very few laws concerning sport. Consequently, the public policy for sport has tended to be formulated in governmental reports (white papers). Despite the fact that major policy changes require the final approval of the Parliament, the major influence on sport policy is exerted by the executive. However, there has been an increasing number of issues placed on the agenda by Members of Parliament in the form of questions to ministers or private members' bills. For example, the change of the Money Game Act distribution formula in 2002 was proposed in the *Storting* by two Members of Parliament who tabled a private members' bill (Dokument nr. 8:16, 2001–2002). There has also been a modest increase in the number of questions on sport in the *Storting* and sport is mentioned more frequently in the parliamentary committees' recommendations (Bergsgard and Rommetvedt, 2004). In addition to the changes in the distribution formula in the Money Game Act, the Parliament discussed, in 2000, the implementation of an EU Directive on TV Rights for Major Sport Events (97/36/EC). As a result of the increase in new types of fighting sports in Norway the Parliament in 2001 established general regulations regarding all combat sports that included the possibility of participants being knocked unconscious. Two doping cases at the Sydney Olympics led to a report on sport policy from the government to the *Storting* being subject to a public hearing in the Parliament (St.meld. nr. 14, 1999–2000; Innst. S. nr. 147, 2000–2001). Occasionally, some Members of Parliament have indicated that the allocation of at least some of the gaming profits to sport should be decided upon by the Parliament, but this proposal has never gained sufficient support to challenge the role of the Department of Sport Policy in the Ministry of Cultural Affairs (Bergsgard and Rommetvedt, 2004; Bergsgard, 2005).

At national level we can conclude that the executive had, and still has, considerably more power by comparison to Parliament regarding sport policy. At local level a somewhat different picture arises as it would appear that changes in political organisations have resulted in municipal councillors being more active in sports and thus constraining the previous autonomy of the local administration. Part of the explanation of the greater assertiveness of politicians at the municipal level might be that the combining of sport with broader services has led to more intense and frequent contests for resources.

Government and sport relations

This section examines one of our key analytic dimensions, the relationship between government and sport organisations and is concerned with both formal and informal relations.

Canada

'We made a policy decision years ago that the NSOs are the primary providers of services, not just for elite sport, but for the sport system.' This statement came from a Sport Canada official and indicates that the NSOs are the primary partner for the government at national level. A close relationship is also evident at the provincial level where specialised sport organisations are considered to be important partners for the government. Although the rhetoric of partnership is often used by officials at both the federal and provincial levels it is very much a partnership on terms set by the governments. In order to obtain funding from the federal government NSOs need to operate within 'the Sport Funding Accountability Framework'. The Framework, which has been in place since the mid-1990s, sets robust criteria with which NSOs must comply before they can receive funding. Criteria include that the organisation has to be a national organisation, it must be the single body responsible for the sport, it has to demonstrate a link with the assembly of international sport organisations or the International Olympic Committee (IOC), it has to be incorporated as a not-for-profit organisation, and it has to be democratically based with volunteer membership. In addition to these organisational requirements sports organisations also have to demonstrate commitment to a series of government policies and incorporate them into their strategic plans. Monitoring of compliance is based on frequent and regular contact between Sport Canada and the organisations. According to one Sport Canada official 'The liaison with officers of those organisations happens on both formal and informal levels. So that officers responsible for athletics would be in fairly regular contact generally with the staff person for athletics – resolving issues, giving guidance, giving advice ... .'

Underpinning the relationship between the government and an individual NSO, is the latter's dependency on the former for funding. Only the most commercial NSOs could survive in the long run without government funding. The heavy requirements tied to the release of government money could be seen as contrary to Canada's liberal tradition of limited government intervention in the private sector. However, as one Sport Canada official explained:

I think government has less involvement now in many respects in guiding the directions of organisations than they did 15 or 20 years ago. 15 years ago people like me would actually go to organisation meetings and help them create strategic plans. And when doing that you help guide the content of that plans. Now we do not take a role in that; that has changed over the last 7 or 8 years. But on the other hand I think the direction has changed a little bit from supporting sport for the value and benefit that sport brings, to more using sport to progress with government objectives. So it is more sport as the vehicle than … as a means in itself … So that would be probably one of the more significant changes that I have seen…

As in other countries, especially England, the intensity of government monitoring and regulation of NSOs, seems to depend on the extent to which the latter are prepared to internalise the values (strategic/corporate plans, audit, performance targets, etc.) which results in an 'earned freedom' from the more intrusive forms of government oversight (Green and Houlihan, 2005).

As noted in the previous chapter there is no confederation of NSOs or other umbrella organisation at national level in Canada. There are several relatively weak organisations like 'Sport Matters,' the Coaching Association and so on that advocate on behalf of sport but there are no strong, unified organisations that include almost all sports organisation at national level. The result is that Sport Canada, a government agency, is also the main lobby on behalf of sport at the federal level. At the provincial level there are some umbrella organisations, like Alberta Recreation and Parks Association (ARPA) but their lobbying capacity is limited by their membership which is often broad, including staff from governmental services as well as academics, students and volunteers, etc. and by their financial dependence on the provincial government. The government then, as discussed earlier, plays a major role in the development of sport policy.

England

The sports councils act as intermediaries between the government and the sport sector. However, as discussed earlier, it is arguable whether the sports councils are in the middle or are an extension of the executive branch, particularly the DCMS in

England. However, their perception of themselves is as a form of internal lobby on behalf of sport in part filling the gap left by the ineffectiveness of the CCPR. Since 1972 lobbying central government and politicians has been the self-proclaimed task of the CCPR but its effectiveness was disputed by a number of interviewees. An official from the British Olympic Association (BOA) stated that if they needed to lobby government it would not be 'through the CCPR, we would go directly ... we would go straight to the minister'. However, the interviewee added that the BOA would encourage other sport organisations to go through CCPR or through themselves, but added: 'Football will go straight to Tony Blair.' This statement identified a feature of sports lobbying that several of our interviewees underlined, namely that the major sports like football, rugby, cricket, tennis and golf go directly to the Minister of Sport or, on admittedly rare occasions, even bypassing the Minister and go straight to the Prime Minister. Lobbying also takes place via Members of Parliament who would be asked to raise questions in the House of Commons and through MPs who sit on the CMSC in the House of Commons. With regard to lobbying of the Select Committee the objective is either to influence the agenda of the Committee or to ensure that their voice is heard via the presentation of evidence when issues that concerns them (e.g. the Olympic Bid and the redevelopment of Wembley Stadium), are being discussed.

At first glance the relationship between the government and the sport sector seems to be based on informal, fragmented, and irregular contact and lobbying. The major sports organisations have the capacity to approach senior members of the government directly on issues that concern them and there is no single organisation that has the authority to speak collectively on behalf of sports interests. Two possible candidates, the BOA and the CCPR, are unsuitable, the BOA because it confines its lobbying to Olympic issues, and the CCPR because of the breadth of interests that it tries to accommodate and represent. However, the CCPR claims to be the 'voice of sport' and has quite close contact with civil servants in the DCMS and can expect to meet the Minister several times a year. The structural weaknesses of the Council notwithstanding it can claim to represent the grassroots level more effectively than the NGBs of sport due to their preoccupation with issues associated with elite sport. While acknowledging the efforts of the CCPR a Sport England official complained that the sport sector did not act collectively and rarely talked with a unanimous voice, and consequently had less influence on policy debates than, for example, the art sector.

In general, contact between the sports sector and the legislature is irregular and weak. For most NSOs the most valuable relationship is with UK Sport and, to a lesser extent, Sport England. However, as was the case in Canada both UK Sport and Sport England have become increasingly demanding of their partners. Both agencies share a twin concern to simplify the structure of NGBs and to modernise their organisational policies. As regards modernisation one representative from UK Sport argued that:

We are trying to persuade governing bodies of sport, many of whom originate in the 19th century ... to take the big step into the 21st century. And that means [modernising the] governance of the organisation, their decision making process of their organisation, the professionalism of their organisation ... and making sure that there is value for money ... If they are going to receive money in the 21st century they have to be accountable.

As in Canada offers of greater devolved power are conditional upon organisational modernisation and the internalisation of the government's policy priorities. Modernisation is also a requirement for UK Sport and the other sports councils part of which involves them adopting a more strategic role and withdrawing from the direct delivery of services which should be the responsibility of the NGBs. However, they are required to deliver results against specific targets regarding elite success and especially Olympic medals as a condition of funding.

The overall picture of the relationship between government and the sports sector is mixed. On the one hand as regards the sports sector as a whole power in dispersed among a wide range of organisations with no significant national level advocacy organisation. On the other hand the sports that are important to government, mainly Olympic sports, have links with the sports councils and have an influential collective voice via the BOA. In summary, there appears to be selective concentration of sectoral power, but within a framework largely determined by the government through UK Sport and the DCMS.

Germany

Despite the emphasis on the self-government of sports organisations and their independence from government, there is, in many respects, a close relationship between the public sector and sports organisations in Germany. One interviewee from the DSB pointed out that, 'Within the tradition of sport in Germany, the main engine of development of sport was always more in the self-organised [voluntary] area rather than in governmental political institutions. Over the years it has changed a little bit. It is a more complex system of interactions, and interest and cooperations.' Recent changes have led to more interaction and cooperation among actors or, one might argue, to a greater interplay between the government and sports organisations regarding the values that legitimate public support to sport. At federal level one interviewee emphasised that the policy objectives that justified support for sport from the *Bundesministerium des Innern* (BMI) were mutually agreed on by the different parties. 'Normally these concepts are worked out together with DSB, NOC, the national sport federations and BMI.' The relatively close network formed by the public authorities and the sports organisation indicates, as Heinemann (1996) points out, that the sports organisations are not as autonomous and independent from the state as the rhetoric claims. According to another interviewee from the DSB, such autonomy as the sports organisations possess is limited by their resource dependency: 'It is very easy to steer developments by giving or not giving money'.

An official from the BMI stressed that regarding the finance of sport the DSB 'has an advisory role. They are our partner as the coordinator of the sport movement'. However, the DSB provides advice, but the money from BMI goes directly to the NSOs, not to or via the DSB. And, as noted in the previous chapter, the NSOs receive around 40–70% of their funding from the BMI. The exceptions to this pattern of resource dependency are the commercial, rich and professional sports like tennis, golf and football that do not receive any funds from the Ministry. As in many other countries access to public funding depends on fulfilling criteria set by the Ministry which include spending money on youth sport and anti-doping activity. However, the most important criterion is international success: 'Of course it could be that if they are not successful they get more money. But no, it is the other way around, they must be successful,' according to a senior BMI official. This policy of 'medals for money' is common across all four countries. However, it is worth mentioning that in England and Canada, though to a more limited extent, the 'medals for money' policy is reinforced by a system similar to the business philosophy of Management By Objectives which is based on the setting of agreed objectives, interim targets and comprehensive monitoring and evaluation. By contrast, in Germany the relationship between the Ministry, the DSB and the NSOs, is more informal and based on close and continuing contact rather than contract.

According to Heinemann (1996, pp. 180ff) this somewhat ambiguous structure stems partly from the coupling of two forms of legitimation of government involvement in sport, the concept of neo-corporatism and the ideal of subsidiarity.

Neo-corporatism implies an obligation on the part of the government to guarantee to the population certain welfare standards in relation to social integration, health and civic engagement and, on the part of the sports organisations to contribute to the fulfilment of these public tasks in return for influence over policy direction and content. It is a situation where the 'state provides juridical security and funds to accomplish the functions; the associations fulfil these functions with less expense and bureaucracy than the state' (Heinemann, 1996, p. 180). The principle of subsidiarity means, as discussed above, that the organisation closest the problem or user group should be in charge of policy and service delivery. This means that the authorities should support, but not control, the activities of sports clubs. So, '[i]f the DSB describes its relation to the state in term of "partnership subsidiarity", then it attempts to link two different kinds of legitimation', claims Heinemann (1996, p. 181).

At federal level one of our interviewees pointed out that the DSB is a strong lobby organisation that at least twice a year takes part in a joint meeting with the Sport Committee in the Bundestag. However, in general there is not a great deal of lobbying by sports organisation directed towards the Sport Committee, perhaps because there is no need. As we saw earlier the Committee acts almost as a 'sport fraction' in the Bundestag, a view confirmed by the President of DSB, von Richthofen, who commented that: 'There is no doubt at all that the Sports Committee has, under various leadership and different (political) compositions, achieved a good reputation in organised sport' (*Deutscher Bundestag*, 2003, p. 9). Further, the Ministry of Interior acts, to an extent, as a lobbyist for the sport sector, with DSB as a guide. One of our interviewees at federal level considered sport to be a very powerful sector with the German Sports Confederation (DSB) and the National Olympic Committee, which recently amalgamated, being particularly influential. He argued that the President was powerful having 37% of the German population (i.e. sports participants) behind him and that sport was probably more powerful even than the church. Further, there is considerable overlap of personnel between leading positions in non-governmental sport organisations and positions in political councils at different levels, political parties and public sector sports bodies.

As regards the influence of sports organisations at the *land* level interviewees from the LSB in NRW claimed that they were a much stronger organisation than the federal DSB. The fact that NRW's funding of the *land* sports organisations mainly goes through the LSB, while the federal funding to the sport federations goes directly from the ministry, albeit in cooperation with the DSB, emphasises this division of power. In general, it seems as if the sports organisations at *land* level are more active in lobbying politicians than the sports organisation are at the federal level. At the municipal level the picture is more varied with an interviewee from one municipality stating that the culture sector is a more effective lobby than the sport sector. While interviewees in another, more typical, municipality reported that the sports committee included representation from the sport sector which collaborated closely and negotiated directly with the municipal government. Major issues such as sport facility development are discussed in the committee before being discussed by the city council.

Heinemann's (1996, p. 181) assessment that 'The sports organizations have considerable potential for influence at all levels of political decision making and administration' is broadly supported by our research. The 'family-relation' metaphor has, as in Norway, been used frequently to describe the relationship between the sports organisations and the government in Germany, 'It is a family because we are fighting for a good thing. We are fighting for a clean and proper sport,' according to an official from the BMI. This interviewee drew a comparison with the culture sector which is fragmented and commented: 'It is different, it is not a family, but sport is a family.'

The relationship between the government and sports organisations is paradoxical. In the post-war years there has been a conscious attempt by the West German and now German government to respect the autonomy of sports organisations while at the same time developing a close relationship on many issues. The ambiguity in the relationship is easily illustrated. Until the 1970s the national sports confederation received public funds to help cover their administration costs. This arrangement was phased out, according to the DSB, because they wanted independence from the government. However, according to an official within the BMI the ending of the funding arrangement was due to lack of governmental control over its use. The arrangement, according to another BMI official, was not 'successful' ... '[b]ecause the Parliament asked us, they did not ask the DSB, what happened to this money. It was also difficult to explain about money which we could not spend, but were responsible for'. A second illustration concerns the role of DSB in the distribution of funding from the BMI to the national sport organisations for development. Interviewees within the DSB claimed that they 'did not want to handle the money' because it could compromise their relationship with the single sport federations. According to the BMI it could not hand over the funds for the DSB to distribute because that would result in parliament losing control of the money. 'It is a legitimate suggestion that the German Sports Confederation (DSB) should get all money and distribute it as it sees fit, but that does not work – It is public money,' stated a representative from the BMI.

As pointed out above, the relationship between the government and the sports organisations are mostly on a personal level, as a type of family relationship. However, some of our interviewees thought that 'family' was too strong a term to use about this relationship, and referred instead to 'friendship relations' indicating a close but pragmatic link as a more suitable metaphor. The nature of relationship has few of the attributes of neo-corporatism and is probably best described as a series of policy communities operating at the federal and *land* levels.

Norway

The organisation of competitive sport in Norway since the end of the Second World War has been rather monolithic. The NIF has had almost a complete monopoly on all the gaming profits allocated to sport. As Goksøyr *et al.* (1996, p. 126) observed: 'Even if NIF did not have a monopoly on the gaming profits granted by law, in practical politics they had little inclination to distribute money to purposes outside their domain. To receive a share of sports' gaming money, applicants had to affiliate to the NIF-system' (authors' translation, see also Tønnesson, 1986; Bergsgard, 2005).

The sport policy-making model that was established in the immediate post-war period facilitated a concentration of public power. It can be argued that the granting of the power to distribute gaming money to sport structured the power relations inside the sport policy sector. In the case of sport, one may argue that the policy-making system resembled state corporatism as defined by Schmitter (see Chapter 2). The organisational monopoly of NIF, the close relations between NIF and the Ministry, and the exclusion of Parliament from the process of allocating gaming profits to sport, closely matched Schmitter's 'strong' version of corporatism (Schmitter, 1979). However, even though Norwegian sport organisations depend to an extent on public funding, they do have a high degree of autonomy *vis-à-vis* the state. Self-government rather than state-government characterises Norwegian sport organisations. Consequently, the label 'state corporatism' should not be used without qualification in this context. In 1988, both NIF and the Ministry agreed to phase out the Sport Council that was established as a corporatist body in 1957 (see above). They argued that the Council was not needed because of the good and close relations between the two organisations. In other words, they did not need a formalised corporatist body in order to cooperate. The relationship that developed between sport and public authorities has been described as an informal 'family relationship' (Selle, 1995). The present procedures for the allocation of operating grants to NIF can be viewed as mixture of administrative corporatism and administrative lobbyism. NIF's yearly applications and the Ministry's letters of award are supplemented by discussions and informal negotiations between the two.

As we have mentioned earlier, the Parliament has no role to play in this process. However, when it comes to decisions regarding the distribution formula of gaming profits to various purposes, Parliament plays a decisive role. The decision in 2002 to give gaming money to sport and culture only, and not to research, was the result of extensive parliamentary lobbying carried out by the Confederation of Sports. According to the President of the Confederation, NIF had a hundred meetings with politicians in order to convince them to give 50% of the gaming profits to sport (Bergsgard and Rommetvedt, 2004). This focus on lobbying politicians may indicate a certain shift with regard to sport policy-making in the same direction as in Norwegian politics in general (i.e. from administrative corporatism to parliamentary lobbyism). However, at the beginning of the new millennium, interviewees in Parliament give us no clear indication of significantly increased lobbying from sports organisations. Parliamentary lobbying is, with some exceptions, still relatively limited partly due to the special arrangement with regard to the allocation of gaming profits to sport. The public hearing initiated by the Parliament in 2000 in relation to the governmental report on sport and the doping cases in the Sydney Olympics, could point in the direction of a more active parliament towards the sport sector. The involvement of some MPs in an intense quarrel between the Ministry of Cultural Affairs and NIF in 2004 over the allocation of gaming profits could also be seen in this light (Bergsgard and Rommetvedt, 2004) although it should be noted that the activism by MPs was short-lived.

Seeing sport as a segment or a relatively tight policy network, as the family metaphor indicates, is also relevant at the local level with the focus on the relationship between sport and individual politicians. There are many cases where local politicians have central positions in sports clubs and associations. These relations seem to be of more importance than the relationship of the sports club to the administration in the municipality. Nevertheless the administration is exposed for lobbyism, especially from the bigger clubs. Further, there are established local Sports Councils (from 1970 and onwards) consisting of the clubs in each municipality (Opedal and Nødland, 2004). These councils interact frequently (at least in a majority of the municipalities) with the sport administration, but also with the local politicians.

Policy objectives and priorities

In this part we examine the formal objectives of government involvement in sport as expressed primarily in governmental papers and reports, with particular emphasis on the intrinsic and extrinsic values of sport and priorities given to high-performance sport and *sport for all*, respectively.

Canada

Already during the Second World War the government in Canada passed the first National Physical Fitness Act that aimed at increasing participation in competitive sport and physical activities (Horna, 1989). Later, in 1961 the Fitness and Amateur Sport Act highlighted both increased physical activity in the population due to the poor level of physical fitness, and the strengthening of the elite performance in relation to the successful Eastern-Bloc countries (Horna, 1989; Macintosh, 1996; Green and Houlihan, 2005). These dual objectives were pursued in subsequent years, however with an emphasis on the latter aspect (see Chapters 6 and 7). This focus resulted in two separate paths, where the fitness and recreation part was more or less driven out of the sport policy area and into the health sector. The recent Canadian sport policy indicates however a reunion of these two objectives – competition/elite performance and fitness/recreation. The government document *Canadian Sport Policy* from 2002, and the *Physical Activity and Sport Act* from 2003 are of particular importance. 'It (*Canadian Sport Policy*) is a landmark document in Canadian sport policy, because it has been approved by all 14 provinces and territories, which in our environment is very difficult to get all the jurisdictions to agree to anything,' observed one Sport Canada official. The *Canadian Sport Policy* established broad aspirations, including both enhanced participation and excellence, and also enhanced capacity and interaction. To enhance capacity implied in this case, that 'the essential components of an ethically based, athlete/participant-centred development system are in place and are continually modernised', while enhanced interaction meant a more connected and coordinated sport system (Sport Canada, 2002,

p. 4). This broadening of scope can, in many ways, be seen as a shift in the balance away from elite sport to mass participation legitimatised by the presumed health benefits.

So we have to justify and rationalise our sport because this is the priority of the day. And now it is health, now we are hanging our hat on health … And there is a new one now … 'social capital' (!) is the big one right now that we are putting our hat on, is the buzz word in the policy halls of government. So sport is capitalizing on that (Sport Canada official).

On the one hand the instrumental view of sport held by government is clear but on the other hand the emphasis on participation and the welfare benefits of sport is, in many ways, a return to the policy priorities of the 1970s and 1980s.

England

According to Houlihan (1996, pp. 379ff) there are three main factors that can explain the genesis of Britain's public sport policy in the 1960s: (1) a continuing concern with 'the association between adolescents and urban disorder', (2) the 'decline in Britain's international sporting success' and (3) 'electoral pressure on government … for an expansion of opportunities for sport and recreation'. We see that sport as both a means to non-sports purposes – social policy and international prestige – and as an end in itself – as a leisure activity – are included as factors rationalising governmental involvement in sport.

Contemporary sport policy also highlights these two pillars, although with a clear emphasis on sport as an instrument for other purposes. *A Sporting Future for All* in 2000 (DCMS 2000), *A Sporting Future for All: The Government's Plan for Sport* in 2001 (DCMS/DfEE 2001) and *Game Plan* in 2002 (DEMS/SU 2002) are the central documents that outline the Blair government's sport policy. The vision for British sport policy is: (a) increased participation by young people through enhancing school sport, (b) life-long participation through sport in the community and (c) talent development through sporting excellence (along with other, more 'technical', objectives such as modernisation). In other words, the Government wants to see: 'more people of all ages and all social groups taking part in sport; and more success for our top competitors and teams in international competition' (*A Sporting Future for All*, 2000). The Government emphasises the problems arising from differential access to sport based on ethnicity, gender and social class. It is further argued that uneven access and exclusion have social and health implications. Finally, the documents emphasise that social exclusion is diminishing the 'pool of talent' available to elite sport.

In December 2002 the Strategy Unit in the Cabinet Office together with DCMS published the report *Game Plan: A Strategy for Delivering Government's Sport and Physical Activity Objectives* (DCMS/Strategy Unit, 2002). This report was an analysis of the state of the sport in Britain and the role of the government and sought to clarify the overarching objectives for public sports policy which were to double the participation in sport from 35% to 70% of the population by 2020, and to have teams and athletes sustain a ranking amongst the top five countries by 2010. 'Scandinavian participation, Australian success,' is how these objectives were expressed in the report (2002, p. 81). The aim of increasing participation was given priority in order to maximise the assumed health benefits. Other overall benefits like reduced crime and greater social inclusion were acknowledged as important, but the report concluded that the evidence of the influence of sport in these areas was less significant, noting that 'the benefits of physical activity on health are clear ... whereas for other areas such as education and crime reduction, sport can best be used as a part of a package of measures to achieve success' (2002, p. 79). *Game Plan* is in many ways a refreshing policy document insofar as it is clear in linking government investment in increasing participation to the availability of robust evidence. However, the commitment to evidence-based policy is replaced by vague rhetoric when investment in elite sport is considered. The report notes that 'creating a "feel good factor" from elite success is the other area where, despite the difficulty in quantifying the impact, there appears to be a positive impact for the nation as a whole'.[8]

Houlihan (1997, p. 92) pointed out that the government's involvement in sport has traditionally been 'reactive rather than the outcome of a strategic overview'. However, recent government documents on sport, especially *Game Plan*, indicate a clear shift to a more strategic approach and a greater willingness to intervene in the activities of NSOs and local government. There has also been an increased and more explicit emphasis on supporting sport as a means for achieving other non-sport purposes especially in relation to health. However, the extent to which the increased focus on mass participation has been reflected in changes in patterns of funding and the structure of the delivery system is debatable. Indeed Green and Houlihan's study of elite sport development in UK (and Australia and Canada) indicated that the focus on restructuring the NGBs in order to produce elite success has altered the balance of both political priority and funding between elite interests and mass interests in favour of the former (2005, pp. 179ff).

Germany

Because of the intense politicisation of sport during the Third Reich period the state has been reluctant to articulate policy objectives for sport apart from those that the sport movement itself has identified. Federal support for sport is primary 'a help to self help' as argued in the introduction to the ninth sports report from the Ministry of Interior to the Bundestag: 'Sport is, in its distinctive and basic form, the free choice of the citizens. They choose themselves their organisations, which are independent from the state. The Federal government endorses the autonomy of a sport system that should be independent from state intervention and rules' (authors' translation, BMI, 1999, p. 9). This position is consistent with the character of the general welfare regime in Germany where the emphasis is on the role of non-governmental and non-commercial associations in delivering welfare services, especially those that are not core issues for the welfare state.

Although respect for the autonomy of sport organisations is an important political value the government has made clear what it considers to be the rationale for continued prioritisation of public funding. Successful elite performances are seen as a means to generate international recognition for Germany and a valuable resource in international relations. The federal government also acknowledges the complementarity between elite and mass. In the last report to the Bundestag (BMI, 2002) the increase in sport participation was emphasised as an important political goal for the Federal government working and cooperating with the state and municipal governments. The Federal government has also highlighted the value of sport in breaking down social barriers and unifying people. However, it is important to emphasise that most of these justifications have been long held values of the DSB. As Heinemann (1997, p. 180) notes: 'We can say, that this declaration of functions is an ideological argument that provides a legitimation of sport and fosters the acceptance of sport by the population.' The strong consensus regarding the rationale for government support for sport and for the autonomy of sports organisations was summed up by one federal official who observed that sport was good for integration, for youngsters, for society, indeed sport was good for 'everything'.

While the federal government has been cautious about increasing direct involvement in sport the *länder* have been less reticent. The Presidium of the Standing Conference of ministers of sport from the *länder* stated in the foreword to the collection of 'decisions and recommendation from the conference from 1977 to 2000', that 'Sport has an important socio-political function. It develops in a diversity of shapes and spreads continually further. The requirements and tasks for sport therefore belong to the public sport development system' (SMK, 2001, p. 1).

In summary, at the federal level there has been an increasing emphasis on sport as a contribution to health policy, while both federal and *land* level justify public involvement in sport in relation to contribution to social policy objectives. However, it would be inaccurate to interpret the increased emphasis on mass participation as indicating a lessening in the policy commitment to elite sport success. Indeed many of our interviewees pointed out that when it comes to elite sport Germany has adopted the (or at least part of the) former East Germany system resulting in an increased focus on elite sport infrastructure (schools, Olympic centres) and on the utilisation of science in elite sport development.

Norway

In the mid-nineteenth century public involvement and support for sport in Norway was legitimated by defence requirements. The first sports organisations that were established in the second half of the nineteenth century were related to military activity. However, from 1929 responsibility for sport was given to the Ministry of Social Affairs and social and health benefits became the dominant public motive for supporting sport (Goksøyr, 1992). After Second World War and the availability of gaming money sport was included in what has been called the social functionalist welfare regime (see Chapter 3). Public support for sport was related to sport's function of cultivating good citizens. Later, in the 1970s, sport became a part of what was called the 'extended concept of culture' (Mangset, 1992). In the period from 1973 to 1983 four different governments presented four different reports (white papers) on culture (Tønnesson, 1986, pp. 281ff), but the views regarding sport that were expressed in these documents did not vary significantly. The essential perception of sport that legitimates public support is the phrase 'sport for all' or 'the opportunity for as many as possible to have equal access to sport', as stated in the first white paper published by a centrist government in 1973 (authors' translation, cited in Tønnesson, 1986, p. 282).

There have been two major government reports on sport prepared for the Parliament. The first published in 1991/1992 and the second in 1999/2000. Both reports emphasised a broad social role for sport. The 1991/1992 report called *Sport – popular movement and popular entertainment*, stated that: 'Sport is legitimated both by its intrinsic value and its utility value. This implies that sport is both an end and a means' (St.meld. nr. 41,

1991–1992, p. 12). The utility value of sport was exemplified by its prominence in voluntary work, its role in social development of children and its capacity to generate health benefits: '[T]he socio-economic benefits of the population's involvement in sport and outdoor recreation is probably significantly higher than the costs that follows such activity' (St.meld. nr. 41, 1991–1992, p. 14). The report emphasised that the overarching objective for public sport policy was *sport for all*, but especially for children, youth and marginal groups.

The second and most recent government report on sport was titled *Sporting life in transformation – Concerning the government's relation to sport and physical activity* (St.meld. nr. 14, 1999–2000). In the introduction it is explained why the government has to justify its involvement in sport: 'Previously sport was seen as a united movement. A detailed definition of the motives for governmental participation in the area of sport has consequently been seen as unnecessary. Today this unity is under pressure from internal and external forces which has resulted in a more ambiguous picture of sport' (p. 5). One key development challenging the unity of sport has been the growing importance of elite sports (Tønnesson, 1986; Bergsgard, 2005). The recent Norwegian government report on sport does not, unlike recent British reports, attempt to quantify elite sporting 'achievements of the country'. However, the arguments for the continued support of elite sport are similar: 'The Government will support Norwegian elite sport financially so that an ethically and professionally qualified elite sport environment is secured, and so that elite sport may still be considered as a means of cultural identification in Norwegian society' (authors' translation, St.meld. nr. 14, 1999–2000, p. 37). Although mass participation remains the key priority there has been an increase in public funding for elite sport, for example, the provision of special state grants to elite athletes, support for building/restructuring national facilities and the Central Sport Centre, support for the Lillehammer Olympics and support for participation in the Olympics. In addition, a proportion of the basic funding to NIF and the sports federations has been spent on elite sport. Since 2000 for example, there has been a specific post related to elite sport within the funding agreement with NIF concerning lottery money indicating central government support for the development of elite sport.

Conclusion

Of the three analytic dimensions explored in this chapter the first was the significance of state structure, and particularly the significance for the sport sector of a federal or unitary, centralised or decentralised state. In general, the sport sector in Germany, Canada and partly England is structured as we suggested in Table 2.1. In Germany and Canada the sub-national state level, the *länder* and the provinces, plays a prominent role in the sport policy system, especially when it comes to sport participation/ recreational sport and school sport. While the sub-national state level is also involved in elite sport in the two countries, the federal level has main responsibility, especially related to international elite sport. In England one can say that the central government plays a determining role both regarding elite sport and mass sport. The establishment of the two sports councils, UK Sport and Sport England, and of the National Lottery in the mid-1990s are evidence of this centralisation. However, it should be borne in mind that roughly 75% of the funding for sport is channelled through the local authorities and that there have been some, albeit limited, reforms aimed at strengthening the regional level of the English sport system particularly in relation to *sport for all*. Although it can be questioned how profound the promotion of regionalisation is, one can argue that there is a degree of ambivalence in the current evolution of the English sport system. The Norwegian sport policy system deviates most clearly from our assumptions presented in Table 2.1. The central government plays a more prominent role than was assumed both by funding sport and by providing policy guidelines attached to this funding. Further the central government is more active in setting general sport policy objectives and in legislating, albeit in a limited fashion in the area of sport. It is acknowledged that the local level has, to a certain degree, discretionary power through the funding of sport clubs, planning and supporting building of sport facility, etc., but is not obvious that the local authorities in Norway have more devolved power in the sport policy system than the local authorities in England, Germany and Canada. In all of these countries the major task for the local authorities in the sport policy system, was to build and maintain the physical infrastructure for sport, with support from the central government. In addition, the capacity of local authorities to determine a distinctive sport policy was substantially limited, primarily by their dependence on central funding and by the publication of more explicit national sport policy frameworks.

In relation to the second analytic dimension, executive-legislative relations one can conclude that the legislature plays a minor role in shaping sport policy while the executive has a much more dominant role. However, we expected the contrary in Germany and Norway. In Germany, in contrast to the federal level, the legislature does have a significant role at *land* level regularly discussing sport policy issues and debating the distribution of the *land's* sport budget. Furthermore, in some *länder* there is a distinct body of sport law setting out general guidelines and objectives for sport policy. In Norway the strengthening of the parliament at the expense of the executive that has generally taken place in the political sphere over the last 20–30 years, is not evident in relation to sport policy. It is still the executive, more precisely, the officials in the Sport Policy Department, that are the major force in shaping the national sport policy.

The third analytic dimension concerned the relationship between sport organisations and the government in each country. In general, there was closer correspondence with the exceptions recorded in Table 2.1 than for the other dimensions. There is a loose policy network for sport in both England and Canada, and even if we can see Sport Canada and the sports councils in England as some kind of advocates for the sport sector within the government, they are far from being corporatist bodies. In Germany the network is fairly closed, both at federal and national level, yet maybe more as a 'friendship relationship' than a 'family relationship'. The 'family-relationship' metaphor has, though, been used to describe the policy community in Norway, indicating a close relationship between the government and the voluntary sport sector both at the national and local levels, but with few formal councils, boards, etc. In addition, the funding of the NSOs, through the dominant umbrella organisation in Norway, NIF/NOC, indicates a strong and close relationship with government. This arrangement contrasts with that found in the other countries. In Canada and England/UK funds for the national specialised federations (NSOs/NGBs) were distributed directly from a public body (council/agency), and the funds from the Ministry of Interior in Germany are mainly distributed directly to the specialised national sports federations, albeit with some cooperation from the federal umbrella organisation, *Deutsche Sport Bund*.

Finally, if we examine the nature of sport policy in relation to Esping-Anderson's typology of welfare regimes we find a degree of discontinuity in each country. Although it is accurate that the commercial sector plays a significant role in sport in Canada and England, it is not the case that the state plays a limited role. In both countries there has been significant government involvement admittedly with some shifts in the nature and intensity of engagement due to shifts in political priorities. However, in recent years there has been a significant intensification in government involvement in sport policy, especially in England with sport being increasingly redefined as an element within the health sector, and consequently a core issue for the welfare state. In

Germany, the non-state voluntary sector plays a major role in the sport policy system, although in close relationship with the government at all levels. In Norway, apart from football, there is a rather limited commodification of sport and there is an active state in the sport policy area. However, the government does not run the actual sporting activity as competitive organised sport is run by the voluntary organisations, while the more recreational sport is seen as a personal initiative much of which takes place within commercial health training centres. The state's role in Norway is to lay the foundation for sporting activity, especially inside the voluntary organisations, rather than undertaking extensive service delivery.

Notes

1 Ben Johnson won the 100 m final at the 1988 Olympic Games in Seoul in a record time, but tested positive for the steroid stanozolol and was subsequently disqualified.
2 See www.ccpr.org.uk
3 From *Sport England Annual Report* 2001–2002, Part 1.
4 From UK Sport (2002). *Summary Financial Statements of UK Sport's Exchequer and Lottery Accounts 2001/2002.*
5 The difference may stem from the fact that Game Plan's figures covers all of the UK, Houlihan and White's England and Wales, while the Carter Report's figures cover only England.
6 In May 2006 DSB and the *Nationales Olymiches Komitee* (NOK) merged and become one organisation, *Deutscher Olympischer Sportbund* (DOSB). Since our field work was carried out in 2003/2004 we will here still use the name *Deutscher Sportbund* (DSB)
7 We will here use the term 'gaming money' in the period from 1946 to 1991, since the profits to sport in that period came from gaming on sport, and 'lottery money' after 1991 since then the majority of the money to sport comes from the state lottery.
8 The reports find little clear cut evidence of economic, social or participation benefits from international success or hosting big events.

CHAPTER 6

High performance sport

Introduction

It may be agreed that to compete with others and try to reach the highest possible level of performance is the main objective and the core rationale of the whole sport system (Tangen, 2004). In this respect sport systems may be compared to *art* systems as both are usually characterised by inexorable selection, competition and hierarchies (Mangset, 2004).[1] While our concern is with high performance sport our focus is less on the fully commercialised sports, such as English football and Canadian ice hockey, and more on the sports, most Olympic sports for example, that depend more on voluntary efforts and state support at the elite level.

The priority given to elite sport varies considerably between countries, due in part to different national cultural values and traditions, political and administrative structures, and relationships between governmental and civil society sports organisations. In contrast it seems as if sports policies, and especially elite sport policies, in different countries have become more similar in recent decades. In this chapter we will compare the values, structures and relationships connected to high performance sport in the four countries. We will build upon discussions in Chapter 2 and ask whether various patterns of organisation of high performance sport reflect the general differences between welfare regimes, described by Esping-Andersen (1999). We will also explore how high performance sport policy is affected by the general homogenising forces identified in Chapter 3, and discuss the implication of the analytical dimensions presented in Chapter 2 (Table 2.1) for this policy area.

The number of medals won in Olympic Games and other international sport competitions offers the most self-evident and transparent measure of success in high performance sport. All four countries in this study have been relatively successful in the most recent Olympic Games (see Table 1.3 in Chapter 1). Germany is still a high performer in international competitions, even if it lost its undisputed leading position following the collapse of communism and the unification of East and West Germany in 1990. Germany ranked 2nd on the medal table of the Salt Lake City winter games (2002), 5th on the medal table of the Sydney summer games (2000), 6th on the medal table of the Athens summer games (2004) and 1st on the medal table of the Turin winter games (2006). Although Norwegian sport policy appears more oriented towards *sport for all* than German sport policy, Norway has still been quite successful at the elite level, particularly when the size of the population (only 4.6 m) is taken into account. Norway ranked 1st in the medal table at Salt Lake

City, 19th at Sydney, 17th at Athens and 13th at the Turin Olympic Games. Canada ranked relatively high on the two last winter Olympics medal table (4th in Salt Lake City 2002 and 5th in Turin 2006) and the UK relatively high on the Sydney (2000) and Athens (2004) summer Olympics medal tables (10th in both). However, when the size of the population (nearly 60 m) is taken into consideration the UK has been less successful than many other countries of similar wealth and population (DCMS/Strategy Unit, 2002, p. 30).

Why are most countries striving to achieve success in international sport competitions and how can the factors that lead to success be identified? The answers are not obvious as there are examples of countries with relatively different elite sport ideologies, for instance Germany and Norway, which have been successful in international competitions. During the last decades high performance sport has been institutionalised in many countries with both public authorities and sport organisations developing specific policies and establishing new organisations in this field. Public or semi-public specialist elite sport policy units have been established; elite sport centres have been created; scientific methods have increasingly been adopted; programmes for the professional education of coaches have been developed; and policies for identification, selection and training of talented athletes have been designed. But the institutionalisation of high performance sport also inevitably awakes dilemmas and value conflicts. The 'dark side' of elite sport which encompasses doping, eating disorders, sexual abuse and hooliganism are regular and increasingly urgent topics for sport policy debate.

It may seem as if the institutionalisation of high performance sport has followed a rather similar pattern in different countries. Thus Green and Oakley (2001, p. 249) ask whether there is a trend towards 'a (globally) uniform model of elite sport development (diminishing contrasts), or whether there is room for diversity (increasing varieties) in national elite sport systems'. Specific events ('focusing events'[2]) may occur and speed up or slow down the homogenisation process. A number of factors, however, seem to support the diminishing contrast hypothesis – at least in the countries[3] studied by Oakley and Green (2001).[4] Later in this chapter we will discuss whether this is also true for the four countries under scrutiny in this study and, if it is, how should we explain it? It seems as if the sport organisations of different countries *imitate* each other. The less successful 'regimes' imitate the more successful – or at least they imitate what they believe to be the most successful – regimes. Green and Houlihan (2005) write about 'policy transfer' instead of 'imitation' in order to describe such processes.

Our study is mainly based upon analysis of policy documents and qualitative interviews with senior personnel in public sport policy units and sport organisations. We particularly focus upon the discursive level, that is upon how agents in different positions and at different levels of the sport system speak and write about high performance sport. Sport systems in most countries are characterised by conflicts and dilemmas between elite sport and *sport for all*. The relative priority of elite sport versus *sport for all* may depend upon profound differences in values and norms between countries, that is upon differences in 'deeply rooted policy orientations and rules of collective actions' (Chapter 3). As noted by Green and Houlihan (2005, p. 61) such ' "deep core" and "policy core beliefs" are assumed to have a high level of resistance to change.' But sports policy discourses should also be studied from another, more rhetorical perspective. Arguments are also used in sports policy debates in order to obtain specific policy effects. Elite sport lobbyists tend to use arguments for support of high performance sport that are acceptable and influential in the political world. Elite sport discourses are therefore often strategic, ambivalent and euphemistic. They tell us that high performance sport should not be supported for its own sake, but rather because of the benefits it brings to public health or international diplomacy. In Chapter 2 we noticed a general tendency towards 'generalisation of interest' in pluralist societies (i.e. that political actors try to broaden their alliances and legitimacy basis). One should also expect this tendency to be reflected in high performance sport discourses.

In this chapter we will therefore give particular emphasis to comparing different elite sport discourses, that is written official policy statements in documents and verbal interview statements from public and sport organisation officials. We will also confront and compare the development of elite sport discourses with the parallel development of elite sport organisation. In this context we will particularly analyse how different sport systems describe and organise the 'pathways to the podium' (Green, 2004), that is the organisation of different phases from talent selection and development to podium success.

Values, priorities and ambivalences

Sport systems tend to celebrate equality and difference at the same time giving prominence to the principle of 'fair inequality' or 'equal chances.' The result of equal chance and competition between athletes with different physical potentials and mental motivations is of course inequality and hierarchy. The top athlete usually achieves a much higher level of performance, becomes more famous, earns more money, and often receives more public subsidy than other athletes. The organisation of sport (associations and clubs) is characterised by similar inequality and hierarchy. But the hierarchical 'pyramid model' is more pronounced in the sport system in some countries than in others. According to the general policy models described in this study (Esping-Andersen, 1999) English and Canadian sport policies should be expected to be more competitive, elite oriented and commercialised than the sport policies of other countries, while German and Norwegian sport policies should be expected to be less competitive and more *sport for all* oriented. We should also expect German and Norwegian governments to be more involved in sport, while British and Canadian governments should be expected to leave sport more to the market.

Sport policy, and particularly public support to elite sport, has been justified in various ways at different periods and in different countries. Government involvement in sport, has for instance, been justified in terms of its contribution to health benefits, military success, national pride, national unity, social peace and the reduction of crime. Such justifications by non-sporting objectives illustrate the on-going politicisation of sport (see Chapter 3). During the 1950s and 1960s the Soviet Union and other Eastern European countries started to use sport systematically to reach instrumental goals. According to Heinemann (1996, p. 169) 'elite sport [in the former GDR] functioned as the symbol of the 'superiority' of the communist economy and the ambassador of the communist political order'. The success of these policies, and particularly the success of Soviet and East German athletes in Olympic Games and other international competitions, prompted increased concern about the need for more active government sport policies in many countries outside the communist bloc, for instance in Australia, Canada and USA (Chalip *et al.*, 1996; Farmer and Arnaudon, 1996; Macintosh, 1996). During the 1970s and 1980s many countries therefore implemented more active sport policies in order to promote high performance sport. Australia's systematic and efficient elite sport policy during the 1980s and 1990s, with the establishment of the Australian Institute of Sport in 1981, served as an example for other countries. Australia, and to a lesser extent Canada, have both adopted policies of elite squad development which are very close to the Soviet model in a number of key respects including the systematic sifting of school-age children as a means of identifying the potential elite, the development of specialist training academies, the subordination of domestic governing bodies to government policy and the use of public money to support individual elite athletes (Houlihan, 1996, p. 6).

During the same period, however, the development of sports policies became influenced by more egalitarian welfare values and a wider range of instrumental rationales including improved public health, economic development and community cohesion. Sports policies therefore usually had to balance between egalitarian and welfare values, on the one hand, and values connected to high performance and international success on the other. The relative impact of these opposing value systems has of course changed from one period to another, partly according to which political movement (liberal, conservative or social democrat) has been in power and partly according to different focusing events in the sports field (such as Olympic successes/failures, hosting of international competitions (mega events) and doping scandals).

Canada

Canadian ambivalence ● ● ●

The Canadian Sport Policy, a governmental plan,[5] states that high performance sport is one of the four pillars of Canadian sports policy. According to this plan it should be a goal of the Canadian sport policy that, by 2012,

the pool of talented athletes has expanded and Canadian athletes and teams are systematically achieving world-class results at the highest levels of international competitions through fair and ethical means (Sport Canada, 2002, p. 17).

International success should therefore be a very important goal for Canadian sport policy both currently and over the coming years. But such goals are not as undisputed in Canada today as they were some decades ago. *The Canadian Sport Policy* also demonstrates that the high performance goals have to be balanced against *sport for all* goals and ethical considerations, at least at a discursive level (*ibid.*, p. 10). The priority given to high performance sport is more ambivalent than before. The extreme power, weight and visibility of professional sport[6] make the dilemma even more pertinent. The professional sport sector hardly abides by the rules of the rest of the sport community. Thus, *the Canadian Sport Policy* states that in professional sport there are 'examples of the distortion of the basic values of sport', which do not always offer good role models for the youth (*ibid.*, p. 12).

This ambivalence in relation to elite sport also appears in face-to-face interviews with Sport Canada officials. It was partly caused by the Ben Johnson affair (see below). According to Sport Canada officials, elite sport was the main objective of Canadian sport policy 'for many years, until "the *Canadian Sport Policy*-[report]"' (2002). They maintain that until then official sport policy favoured a 'pyramid model' with success in international championships as the ultimate performance indicator. *The Canadian Sport Policy*, however, introduced a broader perspective, favouring general participation in sport and 'physical activity', that is a broad approach, just a bit narrower than the European *sport for all* policy. Such a policy may be promoted for two quite different underlying reasons:

One is to create a strong base of people in sport, to give the pyramid more ammunition and more people to hopefully rise to the top, and there is a debate whether that works or not. And the other one is for the good of Canadians, because if they are active in sport they are [more] healthy (Sport Canada official).

Therefore a *sport for all* policy may appear both as a high performance policy in disguise (see below) and as a broad welfare oriented policy for the whole population. This ambivalence within the official Canadian sport policy discourse suggests that the sport system is still haunted by a profound malaise after the Ben Johnson scandal in 1988. However, this ambivalence does not seem to affect significantly the national sports organisations, at least not those that are most involved in international sports competitions, as they do not hesitate to prioritise high performance sport. The Canadian Olympic Committee (COC) is clearly unconcerned, as according to one COC officer, 'We think that the government needs to invest more dollars in development, talent identification, developing those athletes from provincial teams up to national teams. Think of it as a pyramid, it is at the top of the pyramid that we go'. According to a Canadian sport policy researcher other national sports organisations share this elite sport vision commenting that, 'They are almost genetically biased towards high performance'. Sport organisation representatives are generally frustrated because of what they perceive as a reticence on the part of the government in relation to high performance sport in Canada. This frustration was captured in this typical comment from one sports administrator, 'We are very much a culture of make it fair for everybody'.

Historical background of current Canadian sport policy • • •

The Canadian federal government made its first attempts to develop a systematic sport policy in 1961, when the government enacted 'an Act to Encourage Fitness and Amateur Sport' (Macintosh, 1996; Green and Houlihan, 2005). This initiative was motivated by a double concern, both for elite sport and *sport for all*. During the 1950s Canada had suffered bitter defeats in international sporting competitions, especially by the Soviet Union in ice hockey. At the same time there was a growing concern among educators and politicians about the poor level of physical fitness in the Canadian population (*ibid.*). Canadian health policy officials looked to Scandinavia for inspiration and models (e.g. the PartipAction project launched in 1973). An international comparison in the early 1970s seemed to demonstrate that an average 60 years old Swede typically possessed the same fitness level as a 30 years old Canadian resulting in the issue being kept in the public gaze due to frequent references to 'the 60 Year Old Swede and the 30 Year Old Canadian' in the popular press.[7]

An important step in understanding the development of Canadian sport policy is an appreciation of how the policy tension between elite and mass sport was resolved. As already mentioned egalitarian and instrumental rhetoric may sometimes have concealed that the principal objective of a country's sport policy was/is in reality to promote elite sport. According to Macintosh, this was more or less the case with a policy document issued by Health and Welfare Minister Munro in Canada in 1969. Macintosh noted that 'Although this document contained a great deal of rhetoric about mass participation in sports and recreational activities, its recommendations were directed largely towards elite sport' (1996, p. 46). Thus the arguments for *sport for all* were not necessarily inspired first and foremost by egalitarian values. Such arguments rather served as an instrument for promoting elite sport. Mass participation primarily seemed to function as a recruitment base for the selection of high performance athletes. A sport policy researcher maintains that this has also generally been, and continues to be, the case in Canadian sport policy observing that national sport organisations are interested in grassroots development only as a form of recruitment and development:

I would say that from 1970 to 1988 the focus was almost exclusively on high performance. Under a banner of excellence, what I call ... the 'ideology of excellence' – was the overarching goal – getting athletes to the podium. That was justified in the name of national unity, justified in terms of world competitiveness, it was justified in terms of inspiring the youth to be the best they could be, but the focus was on high performance.

Poor performances in international competitions during the 1960s and 1970s (e.g. the Montreal Olympics in 1976) contributed to increased federal involvement in high performance sport in the following years. The creation of the Canada Games during the 1960s, the establishment of Sport Canada as a national government agency for elite sport during the 1970s and the Best Ever campaign during the 1980s (for the Calgary Olympics, 1988) were some of the measures taken to improve the Canadian high performance sport system. Thus, according to Green and Houlihan (2005, p. 63), Canada was among the 'early Western adopters' of 'many of the principles of organisation and administration developed by the former Eastern bloc countries'. They interpret the establishment of professionalised elite sport development structures in Canada and several other countries, including Australia, as a case of 'policy transfer' or 'imitation'.

During the 1980s and 1990s, however, it became more difficult to justify public support to elite sport by appealing to general interests and positive rationales like national unity, public health and/or international diplomacy, because of an increased focus upon the 'dark side' of elite sport. The use of drugs in sport challenged the idea of sport being associated with fair play and health benefits. It appeared that many young and ambitious athletes suffered from eating disorders while the commercialisation of elite sport broke with the idealistic objectives that sport traditionally was supposed to promote. Such tendencies created an international crisis and a need for self-scrutiny within sport policy. The Canadian sport system was particularly afflicted by such a crisis, because of the Ben Johnson affair after the Seoul Olympics in 1988. The disclosure of 100 m winner and world record holder, Ben Johnson's, use of steroids during the Olympics created a national scandal and a period of self-scrutiny that lasted for several years. It appeared that drug abuse was quite widespread among Canadian top athletes. The whole sport system, and particularly the elite sport system, was therefore subject to general mistrust (Macintosh, 1996). According to one sport policy researcher,

Ben Johnson's disqualification for steroids from Seoul was a devastating event. Whereas in other countries similar disqualifications were swept under the rug or even denied, as in the USA, in Canada it was a matter of national crisis. So for 2 or 3 years there was really a very high-level on-going debate about the entire purpose of the amateur Olympic sport sector – and government support to that sector.

The Canadian sport system therefore suffered from a profound legitimacy crisis. The Ben Johnson affair was the 'focusing event' that created the opportunity for a distinct redirection of Canadian sport policy. It was followed by a general public debate sustained by the Dubin Inquiry into the Ben Johnson scandal and doping in Canadian sport. The discussion resulted in a temporary re-consideration of the values underpinning Canadian sport with mass sport (for instance women's sport and aboriginal sport) being reappraised and receiving more attention. However, this is not to imply that public authorities in Canada had not shown any interest in *sport for all* earlier but after the Ben Johnson crises there was a revival of a broader sport policy which was maintained at least over the medium term of 5–7 years.

The Dubin Report was followed by the so-called Best Report,[8] which continued the re-evaluation of Canadian elite sport policy. Among other things it asked the fundamental question, 'Why do we support high performance sport at all?' (Green and Houlihan, 2005, p. 46). According to the above mentioned sport policy researcher the early 1990s was 'a period of transformation of the Canadian sports community' during which sport policy became 'value based'.[9] From another perspective this was also a period of set-backs for high performance sport. A Sport Canada official offers the following diagnosis:

I think there were a number of years where federal officials were afraid to state expectations of trying to accomplish, of trying to win medals. It was almost 'we cannot be asking athletes to win medals, because that would be asking them to use drugs'.

In addition, the dominance of neo-conservative political interests in the mid-1990s caused a substantial cut-back in the public sector finances which affected new sports initiatives severely and led to substantial cuts in Sport Canada's budget (Green and Houlihan, 2005).

During the last 10 years, partly prompted by public concern, efforts have been made to find a better equilibrium between high performance and *sport for all*/public health objectives in sport. However, there are differences of opinion about whether these efforts have been successful. Some Sport Canada officials we interviewed maintain that there has been a change of policy objectives with the one-sided focus upon 'high performance' augmented by a concern with 'participation', 'health' and 'physical activity'. Other Sport Canada officials also argue that Canadian sport policy, unlike Australian sport policy, never had set 'aggressive targets' of a specific number of Olympic medals. The policy aim was to be 'best ever' which could be defined in several ways.

Other observers are less confident about the change of perspective and goals in sport policy towards a more democratic and egalitarian direction. According to Houlihan (1997, p. 83) the revision of elite sport objectives proposed in the Best Report were not followed up by the Minister:

In November 1994 the Minister announced a revised set of objectives for Sport Canada which largely ignored the thrust of the Best Report and its argument for a broader and less elitist approach to sport, and confirmed the priority of elite sport success by making it clear that federal funding would be used primarily to support high-performance athletes.

This view was endorsed by one Canadian sport policy researcher who argued that the transformation of Sport Canada's objectives has not been profound. He acknowledged that the *Physical Activity and Sport Act* (2003) placed greater emphasis on broadly based participation, but observed that as long as Sport Canada channelled most of its funding and activities through the national sport organisations, it would continue to be biased towards high performance sport. Another sport scholar agreed that there has been a revival of elitism in Canadian sport policy recently, but argued that high performance policy is still blurred by profound ambivalence:

I think that the media encourages the government to be more involved in elite sport. I think the government as a rule wants to be less involved in any sport – elite or participation sport. I do not think the government is that interested in promoting sport. And I think there is a reason for that; I think it is because of all the negative things associated with professional sport. The problem is that ... the government is afraid that when people think of sport; they think of professional sport, whereas we are talking more of participation level for all people.

The government also seems to have an ambivalent attitude to specific performance objectives for high performance sport (e.g. number of medals in Olympic Games). It has already been noted that Sport Canada officials denied the existence of such 'aggressive targets' in Canadian sport policy. In contrast to this, however, the former Secretary of State for Amateur Sport, Denis Coderre, in 2001 (as already mentioned in Chapter 3) promoted a 'funding programme focused on high performance sport with the specific objective of achieving medal-winning results' (Green and Houlihan, 2005, p. 49).

While elite sport policy has largely been the responsibility of the federal government it is important to bear in mind that elite sporting success has also been tightly intertwined with separatist politics and consequently features in the policy discussions at provincial level (reflects the 'decentralised federalism' of Canada, Table 2.1). During the last decades elite sport has certainly been a social arena for politicisation and manifestation of Francophone nationalism more or less in opposition to the Anglophone Canadian majority (Harvey, 1999). Green and Houlihan (2005, p. 42) observe that while federal authorities invested more attention and resources in elite sport during the 1970s and 1980s, some provinces, especially Quebec, 'were developing their own elite sport agenda'. According to several interviewees Quebec is actually the province in Canada that invests most in sport. It has become a 'model province' for the Canadian sports world. A (French-speaking) Sport Canada official maintains that 'it is important for the population ... and also for the pride of Quebecers to see Quebec athletes win Olympic gold medals'. According to a sport policy researcher it is also 'very clear' that investment in sport has been 'a vehicle for Quebec identity':

Quebec in the last 30 years has been the most social-democratic in terms of its political composition, and they have seen the state as a vehicle of *social* development, and they have seen the state as a vehicle of *sport* development. So they have invested heavily in sport in Quebec.

Not surprisingly Quebec has been the most successful Canadian province in international championships in recent years. According to a COC official somewhere between 30% and 50% of the Canadian athletes in the Games come from Quebec. It seems as if this province has used sport as an instrument both to manifest national and cultural identity in opposition to the rest of Canada and to develop the province from its relatively weak economic position in the Canadian federation.

The priority given to elite sport in Canadian sport policy *discourse* has fluctuated considerably since the Second World War influenced by shifts in the general cultural climate, changes in political regimes and specific sport policy events.[10] These discursive fluctuations of course have also affected the specific and concrete elite sports policies implemented by the government and the NGOs. But it also appears that this concrete elite sport policy – or the structural elite sport policy – has developed much more steadily and consistently during the same period. Despite all ambiguities and debates it seems as if sport policy in Canada today is, in practice, strongly oriented to the promotion of high performance sport. Thus Green and Houlihan (2005, pp. 49–50) conclude that 'the Canadian federal government has created a centrally planned and bureaucratic elite sport development model which reflects many of the 'rational' organisational and administrative principles evident in the Eastern bloc models ...'.

England

A late starter with an instrumental policy • • •

British sport policy has also traditionally been characterised by ambiguity in relation to elite sport (Green and Houlihan, 2005). It was not until quite recently that public authorities started to prioritise elite sport actively. A significant shift took place in the mid-1990s partly because sport from 1994 and onwards could benefit from support from the National Lottery, and partly because John Major's Conservative government took an active interest in elite sport (*ibid.*). Today, however, international sporting success is unchallenged as an important goal of official British (and English) sport policy. At least this is taken for granted in the most recent policy document on sport from the government, *Game Plan – a strategy for delivering Government's sport and physical activity objectives* (DCMS/Strategy Unit, 2002). In the foreword the Secretary of State for Culture, Media and Sport, Tessa Jowell, discusses what could be done to improve British performance in international sport: 'We can learn lessons from Australia', she writes. Australia has made a 'purposeful pursuit of sporting excellence' after their 'disastrous display at the 1976 Montreal Olympics'. A more systematic and professionalised high performance strategy should be combined with a systematic strategy for increased mass participation. Thus '[w]e should aspire to match both Finland and Australia' (DCMS/Strategy Unit, 2002, p. 7).[11] *Game Plan* does not discuss, however, *whether* international success should be pursued, it only discusses *how* it should be pursued and how it could be justified. *Game Plan* therefore systematically and unproblematically discusses which social benefits high performance sport could bring, such as a more positive image of the country abroad or better economic performance of the country. This kind of justifications by social benefits corresponds closely with the instrumental traditions of British policy more generally (Ridley, 1987; Houlihan, 1996).

In interviews representatives of UK Sport expressed even more explicitly, perhaps not surprisingly, the priority of performance sport. 'In terms of high performance sport [..] we are a high performance agency', commented one UK Sport official. He added that 'our actions are tested to create structures that would produce champions, and we have a very high level mission which is to be in the top five by the year 2012' (and consequently) 'our investment strategies are with primarily [...] Olympic sports'. Thus the yardstick for sport funding is success in international championships. 'There are some sports we are hardly funding at all, because they are not going to make an impact on the medal table'. The emphasis within UK Sport put on elite achievement was recognised by one national sports organisation officer who observed, 'The government wants gold medals. 'Money for medals' is one of their key words at the moment. You are expected to deliver results'. The allocation of the 2012 Olympics to London has certainly reinforced the elite sport focus, both within UK Sport and within wider sport policy.

It is a paradox, however, that *Game Plan*, despite serious efforts, found it difficult to provide robust evidence of the positive effects (social benefits) of international sporting success. The causal relationship between international sporting success and the image of UK/England abroad is unclear, and it is uncertain if sporting success has any substantially positive effects upon the economic performance of a region or a country. The most explicit positive effect (or benefit) seems instead to be a quite vague 'feelgood factor' – a 'sense of euphoria in society as a whole due to an event' (DCMS/Strategy Unit, 2002, p. 62). Except for this, high performance sport can hardly be justified by clearly demonstrated positive benefits. To give high priority to elite sport is therefore finally a matter of political and ideological choice and British authorities have had little hesitation lately in choosing elite sport.

However, British sport policy also tries to broaden its legitimacy by focusing upon general interests like *sport for all*, although not weakening its principal elite sport focus. According to a Department of Culture, Media and the Sports (DCMS) officer 'I think it is a growing awareness that sport can be a way of achieving other targets in term of, for example, social inclusion, a way of involving minority groups … It is not a shift away from elite sport, [it] is just a broadening of the focus'. This illustrates that British sport policy strives to broaden its legitimacy basis and increase the political support to sport (see the discussion of generalisation of interest in Chapter 2). But an active *sport for all* policy can also be justified for elite sport reasons, for example investment in increasing child and youth sport participation may result in elite sport successes later. According to one interviewee from the political field there is a need to focus on the grassroots now, because it is the 12 years olds today that will be the athletes in 2012.

Historical context of current elite sport policy in England • • •

Before the 1970s British sports policy was rather unsystematic, *ad hoc* and reactive (Green, 2004; Green and Houlihan, 2005). An Advisory Sports Council, however, was established by the government as early as 1965. During the 1970s and 1980s public authorities gradually intervened more actively in the sport field although high performance sport was hardly prioritised as the main focus remained mass participation. The Advisory Sports Council was restructured given executive powers and a new name, the 'Great Britain Sports Council' in 1972 (Green, 2004). A House of Lords report on 'sport and leisure' was published in 1973, followed by a White Paper on 'sport and recreation' in 1975 and another White Paper on 'Policy for the Inner Cities' in 1977. These documents illustrate the broad and socio-cultural approach to sports policy that predominated in this period. However, the focus gradually changed from *sport for all* to sport for specific groups (e.g. disadvantaged and inner city youth), with sports policy becoming an integrated part of welfare policy (Green, 2004). However, the Thatcher government, elected in 1979, changed the general direction of policy in a neo-liberal direction, giving greater emphasis to accountability and income generation in sport policy (Green and Houlihan, 2005).

Despite the increasing neo-liberal economic climate the broad socio-cultural direction of sports policy continued in the 1980s reflected in the GB Sports Council strategy document *Sport in the Community: The Next Ten Years*, published in 1982. However, the focus upon high performance sport also increased indicated by the allocation, by the GB Sports Council, of more money to elite sport than to *sport for all* (Green, 2004; Green and Houlihan 2005). Yet funding for elite sport was not an indication of the development of a systematic high performing sports policy. This absence was partly because the sports community was badly coordinated and could not 'speak with one voice' (see Chapter 4). It was not until John Major's new Conservative government following the 1992 general elections that the direction of sports policy changed significantly. Prior to 1992 Britain did not have a ministry with explicit responsibility for sport (or for culture in general). But in 1992 the first British 'Department of Culture', which included sport, was established. In the beginning it was euphemistically called 'the Department of National Heritage', not the 'Department of Culture'.[12] In 1997, however, its name was changed by the incoming Labour government to 'the Department of Culture, Media and the Sport' (DCMS). In the meantime, in 1994, the financial base of sport (and cultural) policy was strengthened significantly with the introduction of the National Lottery. A sports policy plan from the Conservative government, *Sport: Raising the Game* (1995), made the change of policy clear. It meant a sharper focus on elite sport and gradual withdrawal of government support to community sport (Green 2004; Green and Houlihan, 2005). A key strategic priority was the development of elite performers supported by the creation of an elite sports academy and improvements in the role of the educational system in fostering elite athletes.

British athletes were not successful in the Atlanta Olympics (1996). In the words of one UK Sport official … 'The problem with that was that sadly we had an enormous number of fours; but fours don't register on the medal table'. Thus the Atlanta failure became another 'focusing event' that contributed to increased pressure for a more effective high performance sports policy. UK Sport concentrated on developing 'a system and a programme for high performance athletes. It wasn't surprising in one way that – we had only been in existence 2 or 3 years – and suddenly along came Sydney, and 'bang!' we got huge results, which takes us from 30th or so to 10th!' (UK Sport official).

During the 1990s Britain started to develop a network of elite sports institutes, similar to those that were established in several other countries over the same period. Labour presented its sport strategy plan *A Sporting Future for All* in 2000. According to Green (2004, p. 373) this plan was illustrative of the Labour Party's 'modernising, reform agenda' and contrasted with the more trad-itional values reflected in *Sport: Raising the Game*, the policy docu-ment of the Conservative government. However, there was no fundamental difference between the social-democratic and the conservative policy in relation to elite sport. A special plan for the professionalisation of coaching (from 'The Coaching Task Force') was launched in 2002. The above mentioned document, *Game Plan*, which also focused upon improving Britain's inter-national performances in sport, was published the same year. These plans explicitly prioritised the development of a strong high performance sport system, that is more professional talent identification and development, the establishment of specialist sport colleges and more extensive and better quality school sport. Over the last 15 years British (and English) national public authorities have developed from relatively reluctant to whole-hearted advocates of an active and systematic elite sport policy.

Germany

Autonomy, hierarchy and federalism • • •

According to several interviewees in the German sports world, to win as many Olympic medals as possible is the primary objective of German sport policy. In Germany 'sport gets money with medals', says an official from the *Deutsche Turner-Bund*. 'The main task is to earn medals. The more medals, the more money you get'. 'We don't need to look for good results; that is self selling. We have only difficulties when the results are bad, like in Athletic

World Championships in Paris, when we got only two medals', commented an official in the elite division of the German Sport Confederation (DSB). He added: 'The better you are, the more [financial support] you get'. Interviewees from the *Bundesinstitut für Sportwissenschaft* also recognise that there is a tendency, in German sport policy, primarily to support 'the sport disciplines with best chances of medals'. They maintained that this aspect of German sport policy even today is 'equal to the DDR [East-German] system'. According to these sources German sport policy gives priority to disciplines that 'brings medals at Olympic Games and sport championships'. This view is confirmed by another DSB official, 'The major thing is to play an important role in world sport, to be a leading nation among other international sporting nations'. This elitist and competitive value system is also reflected in the hierarchic structuring of athletes who are ranked from category A to category D according to their performance levels. 'You have to have a certain number at each level to be provided with a certain amount of money – plus the results at defined international competitions. That is a clear structure and everybody can calculate if they are in or out', says the DSB official. International team athletes have to be on level A or B (where the 'Bs' are the potential or future international elite level athletes).[13] There is also a division of labour between the different national political–administrative levels, corresponding to the ranking of athletes. According to an official at *land* level:

The *Bundes-länder* are responsible for the C- and D-level of athletes. These are young athletes. The *Spitzenverbände*[14] are responsible for B- and A-athletes, that means national teams and Olympic athletes. We are supporting the ground level. The first steps for elite are financed by the *Bundes-länder* or by the state sport federations. The higher levels are always financed by the *Spitzenverbände* and sometimes by the NOK (National Olympic Committee).

This description of German elite sport policy, however, is presented from the point of view of sports organisations. Germany is a federal state without a separate ministry of sport, where responsibility for sport is, in principle, delegated to autonomous sports organisations (the *Deutscher Sportbund* (DSB), the different federal sports organisations and the *Nationales Olympisches Komitee* (NOK)).[15] The DSB has a joint responsibility both for competitive sport and *sport for all* while the NOK concentrates on the promotion of high performance sport. However, according to Heinemann (1996, pp. 162–163), the principle of autonomy of sport does not mean that sport is not 'the target of governmental policies'. '[T]he shaping of sport, except in schools and sport sciences that lie in the hands of the *länder*, is principally a matter for organised sport itself. The government sport policy is one of financial support' (*ibid.*, p. 163). Since the federal government provides direct financial support to the different federal level sports organisations directly it has the capacity to exert substantial influence over elite sport. In general, there is a division of financial responsibility between the federal level and the *länder*, where the federal level supports elite sport and international competitions, like the Olympic Games, while the *länder* support more socio-cultural sporting activities. This division of labour is not, however, clear-cut as the *länder* also provide some support to elite sport. At the federal level it is the Ministry of the Interior that has the principal responsibility for sport; at the *länder* level it is usually the ministry responsible for culture. A permanent Sports Minister Conference (between the ministers at the *länder* level) also plays a role in the coordination of elite sport.

Because of the relative autonomy of the sports movement in Germany it is difficult to detect the official German sport policy, the goals, values and discourses, from federal documents. The Ministry of the Interior presents federal German sport policy in quite general and pluralistic terms, emphasising the autonomy of sport, the dual objectives of high performance sport and *sport for all*, the importance of the fight against doping in sport and commitment to high ethical standards.[16] But in a White Paper to the Parliament the government (i.e. the *Bundesministerium des Innern*) expressed more explicit elite sport goals and discourses (BMI, 2002). The White Paper discussed several aspects of sport policy, both elite sport and *sport for all* and emphasised the impact of sport upon economic development and upon the prestige of Germany abroad, and maintained that high performance sport also stimulated *sport for all* (*ibid.*, p. 10). In addition, the White Paper discussed the organisation and promotion of elite sport in more detail and stressed the financial contribution from the federal state to the preparations for recent Olympic Games and the general success of Germany in terms of position in the medal table at the last Olympics (*ibid.*, pp. 27–29). The prioritisation of elite success in the 2002 White Paper was reinforced by the publication of a separate policy document about competitive sport from the ministry. It confirms the impression of a strong and explicit ambition of the federal government to promote a professional and structured elite sport policy, where German medals in Olympic Games have the highest priority (BMI, 2006).

However, despite the evidence from policy documents a BMI official denied that international success was the primary criterion for the allocation of federal money to sport. In the former GDR this was the case, he says, but not in unified Germany, 'Nobody in the government would cut money because of bad results'. However, an official in the German Sport Confederation was not so sure and argued that if a sport does not succeed in international competitions the Ministry may at least ask unpleasant questions: 'Then the Ministry is asking, what have you delivered? You have spent so many millions, and we want to know what you are doing to improve the situation'.

Historical background of today's elite sport policy in Germany • • •

The decades after the separation of Germany into two states (1949) elite sport policies took quite different directions in East and West Germany. West Germany (the Federal Republic of Germany FRG) developed a structure with strict separation between autonomous sport organisations and government policies. Public sport policy was very much a *länder* responsibility. The FRG also developed quite a broad sport policy, where high performance sport was prioritised in connection with, and in parallel with, more socio-cultural sport policy issues such as health related sport (Heinemann, 1996). East Germany (the German Democratic Republic, the GDR), in contrast, developed a much narrower policy, where high performance sport was used as an instrument to demonstrate the superiority of the communist model. The GDR had no independent sport club structure like that in the FRG and many high performance athletes were selected, trained and paid by the army. Resources were very much concentrated in high performance training centres in Berlin where there was a substantial 'overemployment' of support personnel. A DSB official reported that 'when we took over, in East Berlin in track and field, we took over 65 physiotherapists. Each individual athlete had his own ... Now we have [only] 8 [physiotherapists]'.

East German sport policy also tried to stimulate broader participation, but according to Heinemann (1996, p. 170), 'Sport for All did function to a large extent as an instrument for selection of sport talent or paramilitary education' (Heinemann, 1996, p. 170). The different priorities given to *sport for all* in the two systems also implied a much broader development of sport facilities in the FRG than in the GDR (i.e. more sport grounds, sport halls and swimming pools). Subsequently, the proportion of the population who participated in sport was much higher in the FRG than in the GDR (Heinemann, 1996, p. 170).[17] The unification of two different sport cultures and sport structures after 1990 was difficult. However, according to an interviewee at the *Bundesinstitut* 'the former GDR system is step by step being made part of the Western sport system'.[18] The East German sport system had to accommodate to the West German model. This view was endorsed by an interviewee from the Ministry of the Interior who stated emphatically that 'we did not accept the state sport system of East Germany … we did not adapt; they had to adapt'. The biggest change was the abolition of the systematic and centralised practice of doping in high performance sport. The general impact of science in sport may also have been somewhat reduced with, for example, the former sport university in Leipzig now integrated as a faculty at the University of Leipzig.[19] The GDR tradition of very early talent identification and systematic training, often by the age of 6 or 7 years, also seems to have been weakened. However, the focus upon talent identification among youth and children and upon elite sport in general is sharper than it was in West Germany during the 1970s and 1980s. The tradition of concentrating support on those sport disciplines with chances of winning Olympic medals and other championships also persists in the unified Germany.[20] Furthermore, the GDR model of Olympic training centres (*Olympiastützpunkte*) and elite sport schools (*Elitenschulen des Sports*) has been retained and adapted to the new German sport policy although, it is claimed, these adaptations have been sensitive and cautious. In the words of an official from a federal sports organisation,

We have 20 Olympic training centres. That was an idea that we gathered from former East Germany when it still was there. We invented them in '85–'86 when Germany still was divided. This was a new element in elite sport in Germany. They had it already in GDR in a different way which we could not copy because of different mentality and different political needs and systems. We tried to see what the positive aspects were [..] that we could introduce in West Germany. After reunification we adapted it as far as we could; including elite sport schools. Thirty-eight elite sport schools with talent promotion and so on. [This is] also something that stems from the former GDR.

Thus the sport policies of the eastern and the western part of Germany are slowly being fused although the spectre of the former GDR system continues to inhibit the process. Nevertheless, substantial aspects of the former East German elite sport policy have been absorbed into the West German model and it is certainly appropriate to refer to a degree of 'policy transfer' or 'imitation'.

Norway

Contradictions in relation to elite sport • • •

Many researchers and essayists maintain that Norway is characterised by particularly egalitarian values and social structures

(Enzensberger, 1984; Lunden, 1993). Egalitarian values are also strongly reflected in Norwegian sport policy discourses. Consequently, it may be argued that one would not expect elite sport to be prioritised by public authorities. However, it could also be argued that as Norway is a relatively young country with quite strong nationalistic values a focus on elite sport is to be expected in order to enable Norwegians to manifest national pride by winning international sport competitions. The tension between these two value systems has caused a somewhat schizophrenic sports policy in Norway. It is difficult to combine an unreserved commitment to the values of *sport for all* with the values of 'Olympic success'. This has also contributed to rather euphemistic sport policy discourses which conceal the inherent inequality and competitiveness of the sport system.

The difficulty of resolving the tension between the goals of *sport for all* and elite achievement may be the reason why the latest Norwegian White Paper on sport policy pays relatively little attention to high performance sport (St.meld. nr. 14 (1999–2000)). High performance sport is not mentioned among 'the principal challenges' of Norwegian sport policy in the years to come (*ibid.*). The principal challenges, and the justifications for public support to sport, are partly connected to the intrinsic values of sport, such as the pleasure of physical activity, and the generation of social capital within sport communities and partly to the instrumental values of sport, such as health benefits. When elite sport is discussed in the document it is often in relation to problematic tendencies and consequences, like commercialisation and professionalisation. This does not imply that the Norwegian government does not support high performance sport in practice or even that it offers relatively less support to it than that provided by other countries. The White Paper indeed states explicitly that high performance sport should be one of three main priorities when gaming money is allocated to sport. It is argued that high performance sport deserves public support, particularly for its contribution to 'cultural identity':

The government will support Norwegian elite sport financially so that an ethically and professionally qualified elite sport environment is secured and so that elite sport may still be considered as a means of cultural identification in Norwegian society.

The White Paper also states 'the justification of governmental support for high performance sport is primarily due to its effects upon the experiences and the identity of the whole population'

(St.meld. nr. 14 (1999–2000) p. 54). However, while high performance sport is mentioned it receives less space and attention in the Norwegian White Paper than in similar official documents from the other countries in our study. Moreover, public authorities in Norway do not set explicit performance objectives in international sporting competitions, such as a specific number of Olympic medals or a specific ranking on the medal table. This does not imply that such goals are not present in Norwegian sport policy debates. On the contrary, the sports pages of Norwegian newspapers and sport programmes on television often discuss such goals and aspirations. But in public documents such discourses seem to be muted or euphemised.

One of the reasons why high performance goals are more or less absent in public sport documents in Norway, may be that elite sport is considered to be primarily a sport *organisation* responsibility, as in Germany. The Ministry states that: 'High performance sport is an important priority for organised sport' (St.meld. nr. 14 (1999–2000) p. 54)). Thus the Ministry supports high performance sport through the general subsidy to the organised sport system. The umbrella sports organisation, The Norwegian Olympic Committee and Confederation of Sports, NIF/NOC, for its part, has formulated explicit high performance sports objectives in its applications for state subsidies. According to the application for 2006 it was NIF/NOC's ambition 1) to be among the three best European nations on the medal table in [winter] Olympic Games, and 2) to win at least 25 medals in the 2006 Turin Olympics (NIF/NOC 2005). These aspirations proved to be significantly over-ambitious.[22]

The public statement by the NIF/NOC of its Olympic ambitions masked strong divisions and conflicts about the priority of elite sport within the organisation (Hanstad 2002; Bergsgard, 2005). The regional and local levels of the organisation have criticised the central NIF/NOC for being too 'top level oriented', while proponents of high performance sport have felt burdened by the democratic processes of the organisations. '[T]he widespread democracy in Norwegian sport contributes to restraining our work', according to the head of the Norwegian Olympic Committee (NOC), Arne Myhrvold, after the unsuccessful 1988 Calgary Olympics (Hanstad, 2002, p. 185). Since then high performance sport in Norway has become much more prioritised and professionalised, partly with Myhrvold as the President of a united NIF/NOC. But the present head of the elite sport unit of NIF/NOC, *Olympiatoppen*, is still very critical because NIF/NOC does not prioritise elite sport enough. He has asked for 'a more extreme culture of high performance in sport' (Aambø, 2005,

p. 168). He was also very disappointed with the last general assembly (2003) of the NIF/NOC:

They said 'no' to prioritising economic resources more strongly towards the top. Now it was time for mass sport. The Assembly said 'no' to high altitude chambers, one of the areas of competence where Norway has been successful. The Assembly said 'no' to softening up the 'Regulations of children's sport',[23] where the potential for future high performance sport lies. They only voted unanimously in favour of the goal to become among the best in the world! (*ibid.*).[24]

The statements in this article reflect the contradictions within NIF/NOC about how much priority should be given to elite sport. As a head of NIF/NOC's elite sport unit he criticised severely the NIF/NOC general assembly arguing that even the general assembly seemed hesitant to prioritise high performance sport! As far as he can see the advocates of very explicit elite sport goals are currently on the defensive in Norwegian sport policy debates.

Historical background of the current elite sport policy in Norway • • •

The cleavages between advocates of *sport for all* and decentralisation on the one hand, and advocates of specialised sport and international sporting success on the other have existed for some time in organised sport in Norway (Goksøyr, 1992). Rolf Hofmo (1898–1966), the 'founding father' of post-war sport policy in Norway and the head of the first governmental 'Sports and Youth Office', was an entrepreneurial and unconventional bureaucrat who primarily promoted *sport for all* and 'sport for health' values.[25] He also explicitly warned against the negative effects of elite sport (Goksøyr, 2005). During the first decades after the Second World War, Norwegian sport policy was characterised by conflicts of legitimacy between the government's Sports and Youth Office and the Norwegian Confederation of Sport (NIF). However, these conflicts took place within a generally strong commitment to sport and a pronounced scepticism towards elite sport.

According to Augestad *et al.* (2005a: 7) a 'process for establishing a unified, coordinating organisation for elite sport across various associations in Norway' emerged in the early 1970s. But this process was hardly reflected in relevant public policy documents of the period. The 1970s represented an important turning point of Norwegian *cultural* policy and therefore indirectly of *sport* policy (Mangset, 1992). The so-called 'new cultural policy', launched in the middle of the 1970s, was characterised by strong socio-cultural, decentralist and egalitarian values and the inclusion of sport under an 'extended concept of culture' was an important aspect of this new policy. The first White Paper on the 'new cultural policy' published 1973 therefore also defined the government's general principles for sport policy. The sport chapter of this document focused mainly on *sport for all*, that is sport as leisure, sport for health and the role of local organisations in sport. It also warned against the negative aspects of elite sport. Thus the Ministry prioritised modest regional and local sports facility development over costly national facilities.[26] It also stated that a 'centrally directed sports culture which principally emphasised one-dimensional, extreme standards of achievement could hardly stimulate anything other than a passive interest in sport as an entertainment phenomenon' (St.meld. nr. 8 (1973–1974) p. 78).[27] This general emphasis on *sport for all* did not imply that the Ministry totally neglected elite sport, but it indicated that its support was rather reluctant. The policy maintained that as long as the central units of the sport organisations focused predominantly upon high performance sport, public authorities should prioritise regional and local *sport for all* activities and investments.

This White Paper was promoted by a government from the political centre in 1973. The subsequent social-democrat government endorsed the main principles of the sport policy of its predecessors in a new White Paper on cultural policy (St.meld. nr. 52 (1973–1974)), but had to respond to harsh criticism from the organised sports movement because of the former government's negative attitude to elite sport. In this second White Paper the government confirmed the general priority of *sport for all*, but also stated that 'even the champions belong to 'all'; to offer them special opportunities should not be considered an illegitimate part of sport policy' (*ibid.*, p. 44).

At the same time there was a growing concern about high performance sport within the sports movement itself with various factions having different opinions about how it should be organised. From 1974 and onwards the NIF and the NOC started to cooperate more closely in order to promote high performance sport more systematically. A 'Council for coaches and leaders' was established in 1974 which was more or less transformed into a 'Working group for high performance sport' in 1976. This was followed by a 'Committee for high performance sport' in 1978 and an 'Elite Sport Committee' in 1980 (Augestad *et al.*, 2005a, b). NIF also planned to triple its financial support to high performance sport between 1980 and 1983 (St.meld. nr. 23 (1981–1982) p. 121).

These lines of conflict and the general egalitarian cultural climate in Norwegian politics still made it difficult to develop a strong high performance sport policy in Norway in the 1970s and early 1980s. The traditional scepticism towards elite sport was also reflected in the White Paper on culture published by the social-democrat government in 1981, despite the fact that the actual minister of culture, Einar Førde, was a former top athlete.[28] The White Paper first and foremost reaffirmed the priority of *sport for all*, especially for minority groups. But it paid more attention to what the government considered to be disturbing developments in international elite sport, especially increasing professionalisation and commercialisation, and especially the risks of doping and early specialisation (*ibid.*). However, it also stated that 'elite sport must, at the same time, be provided with good and sound conditions' (*ibid.*, p. 116). The White Paper stated that public authorities were about to develop concrete and specific measures in the field of elite sport including facilitating professional education and training at the Norwegian School for Sport Sciences for elite athletes. It was also noted that since 1978 the government had allocated grants to top athletes and that a substantial number of international standard sport facilities had been constructed in recent years with support from the football pool (gambling) money. Most important, however, was the announcement in the White Paper of support from the government to establish a 'national training centre' for high performance sport (*ibid.*, p. 122).

A subsequent White Paper from the following centre-right government signalled a more positive attitude to elite sport.[29] It stated that 'Elite sport has a legitimate and important function in the Norwegian society' (St.meld. nr. 27 (1983–1984) p. 27). But when the culture committee in the Parliament discussed both White Papers the majority (centre/left) reaffirmed its relatively strong support to *sport for all* and its traditional scepticism towards elite sport (Innst. S. nr. 132 (1984–1985)). Even the Conservative Party's advocacy of high performance sport seemed to have been silenced.

In the organised sports movement there were still disagreements about how and the extent to which elite sport should be professionalised. A key debate concerned the desirability of creating a united independent, professional and national organisation to promote high performance sport, similar to those organisations established in other countries (e.g. the Australian Institute for Sport). A series of 'focusing events' during the 1980s and 1990s contributed to a weakening of opposition to such an organisation (Augestad *et al.*, 2005a). The first focusing event was that Norway was relatively unsuccessful in both the Summer and Winter Olympics in 1984 (Los Angeles and Sarajevo). This perceived failure contributed to the establishment of a new elite sport organisation in 1984, 'Project 88', jointly by NIF and NOC. This relatively independent and centralised organisation was intended primarily to support athletes within the context of their sports organisation. Although 'Project 88' failed to increase the number of medals in the 1988 Olympics (Calgary, Seoul) it was still evaluated as promising. In 1988 'Project 88' was renamed *Olympiatoppen* and, after the General Assembly of NIF in 1990, it was accorded a more permanent and financially secure foundation, mainly because it was attached to NIF/NOC (St.meld. nr. 41 (1991–1992); Bergsgard, 2005).

The second focusing event occurred in 1988 when the Winter Games of 1994 were awarded to Lillehammer. This decision certainly gave a strong impetus to high performance sport in Norway, both to athletes and support personnel. Already a couple of years earlier the government had supported the new elite sport policy by subsidising the building of the national elite sport centre and acting as financial guarantor for Lillehammer as a future host of the Winter Olympics. Government subsidies were mainly justified by regional development arguments (see discussion of generalisation of interests, Chapter 2). However, contrary to several other western countries, the development of a centralised and independent structure for the promotion of high performance sport was not initiated and carried through by the government (Augestad *et al.*, 2005a). In Norway it was the organised sports movement itself (NIF and NOC) that was the 'operative agent'. In 1996 NIF and NOC finally merged into one organisation, with the former NOC President as the first President of the joint organisation. From one perspective this merger reflected the decreasing scepticism, and the symbolic victory, of high performance sport in the organised sports movement. From another, alternative, perspective it reflects the domestication of NOC (an elite sport unit without a democratic basis) by the organised and democratic sports movement (NIF). It may still be said that Norway 'copied' other western countries in developing a strong, centralised and professional organisation to promote high performance sport (*Olympiatoppen* and NIF/NOC), but it did it in accordance with the specific national policy traditions of an autonomous umbrella organisation in close cooperation with public authorities.

The third focusing event was that Norwegian athletes were successful in the following Olympic Games, especially in the Albertville (1992) and Lillehammer (1994) Winter Olympics. The new, centralised organisation of high performance sport, *Olympiatoppen* finally seemed to demonstrate its efficiency! In addition, the successful organisation of the Lillehammer Olympics contributed to the legitimation of elite sport both among politicians and the general public in Norway.

Despite the increased prominence of elite sport policy within overall sport policy debates *sport for all* discourses have still dominated the government's sport policy documents since the early 1990s. According to the 1992 White Paper on sport policy, sport should be supported mainly because of its 'intrinsic values', its function as 'popular movement and entertainment', its role in the education of children, its effects on people's health and its effects on employment (St.meld. nr. 41 (1991–1992) p. 12–14). But this White Paper also offered a small chapter on high performance sport and confirmed the government's support for further institutionalisation. However, the next White Paper on sport policy, as we have already noted, seemed to reduce the priority given to high performance (St. meld. nr. 14 (1999–2000)). This seems paradoxical as the sport policy rhetoric of the government continued to be oriented towards *sport for all* at the same time that high performance sport was becoming more institutionalised. Although NIF/NOC was the principal agent behind the institutionalisation process there was clear government support. The profound and continuous ambivalence in Norwegian sport policy towards elite sport is combined with an important division of labour between organised sport and the government in relation to elite sport. The sports organisations (especially the central umbrella organisation), on the one hand, 'take care of' elite sport. NIF/NOC has developed an increasingly strong elite sport policy and organisation more or less similar to the elite sports organisations of other western countries. The central political authorities (Ministry of Culture, Culture Committee of the Parliament) on the other hand 'take care of the legitimacy work', that is they stress the egalitarian and social benefits values of sport as strongly as is required in order to maintain political support. But similar ambivalences also characterises the sports movement (NIF/NOC) itself. According to Bergsgard (2005) there is a similar division of labour and there is an explicit tendency to 'double talk' or 'double book-keeping' within the organisation. Bergsgard also notes that the NIF/NOC justifies itself by democratic *sport for all* values in relation to the general public and political authorities, while the organisation in practice often prioritises top level sport and central led administration.

Pathways to the podium

One of the most important challenges for the high performance sport system seems to be to organise the best possible 'pathway' from talented child to successful adult athlete. How this pathway is organised and described in the four sport systems reflect important cultural differences between the countries, differences that are related to the specific cultures of socialisation, education and bodily discipline that predominate in these countries. Within the context of this chapter we cannot treat all relevant aspects or phases of the pathways, but we will discuss the most important ones (i.e. early talent identification and selection; organisation of/arenas for training (school, club, etc); coaching; use of sport science methods; and the organisation of elite sport centres/institutes). This will be discussed in relation to the general approach in this chapter, namely whether the different 'pathways to the podium' in the four countries are characterised by 'diminishing contrasts' or 'increasing varieties' (Green and Oakley, 2001), whether they vary according to general differences between welfare models (Esping-Andersen, 1999).

The ambivalence between elite sport and *sport for all* values may appear particularly salient when it comes to talent identification and training of children and youth. How early should the talent identification start? At what age can systematic and specialised training begin without violating the integrity and potential of the child? Should one follow the Australian example and develop an ambitious and comprehensive 'Talent Search Programme'? Such programmes may evoke cynicism, because they seem to reflect the former East German procedures of systematic and early talent selection based on genetic tests (Green and Oakley, 2001). At the same time it may be tempting to imitate such programmes because of their alleged efficiency (Green, 2006). Western culture since Rousseau (1712–1778), however, has been strongly influenced by humanistic values that stress a more holistic, non-specialised development of the individual from early childhood to adulthood. Therefore, many educators in western countries have defied early specialisation and systematic training and tough competition among children. In addition social-democrat egalitarianism, especially in the Nordic countries, tends to strengthen scepticism towards early specialisation in sport.

The sport systems of different countries also vary substantially concerning which 'channel' or 'arena' is the most important for the identification, selection and training of recruits to high performance sport. Is it primarily the club structure, the school structure, the professional (commercial) sport structure or possibly the army that plays the most important role? Different 'channels' may represent quite different values in relation to sport. Within the world of high performance sport one often discusses how the different phases of the development of the recruits from early childhood to adult professional athlete should ideally be connected. Is there a good connection – or are there rather detrimental disconnects – between the institutional arrangements responsible for the training of the athlete at different development stages? This is the central issue when the problem of the 'sports path' or the 'pathway to the podium' is discussed. The search for the ideal pathway, the most efficient system that can lead from early talent identification to adult podium success may also be considered from another, more social constructivist, perspective. Sports people tend to construct rational and coherent 'pathways' through a landscape characterised by various and accidental individual careers. The idea of the perfect pathway has the attraction of attempting to construct order out of chaos, but also has a chimerical quality.

Canada

In order to achieve world-class results in future international competitions Canadian sports policy will devote greater attention to 'a systemic approach to ensure the development of a constant stream of world-class athletes, coaches and officials in a sport environment characterised by the highest standards of ethics and values' (Sport Canada, 2002, p. 17). Public authorities at different levels should therefore 'identify and recruit talented athletes into the sport system and provide for their systematic and holistic development towards internationally competitive levels' (*ibid.*). Thus the athlete needs a long-term 'sports-specific pathway' for his or her athletic career, including 'a variety of programming components, such as coaching, athlete support, training, competition, equipment, sport science and medicine, research and access to facilities' (Sport Canada, 2004a, p. 3). How are these goals pursued in practice, and how do different actors in the sports world perceive the talent identification, selection and training system?

Children and youth in Canada can be identified and trained to become high performance athletes through three different 'channels', that is through the club structure, the school structure, and, in some sports, the professional (commercial) sport structure (especially hockey). From the point of view of the COC 'podium success' is without doubt the ultimate goal, therefore 'our dollars should go to them that have most chance.' The COC looks upon the identification and selection process as a 'pyramid' according to which, in order to reach the top, you need 'great programmes' and 'great coaches'. This approach may seem almost as systematic, instrumental and technocratic as the sport policy of the former East Germany, but it is moderated by the dominant 'cultural norms' in Canada that make it difficult to identify talented athletes for specific sport disciplines when the children are very young. These norms prescribe that children's freedom to choose whatever sport they want should not be limited too greatly or too early, says a provincial sport organisation officer. A child with excellent abilities to become a swimmer might perhaps rather choose to, and should be allowed to choose, to become for instance a snowboarder.

Elite sport interviewees maintain that talent identification and systematic training could and should have started a lot earlier than prescribed by dominant cultural norms. The appropriate age for specialisation depends on the sport: 'In some sports you can do it probably very, very early. Gymnastics – 8 years old. Track and field, [it] depends on the type; in running, the early teens. It is very sport-specific', according to one COC official. A provincial sport organisation official for swimming observed that: 'We could start doing talent identification at the age of 6 years if we wanted, depending upon your sport, whether it is gymnastics or swimming, which tends to be slightly earlier than a lot of the other sports'. But both these informants reluctantly acknowledged that it was unrealistic in the present cultural and political climate to identify and systematically train children as early as they could have wished. The Ben Johnson affair and the public debates about detrimental effects of elite sport have contributed to the creation of strong cultural obstacles against such a child sport policy.

Schools are further potential arenas for encouraging and identifying talent. But sport organisation officials in Canada are not satisfied with the interplay between organised sport and the school system. 'There is a very large disconnect in this country, I think, between 'school sport' and 'the sporting system' [...] They are not linked, to be quite honest', says the swimming organisation official. The problem is partly caused by the pressure for more focus upon the 'core subjects' in the school curriculum, commented another provincial sport organisation official (athletics). Consequently sport organisations have attempted to apply pressure to the school system in order to make sporting activities ('the run-jump-throw program') mandatory in the curriculum.

The 'disconnection' between organised sport and schools is also caused by a lack of coordination between competitions within and outside the school sport system. According to one swimming organisation official a young and talented swimmer cannot easily combine school sport competitions with regular competitions outside school. 'If you are a competitive swimmer – if you are someone who participates in year-round swimming – you are not eligible to be in regular high school swimming. You have to compete in a separate category, because it is (i.e. considered to be) an unfair advantage'. The 'disconnection' in the system for identification, selection and training of talent is not limited to the relationship between sport clubs and schools. A provincial swimming organisation official maintained that there are other kinds of disconnections in the 'sports path'. There is no clear division of responsibility between the political–administrative levels and between the national and the provincial levels of sports organisations:

One of the things this country is lacking, is a clear holistic leadership. I can say that in swimming, and I can say that in a number of the other sports that I have worked with or consulted with. There is a real disconnect most of the time between where your national association is, and where your provincial association is. Most groups have not clearly articulated the responsibility set. There are a few sports that are doing a much better job of it. Skiing Canada has made some large strides in what we would call here a 'sports path'. So *this* is how a child starts in the system, and *this* is how it finishes at the top end. And the path is laid out with the roles and responsibility for each level (provincial sports organisation official (swimming)).

Colleges and universities are relatively important arenas for high performance athletes, but less important in Canada than in the USA. The role played by colleges and universities, also varies from one sport discipline to another. Hockey players in universities and colleges tend to be older (22–24 years) than their fellow students in other sport disciplines, like ball playing and cross-country skiing (18–20 years). That is because talented hockey players often first try 'to make it as professional players. So they will, before going to school, … university or college, … try to pursue that direct route to the National Hockey League', according to a college sport organisation official. The young hockey players therefore tend to 'postpone their post-secondary education to pursue that hockey dream'. They will play in the Junior Hockey League and go on playing in a semi-professional league. 'Then by the time they are 22, 23, 24, they realise that 'I am not going to make it as a professional hockey player; I had better go and get my education'. So they will come back to school'. Consequently, these hockey players have adjusted their ambitions to a lower-performance level. Therefore, Canadian universities and colleges are not really very important recruiters to professional sport in this discipline. The most talented and ambitious young (18–20 years) hockey players may instead go to the USA and get free education (scholarship) there for 4 or 5 years. Several young athletes in other sport disciplines also go to the USA, because of a more generous American scholarship system. In the USA a scholarship permits the athlete to devote himself or herself almost totally to a top level career. To be eligible for scholarships at home in Canada, on the other hand, students have to devote more of their time to regular (non-sport) courses. They cannot train full time. But according to a college sport official if you want to

compete at that Olympic level, you almost need to work at it the year around. That is why a lot of our top athletes, in particular in track and field, go to the USA for scholarships, because it is just more of a full-time professional programme, even though it is 'amateur'. They work at it full time. And for those athletes I think their education is secondary to their athletics. For 99.9% of *our* athletes their sport is secondary to their education.

All in all it does not seem as if Canadian universities and colleges consider it to be their primary responsibility to develop high performance athletes. They are rather devoted to a broad and holistic conception of sport education. Therefore few college athletes seem to be aspiring to professional or top level sport. In the words of a college sports official,

For the most part those 2000 athletes[30] are playing because it makes them a well-rounded person ... and because many of those 2000 athletes will graduate, will then become the coaches and the teachers, who will teach our young people about sport. That I think is our major mandate, preparing people to be leaders in sport. I think that is what we do. Not to make professionals, not to make national teamers, that is nice, that is great and we take pride in those people, who accomplish that. But more we are interested in developing 'the whole person'.

The educational system is clearly not an unconditional contributor to high performance success. While the sports organisations, despite some internal differences, tend to regret the absence of a clear and rational pathway to podium success, broader and more 'holistic' academic and educational values seem to dominate Canadian school sport.

There is a need for 'world-class' coaches in order to reach the sports policy goal of developing 'world-class athletes'. But coaches are not necessarily professionalised in Canada and there is considerable variation regarding the level of professionalisation between sports. Local clubs usually have voluntary coaches, at least in track and field ('local clubs rarely have paid coaches'[31]). However, swimming seems to be more professionalised, even at the local level, than track and field in part because 'they [swimming] pay their coaches for the most part'.[32] At the universities there are paid coaches in several disciplines who may cooperate with the sport organisations. But according to a national athletic organisation official they are not always 'working at the high-performance stream'. Sport Canada officials also maintain that the universities 'are not as important as they should be in sport', especially for coaching education, where they 'do not necessarily have the same curriculum as would be in the national coaching certification programme that the Coaching Association operates'. These statements demonstrate once again the different ideological attitudes to high performance sport in the sports organisations and the academic world.

Since the 1980s the Canadian Olympic Committee (COC), the Coaching Association of Canada (CAC) and Sport Canada have joined forces to fund and develop a more professional approach to *coaching education* and to create a network of *national elite* sport centres (Sport Canada, 1999, 2004a; Green and Houlihan, 2005). The purpose of these centres is, of course, to promote high performance sport with the help of professional coaches. The establishment of sport centres also includes more systematic use of *sport science* to enable athletes to 'go to those centres to get nutrition advice, get sport science testing in conjunction with their coaching plans,' according to one Sport Canada official. Sport science here may imply 'physiological testing', 'sport psychology', 'altitude studies' and 'heat studies', reported one national sport organisation official. By 2004 nine such centres had been established in the larger cities around Canada. Most of them are multidisciplinary, but they have also developed specialist expertise in particular sports (e.g. long track speed skating in Calgary, short track speed skating in Montreal). Some of the centres are located in a university and others in a separate sport facility.[33] According to Sport Canada officials the establishment of these centres was partly inspired by foreign models, for instance by similar centres in France, Australia and Germany. The Canadian elite sport centre structure is relatively decentralised, because of the vast size and regionalised political structure of the country. From a strictly high performance perspective there is no real need for so many elite sport centres, according to one Sport Canada official. It seems as if pressure or demands from the provinces have resulted in 'excessive' (from a strictly instrumental/technocratic point of view) number of centres. This demonstrates how a general international elite sport structure has been adapted to the federal political structures and traditions of a specific country.

England

Game Plan tells us that the British government will 'be more systematic in spotting and developing talented competitors' in order to improve the country's performances in international sport (DCMS/Strategy Unit, 2002, p. 9). The relevant governing bodies should lead this work 'against a talent development plan which avoids the damaging effects of over-specialisation and over-competing at too early a stage, but recognises the different requirements of individual sports when it is appropriate to do so' (*ibid.*). The government therefore wants closer cooperation between schools and sport clubs. It looks for measures to 'improve support for gifted and talented pupils' in schools, and it wants to forge 'closer links between schools and sports clubs', for instance by the help of 'talent scholarships' (*ibid.*). The government is particularly concerned with 'bridging the talent identification and development gap' (*ibid.*, p. 123). *Game Plan* tells us that this is necessary because England, at present, 'has no recognisable system for supporting young people who aspire to sporting excellence' (*ibid.*). A UK Sport official confirmed that there was 'no system' for developing the young athletes to top level performers. These complaints about the talent identification and development gap have much in common with the Canadian discussion about a 'disconnection' in the 'sports path'. What UK Sport wants is 'a culture of wanting to do better with coaching, with team preparation, and the sport science and sport medicine preparation programmes, the use of exercise physiologists and so on, all of these scientists, utilising a network of facilities that we are coordinating, called the UK Sport institutes' (UK Sport official). The aim was to build a coherent and strong high performance sport pathway, to 'put in place [...] not a system that *supports* champions, but a system that *produces* champions.'

British sports policy seems to be particularly concerned about the 'talent loss' aspect of the 'sports path' or development system. A key concern is to expand the talent pool, but: '[T]his pool will not feed into the high performance system if there is no talent development pathway' (DCMS/Strategy Unit, 2002, p. 123). It is consequently argued that increased participation in sport should be encouraged in order to expand the talent pool. However, it is also argued that an expanded pool is of little value unless 'those with ability are helped to optimally develop their potential' (*ibid.*, see also DCMS, 2000). These opinions and observations reflect a sports policy discourse that resembles the technocratic-instrumental sports policy of the former GDR. Some of the UK Sport officials talked in similar ways in interviews, while dissociating themselves from the GDR heritage:

We are actually putting into place *a system* which will, I hope, get stronger and stronger in the years ahead, whereby a youngster will be picked up and identified. Not in an East-German way of measuring backs of hands: '[If] you are being three foot six, you are becoming a gymnast; [If] you are becoming seven foot two, you are becoming a basket ball player.' No, not as crude scientifically as that, or through gene therapy or some of the more outrageous processes. But [it has] much more to do with skill levels, coordination; body shape certainly can have a part to play.

Some UK Sport officials believed that the present 'talent loss' amounts to at least 50%. It is a 'moral and educational obligation to help people to achieve their potential whatever they want to do'. In this way an elite-oriented technocratic-instrumental justification is combined with a democratic and meritocratic justification, stressing equal access for all. According to both these views one should put children with special talents together in specialist colleges 'where they will get the same quality of education, but with a bias'. If this is successful

then that means you are in the business of talent identification at a much, much earlier age, which means that they are then fed into a club network, a club structure; the structure is then picked up by a governing body and put into a talent programme; [the] talent programme leads into a [World Class] Potential programme; Potential leads into World Class, and then they are [knocking the table] with a gold [medal] around their neck, waiving to the crowd on the podium!

The British government has responded to accusations of a talent identification and development gap through programmes that try to bridge the gap between the school system and high performance sport. For example, the *PE, School Sport & Club Links strategy* (PESSCL)[34] aims to:

enhance the take-up of sporting opportunities by five- to sixteen-years-olds by increasing the percentage of school children who spend a minimum of two hours each week on high quality PE and school sport within and beyond the curriculum from 25% in 2002 to 75% in 2006 and 85% by 2008.[35]

At the higher education level the Talented Athlete Scholarship Scheme (TASS)[36] provides 'funding to the very best athletes with the potential to achieve success towards and in 2012'. It also aims to bridge 'the gap in sport's talent development pathway between junior representative sport and world-class levels for our most talented 16 to 25 years old sportspeople'.

Coaching is also a key factor in British elite sport policy, but until relatively recently the development of coaching in Britain was 'piecemeal and hardly strategic' (Green and Houlihan, 2005, p. 149). A consequence of the relatively recent emphasis on elite sport policy, is that professional coaching, sport science and sport medicine now play a more significant role in British elite sport (ibid.). The DCMS ordered a special report on the coaching issue from the 'Coaching Task Force' (2002) which reported both a growing demand for volunteer coaches at the grassroots level and a growing number of sports organisations 'with clearly defined talent development pathways requiring increased commitment and skills from coaches at local, regional and national level to work with talented people and gifted young people' (DCMS, 2002, p. 4). A more structured approach to elite sport also increases the demand for 'full-time coaches working alongside full-time athletes' (ibid.). Consequently, UK Sport has invested in 'world class coaches and performance directors', says a UK Sport official.

Like many other countries the UK has recognised the need for some kind of elite sport institutes. The establishment of such institutes (UK Sport institutes, UKSIs) has certainly been influenced by international models, especially by the Australian Institute of Sport (1981) and indirectly by the former Eastern-bloc countries (Green, 2006). According to an official from UK Sport, there was a period when they thought that they would get a big institute like Canberra in Australia. This kind of 'massive, great construction' was what many politicians wanted for some time: 'But it became fairly clear [...] that although that was a political momentum, sport did not want that. What sport wanted was ... a network of structures. That is how the UKSI has grown now.'

Thus sports institutes have been established in all four home countries. In addition there is a regionalised structure of institutes in England similar to those found in many other countries. To a certain degree it is a case of 'policy transfer' or 'imitation', but the sports institute structure in Britain was not copied without reservations. You could even say that they 'rejected the Australian model' (UK Sport official) – or rather that they adjusted it to the political structure of the UK. Thus Green and Houlihan (2005, p. 60) conclude that 'although the UK is at a relatively early stage of developing a coherent model/system for elite sport development, an organisational, administrative and funding framework is clearly emerging'.

Germany

German sports policy is also very explicit about the need for a systematic pathway to international success. The Ministry of the Interior stresses that schools and sports clubs 'should cooperate closely in order to identify and promote talent at an early age'[37] (BMI, 2006, p. 14). The search for an efficient pathway to international success seems to be supported quite unanimously by representatives of the German sports community. An official from the German gymnastic federation, for example, described a 'national concept for how to develop elite sports', which included 'support centres'[38], training systems and coaching systems. A NOK official maintained that the main objective of, and the major challenge facing, the NOK and DSB is

the promotion of talent; getting the most successful young kids up to the senior squad. The problems nowadays are that we have many [who are] successful at the junior level, as world or European champions, but they don't get over the gap to the senior level. We have a lot of dropouts.

As long as the procedure for selection and training is not too closely associated with the former GDR system such discourses do not seem to meet much opposition in the German sports world. An official from the elite sport division in the DSB describes a quite systematic organisation of talent identification and selection, from the *land* level to the national (federal) level. There are elite sport committees at the *land* level, and 'Each state wants to get athletes into the national team. That is why they prepare athletes in the D-squad (14–15 years), and try to bring them on higher level'. This extensive system for talent search, selection and training includes coaches, competitions, talent-spotting programmes and state training centres: 20 national (federal) Olympic support centres (*Olympiastützpunkte*), 154 regional support centres for summer sport, 34 regional support centres for winter sport, and 38 elite sport schools are important elements in the whole system (BMI, 2006).

Interviewees from one city – Paderborn in Nordrhein-Westfalen – described the institutionalisation of a systematic talent identification procedure at their local level. All children in this city (and region) are tested as early as the 3rd grade in order to detect their talent for specific sports. This system of early talent identification and selection did not seem to have been subject to strong criticism, partly because it was not limited just to the development of the most talented children as children with special needs also received advice about appropriate training procedures. In a comprehensive school in the same city, which children attend from the age of 10 years, talented children receive training advice and homework support. This programme of support is based upon cooperation between the comprehensive school and the medical institute of the university nearby. There are also institutionalised meetings between representatives from the city administration and the sports organisations (which includes talent scouts) in order to discuss common problems and objectives.

Such an elaborate system for early talent identification and selection within the education system may appear to be a direct reflection and continuation of the elite sport system of the former GDR, but as already noted today's German sports policy does not accept the GDR system without limitations and reservations. As one interviewee commented,

Many members of the DSB say, let us transfer the former talent system of DDR [GDR] to Germany, and we will get a lot of medals. And let us only pay for disciplines like canoeing etc, where we get a lot of medals. But the BMI would say that sport in Germany [also] has a lot of [non-sport] social benefits.[39]

It is argued that the pursuit of medals is moderated by a broader and more holistic policy than that of the former GDR. Although the school system makes a contribution to the talent identification and development process not all observers see its contribution as crucial or even significant. 'The school is not an arena for talent searching in Germany', observed an experienced sports policy researcher. It is the clubs, not the schools, that are the most important pathways to elite sport success in Germany. The army also still plays an important role. According to the sports policy researcher, 'In winter sport in Germany 60–70% are in the military; the national army is providing more than 700 positions. You are a formal member of the family, but are free to do your training and competition.' Universities, on the other hand, are not very important for elite sport, as scholarships for elite sport are not available. There seems to be a similar disconnection and cultural distance between elite sport and the academic world in Germany as in Canada. According to one academic observer, 'It is nearly impossible to study and participate in elite sport, it is not coordinated'. An official from the elite sport division of the DSB commented, 'The university is too scientific oriented, not high-competition oriented'. This general lack of interest in elite sport in German universities explains why elite athletes rely more directly on two specialised applied academic institutions, the Institute for Advanced Training Sciences in Leipzig and the German Sport University in Cologne. These two institutions are important partners in the German elite sport structure. The Leipzig institution aims 'to link scientific knowledge to the training process' and the coaching academy in Cologne provides 'top level coaches, diploma coaches, for the federation just in their specific sport', according to an official from the elite sport division of DSB.

Outside the education system, clubs and the military the 20 Olympic Support Centres are important institutions in the overall German elite sport structure. According to an official from the DSB,

They provide services for the athletes living in the region where the Olympic centre is located, including coaches, physiotherapists, psychologists, career advisers, diagnostic support, and they are a kind of hub … Adjacent to an Olympic support centre are training centres related to the different federations.

The idea of establishing the Olympic support centres was more or less inherited from the GDR, but they could not be directly copied, because they partly reflected outdated communist and centralist mentalities and structures and partly because there were too many – 42 in total (NOC official). In addition, the East German elite sport organisation was perceived as a very technocratic, rational and efficient system. However, in reality, it seemed to have been rather over-bureaucratised and inefficient. Therefore there was a need for concentration of resources after unification. 'You do not need to have a centre for sailing both in Hamburg and Rostock', said a BMI official who also added that Germany needed just 15–17 of the present 20 centres in the future. Such a number of centres would indeed correspond quite clearly to the federal political and geographical structure of Germany. From a federal point of view these centres, together with lots of sub-centres at the regional level, are the most important parts of the government's elite sports policy for children and youth.

The current network of German elite sport centres was certainly inspired by similar centres in the former GDR and by models in countries like Australia. Such elite sport centres, in Germany and elsewhere, also continuously try to pick up medical knowledge, training principles and organisational models from similar centres in other countries. 'There is a lot of spying going on', especially in order to improve material, reported one DSB official. International cooperation within the International Olympic Committee (IOC) system may also contribute to the exchange of ideas and subsequently to the international homogenisation of elite sport organisations. 'We cooperate with

NOCs worldwide in development projects, sending German experts to other countries to educate coaches, teach doctors, physiotherapists...', reported a German NOC official. However, as in other countries imitation or policy transfer, especially of organisational models and procedures, is also limited by national cultural traditions and political structures.

Norway

It is more difficult to find explicit descriptions of a systematic 'pathway' to international success in Norwegian sports policy documents than in similar documents from the three other countries. We have already seen that Norwegian sports policy documents, from the 1970s to the present, are much more concerned with *sport for all* than with high performance sport (St. meld. nr. 41 (1991–1992), St.meld. nr. 14 (1999–2000)). Even though there has been a significant strengthening of high performance sports structures in Norway, the corresponding discourses have not changed to the same extent.[40] Very little, if anything, is written explicitly in these documents about talent identification, selection and training for high performance success. Nevertheless, an institutional structure (coaching education, elite sport institutes and elite sport schools) has been established in order to support and develop top athletes in Norway during recent decades, which is not so very different from the corresponding structures in other countries.

In Norway a well-organised sports club system plays the principal role in the identification, selection and training of talented athletes. The general school system, by contrast, is not very important. Between 1925 and 1960, however, the relationship between physical education and competitive sport was much closer. Competitive sport played an important role both in primary schools and comprehensive schools (i.e. intra- and inter-school competitions and the pursuit of sporting proficiency awards). Young talented athletes were often identified and inspired by school sport, before entering the regular club system. However, since the 1970s this close relationship between physical education and competitive sport has weakened, primarily due to the influence of a new generation of educationists who considered that school sport that created 'winners' and 'losers' was detrimental to the personal and social development of children. As Augestad (2003a, p. 198) observed 'Competitions became more or less a taboo'.

These reservations about children's participation in competitive sport were institutionalised within the sports movement when the 'Regulations for children's sport' received approval in a vote at the NIF in 1987. The Regulations are still valid in a slightly modified form (NIF/NOC, 2000). Versatility is the main principle for children's and youth's sport, according to the Regulations. The regulations also require that children should not be exposed to specialised and competitive sports activities at an early age and that sport should have an educational and holistic function which contributes to the development of the whole personality. All children should therefore learn various physical activities in order to master their own body (e.g. develop coordination and balance). Specialisation should not begin before the age of 10–12 years, and even at this age the organisation of sport should be guided by the principle of versatility with the child continuing to practice several sports. Children should not participate in competitions outside the local club before the age of 10 years. From 10 to 12 years they could compete at the local and regional level, but not in regional championships. At 11–12 years an athlete and his/her club might participate in nation-wide competitions just once a year. Children should not compete abroad and not against foreigners at home before the age of 13 years.

It should be noted that it was the sports movement itself not the government that established these principles for children's sport, although they certainly had the support of public authorities (St.meld. nr. 41 (1991–1992) and nr. 14 (1999–2000)). There has been, perhaps not surprisingly, a certain degree of opposition to the Regulations within sports organisations. We have already seen that the head of the elite sport unit of NIF/NOC, Jarle Aambø (2005), wanted to 'soften' them. There have also been several incidents in some NIF/NOC federations that demonstrated an opposition or negligence in relation to the Regulations. For example, a local kickboxing club sent a 9-year-old girl to a world cup competition in Italy which resulted in the club being sanctioned both by the central NIF/NOC and by the kickboxing federation.[41] The 'head of development' in the Norwegian football federation considers the Regulations to be characterised by 'good intentions' but in practice they are too 'comprehensive', 'complicated' and 'unclear'. He also considered that they focused too much upon versatility.[42] This and other cases of criticism in relation to children's sport, as well as the incidence of breaches of the Regulations, reflect a degree of internal opposition to the traditional sports policy in this field. There are certainly officers, coaches and parents in the sports family that would like to soften up the Regulations and develop a more 'efficient' system with earlier talent identification, selection, training and competition. It is difficult, however, to say how strong this opposition is as it is not often aired publicly due to the existence of clear limitations regarding what it is possible to say in relation to the Norwegian high performance sport discourse. To develop a clear and efficient pathway from early childhood to adult international elite sport success, including early talent identification, selection and training is not part of legitimate sports policy discourse. However, it should be emphasised that there are also some spokespersons for high performance sport who would argue that the broad and democratic late specialisation policy really represents the most efficient pathway to high performance success.

Despite the more inhibited public discussion of pathways to elite success Norway has developed a relatively similar high performance sport system, and thus a more or less similar 'pathway to the podium,' to that of many other countries. As already mentioned the Norwegian centre for high performance sport, *Olympiatoppen*, was established in 1990. The activities of the centre are very much science based, with special divisions for training and testing, endurance knowledge and health expertise. This reflects the international models that we have already described, but because Norway is a country with a small population there is not the same need for a large number of regional elite sport centres as in the three other countries. Nevertheless, the NIF/NOC has decided to establish three such regional 'centres of competence' – in Bergen, Trondheim and Tromsø. The regional centres are connected to *Olympiatoppen* at the central level, and to universities at the regional level (NIF/NOC, 2006).

Olympiatoppen has also developed a coach education programme for high performance sport in cooperation with the University of Trondheim and several regional university colleges have developed flexible programmes so that athletes are able to combine sports studies with high performance sport. Four (more or less specialised) comprehensive schools for high performance sport have also been established in different regions, while many other comprehensive schools offer more general sports programmes.

Conclusion

Our analysis suggests a significant degree of homogenisation as all four countries have developed, or are in the process of developing, relatively similar high performance sport structures. The sport systems of all countries focus quite strongly and consistently upon success in international competitions, strong and relatively centralised elite sport organisations, systematic and professional coaching, the establishment of elite sport centre(s), and the use of scientific methods to improve the functioning of the whole elite sport system. However, the policies for early talent identification and selection do display a greater degree of variety than other aspects of high performance sport systems. Norway is more cautious than the other countries and does not expose children to intense selection and competition at a very young age. In Canadian, English and German sports policies the search for the best 'pathway to the podium' is a more explicit and, possibly, overriding concern. While it may be that Norwegians just talk differently, more euphemistically, about the search for the best pathway the organisation and delivery of children's sport in Norway is substantially different from the three other countries. However, it is not clear whether Norway has lost many Olympic medals because of its more *sport for all* oriented policy and its more restrictive approach towards the involvement of young children in the talent development process.

It also appears quite clear from the analysis that the sport systems of different countries imitate each other. Australia and Canada certainly picked up ideas about how to organise high performance sport from the communist bloc countries during the 1960s and 1970s. Since then Australia, and especially the Australian Institute of Sport, has been a powerful model for many other countries. Do the sport policies of different countries really succeed in copying the most efficient elite sport organisation or are imported processes altered through adaptation to different cultural and social conditions? The evidence does not support the view that the homogenisation process is just a consequence of rational international competition seeking the most efficient high performance sport system. A more persuasive analysis is one that emphasises the search for the best possible high performance sports policy as the outcome of a process of mutual exchange of values, norms and knowledge, that is as a neo-institutionalist explanation involving a process of cultural adaptation.

Whether one sees differences or similarities in comparative research often depends upon the perspective. A more detailed examination will emphasise differences between the elite sport systems of these four countries, especially related to the centralisation/decentralisation of the elite sport structures, the policy for children's sport, and the policy for early talent identification and selection. If a broader perspective is adopted structural and policy similarities will become more prominent. However, irrespective of the sharpness and breadth of the comparative perspective it is apparent that elite sport systems are not entirely consistent with Esping-Andersen's regime typology. It is certainly true that Norwegian sport policy is less competitive, more *sport for all* oriented and less commercialised than the sport policies of the three other countries and is therefore consistent with the social democratic type. However, linking elite sport systems to the dominant welfare type in the other three countries is much more difficult. For example it is not obvious that German sport is less competitive and less elite oriented than English and Canadian sport. It is also difficult to argue that the German and the Norwegian governments are more directly involved in sport, while the British and Canadian governments are less interventionist in this field.

Thus the division of labour between different public institutions in relation to high performance sport is only partly consistent with the expectations traced in Chapter 2 (Table 2.1). In all countries, whether federalist or unitary, it is mainly the central government that is responsible for high performance sport. But provinces are increasingly involved, especially in federalist Germany and Canada. This is particularly significant in the province of Quebec, Canada, which appears to use elite sport as a vehicle for Francophone nationalism. It is also the government, not the parliament, that plays the most important role in relation to high performance sport in all countries. There are more significant differences between the countries regarding the relationship between the government and the sports organisations. In Germany and Norway strong national umbrella organisations have the main responsibility for sport and play a significant role in sports policy, including high performance sports policy. Sports organisations are also important for high performance sports policy in Canada and England, but because the organisational landscape is more fragmented government plays a more significant role. In all countries, however, the governmental impact upon high performance sport is increasing although in the two countries with strong national umbrella organisations – especially in Norway – it seems as if the government gives less priority to elite sport than in the two other countries, at least on a rhetorical level. Finally, in all countries it appears that the 'policy communities' of high performance sport are increasingly opened up for external values, interests and justifications (i.e. business, health/fitness and community development). This reflects general tendencies of pluralisation and/or generalisation of interest. These developments are particularly evident in relation to the construction of sports venues and the organisation of big events (i.e. international championships). But these pluralisation processes take different directions and find different expressions depending on the cultural traditions of each country. Market oriented discourses are more legitimate in Canada and Britain, while health, fitness and community development discourses are more legitimate in Germany and Norway. All in all, the systematic search for instrumental justifications of sport is particularly strong in British sports policy.

It is important to acknowledge impact differences in the historical development of the high performance sport systems of all four countries. These differences should be understood both in relation to specific cultural and political traditions and values in each country and in relation to specific 'focusing events'. Canada was an 'early adopter' of the Eastern-bloc system. Canadian defeats in international competitions and the country's political need for nationally unifying symbols are important historical explanations of this early institutionalisation of elite sport, while the Ben Johnson affair explains the temporary set-back of the process during the late 1980s and 1990s. England was a late adopter in the development of a high performance sport system, due to strong liberal non-interventionist political traditions and strong amateur sport traditions, but poor international sport performances during the 1980s and 1990s, the introduction of National Lottery, a Prime Minister, John Major, interested in sport and an instrumental government policy towards sport contributed to an acceleration of the institutionalisation of high performance sport. The strong East German elite sport legacy has both strengthened and hampered the institutionalisation of high performance sport in the united Germany. While the strong egalitarian cultural and political traditions in Norway have for long influenced sports policy, including the institutionalisation of high performance sport, strong nationalism has contributed to populist pressure upon the sport system to produce success in international competitions. Thus Norwegian failures and successes in international competitions during the 1980s and 1990s contributed to the acceleration of the institutionalisation of high performance sport in Norway. In all four countries the pressures for homogenisation were strongly mediated by specific national cultural and political conditions. However, the evidence of the impact of cultural and potential mediations was manifest more clearly in the pace of change rather than in the direction of change.

In all four countries there is a strong and consistent drive to institutionalise a strong and efficient high performance sport system, based on a pyramid model. The organisation of elite sport in the four countries therefore develops more or less in the same direction, even allowing for some adaptation to specific national conditions such as federal structures, geography and population distribution. However, the corresponding discourses presented in policy documents, interviews and sports policy debates, still vary considerably. They vary between the countries and from period to period within the same country. This may partly be caused by a form of 'cultural lag' between the development of organisation and discourses, and partly by different discursive legitimacy strategies and relations between different sports policy actors in the different countries. Thus it may be appropriate to conclude that structures converge, but discourses vary in the field of elite sport.

Notes

1 In this chapter the terms 'high performance sport' and 'elite sport' will be used synonymously.
2 Oakley and Green (2001, p. 88) have borrowed this concept from Chalip (1995). They use it about both traumatic and significant events that influence the direction of policy. In our context it should identify 'the key forces behind different nations' elite sport development'.
3 UK, France, Spain, Canada and USA.
4 It is of course also possible that quite different, but parallel, elite sport structures in different countries may be equally 'efficient instruments' for Olympic success. They may be 'functional equivalents'.
5 'The Canadian Sport Policy' has been developed by Sport Canada in cooperation with the ministers responsible for sport, fitness and recreation at the federal and provincial/territorial levels of government – in cooperation/consultation with the sport organisations/community (Sport Canada, 2002).
6 Described as part of the 'entertainment business' by Sport Canada officials.
7 Sources: http://www.usask.ca/archives/participaction/english/home.html and a sport organisation official.
8 Sport: The Way Ahead. The report of the Minister's Task Force on Federal Sport Policy. Ottawa: Minister of Supply and Services Canada (1992) (Chairman, J.C. Best).
9 He probably refers particularly to democratic and humanistic values.
10 That is 'focusing events' like success and/or failure in international competitions, the hosting of specific international competitions in Canada and – especially – the Ben Johnson affair.
11 Finland scores particularly high on mass participation; Australia has been particularly successful with its high performance strategy.

12 There have been strong reservations in British political traditions against establishing a separate ministry of culture
(Ridley, 1987).

13 According to a couple of informants the Canadian Olympic
Committee uses a similarly hierarchical 'carding system'
(A-, B- and C-card) as a basis for allocation of financial sup-
port to athletes.

14 Federations for specific sports.

15 The DSB and NOK merged into one organisation – *Deutscher
Olympischer Sportbund* (DOSB) – May 20th, 2006.

16 http://www.bmi.bund.de/nn_662928/Internet/Navigation/
DE/Homepage/Home.html__nnn=true

17 This appears to be an ironic contrast to the idealistic celebration of the masses in the communist tradition.

18 E-mail from the *Bundesinstitut*.

19 The Institute for training science in Leipzig is still, however,
important for German elite sport together with the coaching
Academy in Cologne (see later in this chapter).

20 E-mail from the *Bundesinstitut*.

21 Authors' translation.

22 The Turin Olympics became a relative deception for
Norway. Norway ended 13th on the medal table (10th best
among European nations). Norway won 19 medals in all;
only two of them were gold medals.

23 *Barneidrettsbestemmelsene*.

24 Authors' translation.

25 Hofmo was not, however, an unequivocal opponent to high
performance sport. It was indeed Hofmo who, in his capacity of vice-mayor, proposed that Oslo should host the
Olympic Winter Games in 1952 (Goksøyr, 1992).

26 In practice the constructions sponsored by the Ministry
became more adapted to high performance standards.

27 Authors' translation.

28 Track and field, 800 m and 1500 m, top level in Norway as a
junior and young senior in the early 1960s.

29 Prime Minister Willoch's conservative (right wing) government (1981–1983) was followed by a centre-right government (1983–1986).

30 Those 2000 athletes who are organised in this college sport
organisation.

31 Interview with national sport organisation official (athletics).

32 Interview with provincial sport organisation official (athletics).

33 A Sport Canada official ironically described the centres as
'virtual centres', probably because they are not necessarily
very distinct organisations – but instead may be integrated
into another institution, often a university.

34 Launched 2002; http://www.sportengland.org/
35 http://www.activesurrey.com/content-1153
36 Established 2004. http://www.sportengland.org/index.htm
37 Authors' translation.
38 *Stützpunkte = Olympiastützpunkte.*
39 E-mail from the Bundesinstitut für Sportwissenschaften.
40 Here Norway differs from England/Britain, where the sports policy discourses changed significantly from *sport for all* and amateur sport into a more positive attitude to elite sport during the 1990s.
41 http://www.aftenposten.no/nyheter/sport/article 1335369.ece.
42 http://www.trenerforeningen.no/Default.asp?layout= article&id=148.

CHAPTER 7

Sport for all

Introduction

Sport for all policy is far from easy to define but may, initially at least, be defined as a government strategy designed to increase physical activity among the general population. The idea that government should support physical exercise among ordinary people has deep historic roots. In 1863 the Norwegian Parliament granted money to a voluntary association founded to promote physical exercise and the use of military arms (Goksøyr, 1992). In 1934 in British Columbia a substantial programme was launched to offer physical training for the unemployed in order to strengthen their position in the labour market (Kidd, 1996). In this early phase the promotion of sport participation was mainly intended to strengthen the employability or military capacity of young male adults. In England *sport for all* as a policy issue has its precursors in the discussions on the content of the physical education curriculum and the establishment of a youth service for adolescent youth based on cooperation between local education authorities and voluntary bodies such as the Boy Scouts Association and the Girl Guides Association (Houlihan and White, 2002). Early sport participation policies were mainly directed towards certain segments of the population especially the young and those of military age, and were based on instrumental values and specific social objectives.

The idea that it was a governmental concern to get everybody to exercise is much more recent gaining strength in industrialised countries in the 1960s and early 1970s. The concept of *sport for all* became familiar in the 1970s when the Council of Europe's Sports Committee presented the 'Sport for all' Charter which asserted that participation in sport was an individual right. The term *sport for all* had, however, appeared earlier in a report from 1968 which argued *sport for all* must provide 'conditions to enable the widest possible range of the population to practise regularly either sport proper or various physical activities calling for an effort adapted to individual capacities' (Marchand, 1990, p. 3). If the concept of *sport for all* is difficult to define with precision it is partly because sport is a rather fluid concept. The European Sport Charter provided the following definition of sport:

Sport means all forms of physical activity which, through casual or organised participation, aims at expressing or improving physical fitness and mental well-being, forming social relationships or obtaining results in competition at all levels.
(Council of Europe Committee of Ministers, 1992, revised 2001)

This broad definition reflects and is reflected in the variety of ways different countries conceive sport. In some countries, such as Germany and Norway, sport is conceived as physical exercise in whatever form while other countries, such as Canada and, at times England, adopt a narrower conception of sport and sport participation. Their idea of sport is narrower insofar as greater emphasis is given to competitive games by comparison to non-competitive physical activities. To an extent the differences between the countries reflect two distinct sports traditions, one influenced by the German '*Turnen Bewegung*' where sport is seen as an integrated part of developing one's personality and the other influenced by the English competitive conception of sport with its focus on achievements and records (Heinemann, 1996). Hartmann-Tews (1999) argues that the competitive conception of sport became dominant, at least in Western countries. 'Its prevalence is due to the fact that this concept of sport is tightly in accordance with the common pursuits of the performance societies of the West, shared by spectators, reinforced by the vicarious public interest of spectator sport and by the mass media as well by economic interest'. She points to the fact that this concept of *sport for all* is not in accordance with the traditional ways of looking at sport and represents a focus on free spontaneous physical effort engaged in during leisure time and on individual needs like fitness, health, pleasure and well-being. It should already be clear that *sport for all* is a rather imprecise concept, capable of including competitive activities, sport serving wider societal goals, as well as sport and recreation mainly for individual pleasure and benefit. Rather than attempt to impose a definition of *sport for all* for the purpose of this study we see it as more useful to accept the ambiguity and fluidity of the concept. The questions to be posed are not only whether different countries have a policy focused on increasing sport participation, but also what they mean by sport participation in terms of target groups, use and direction of policy instruments.

The chapter is organised around three themes:

1 Overall changes in government policy in *sport for all*.
  How has *sport for all*, as an overall government policy, developed? How active is government? Has the significance of this policy area increased, decreased or remained fairly stable over time with regard to political/governmental attention and allocation of resources? What is the actual policy, what are the main changes that have taken place and how might the changes be explained?
2 Structures of implementation.
  The implementation of *sport for all* policies takes place at different government levels, and by different means. In one sense *sport for all* can be conceived of as a task for local government

as people mainly exercise locally, but as in most policy areas, other levels of government can be expected to play supporting roles. Which policy instruments and delivery mechanisms are actually used?

3 Factors influencing *sport for all* policy.

The concern here is to identify the impact of cultural, historical and political factors in shaping the policy process for *sport for all*.

The analysis of these three themes will be informed by reference to the discussion of typologies of the welfare state and the analytic dimensions discussed in Chapters 1 and 2. Regarding the state structure it is important to determine the extent to which state structure (federal–unitary, centralised–decentralised) mediates both policy development and service delivery. The role of voluntary sports organisations is especially important both in terms of policy-making and as agents of policy implementation. As to government systems Canada and England are characterised as more pluralist than Germany and Norway which are seen as more corporate systems. Consequently, we might expect the voluntary sector to play a more central role in *sport for all* in Germany and Norway than in the other two countries. Regarding generalisation of interests and coalition building, it is important to explore how *sport for all* policies are justified in different countries and how the justifications have changed over time. Moreover, it is also important to examine the way in which justifications for government involvement in *sport for all* have been shaped by endogenous factors, for example history and culture.

The development of *sport for all* policies

As we shall see the salience of *sport for all* policies has exhibited considerable volatility over time. The 1960s and 1970s were a 'golden age' for *sport for all* policies. Many governments were investing heavily in facility development and were rewarded with a substantial increase in participation. However, since the late 1980s, when the increase in participation began to stutter and then stall, *sport for all* policies began to drop down the political agenda or experience radical redefinition.

Canada: fluctuating policies

In the early years of its involvement in sport the federal Canadian government was mainly concerned with regulation and had only a limited set of policies intended to stimulate fitness and mass participation. In the 1960s the government supported, albeit modestly, general sport activity by cost-sharing agreements with the provinces and the provision of small grants to sport organisations. The emphasis on elite sport was, at this time, marginal, as reflected in the 1961 *Fitness and Amateur Sport Act* which gave considerable emphasis to mass participation. However, Macintosh *et al.* (1987) in their analysis of federal Canadian sport policy made clear that around 1970 the focus of policy shifted from support of general physical activity and mass sport to support for elite sport development.

Policy changes had consequences within the machinery of government. Sport Canada had, in the early 1970s, a parallel division, Recreation Canada, within the Fitness and Amateur Sport Directorate. Recreation Canada was created as a result of complaints that sport policy had become elite oriented. However, Recreation Canada, created in 1971, became progressively redefined and marginalised. First the organisation was renamed Fitness and Recreation Canada, and later in 1980, the word Recreation was dropped. As part of a major government restructuring and downsizing in 1993 the post of minister for fitness and sport was abolished and Fitness Canada was absorbed into Health Canada. In the early 1970s the finances for Sport Canada as compared to those for Fitness Canada were in a ratio of 3:1, by the late 1980s it had increased to 7–9:1 (Bercovitz, 1998).

In the mid-1980s Fitness Canada developed an Active Living Strategy (Bercovitz, 1998) which marked a shift away from service provision to strategic leadership. Fitness Canada defined its role as reconciling tensions in the federal–provincial relationship and in facilitating cooperation across ministries and with the corporate sector. The idea was one of focusing not on sport and physical exercise *per se*, but on daily activities as gardening, walking or cycling to work, taking the stairs and so on. There was also a concern to shift the focus away from state provision by emphasising individual responsibility. Bercovitz (1998) highlighted the paradox at the heart of the Active Living concept: a government driven, top down policy supposedly 'owned' at community level. The tensions inherent in this paradox were among the reasons why the recreation policy area became fragmented and later marginalised at the federal level. The claim by the provinces that the recreational area was within their jurisdiction was reinforced, in the eyes of the provinces at least, by the claim that federal support in cost-sharing agreements was small compared to the service needs. Such claims added pace to the process of marginalisation. A further factor contributing to the government's decline in interest was its increasing concern with competitive sport and elite sport development. Finally, the deterioration in the national general economic and financial situation made investment in *sport for all* policies more problematic.

The remaining focus of federal involvement in, and residual commitment to, *sport for all* can be found in the Physical Activity Unit in Health Canada. This Unit has a small budget and defines its mission as being, 'To improve the health and well-being of Canadians through regular physical activity' (www.phac-aspc. gc.ca/pau-uap/fitness/about.html, November 2006). Its main concern is strategic leadership for the promotion of physical activity with a particular focus on target groups such as the disabled, girls and women, older adults and aboriginal people. However, its impact has been modest both within Health Canada and also within the wider sport policy sector.

Much of the recent history of federal policy towards *sport for all* is one of neglect, though generally benign neglect, by comparison to the priority given to competitive sport and elite sport development. However, recent years have witnessed some signs of change, best indicated by the treatment of *sport for all* in the 2002 document 'The *Canadian Sport Policy*' and in the subsequent legislation which indicated a significant shift away from the prioritisation of high performance sport. The 2002 objective was to increase the level and quality of active participation and more particularly to:

(a) promote physical activity as a fundamental element of health and well-being
(b) encourage all Canadians to improve their health by integrating physical activity in their daily lives, and
(c) assist in reducing barriers faced by all Canadians that prevent them from being active.

The Federal government gave substance to these policy objectives by allocating $Can 45 million to support the participation strategy over a 5-year period and a further allocation of $Can 5 million was increased to $Can10 million a year in the subsequent 4 years. Interestingly, this expenditure came from the Health Ministry budget and was defined as an investment in Canada's Health Care System (Department of Finance, 2003), although channelled through Sport Canada. That Sport Canada has been given responsibility for the allocation of this money was ironic given that since its foundation it had focused almost exclusively on elite sport development. The emphasis on participation within the 2002 Canadian Sports Policy was acknowledged by a representative of Sport Canada as marking a refocusing for Sport Canada away from an almost exclusive concern with excellence and capacity building. However, he emphasised that the participation pillar, as defined by Sport Canada, is closer to sport than recreation in the sense that the activities should have a competitive element, and operate within a recognised set of rules. The Sport Canada official argued that the organisation's motives for supporting participation strategies was not only to calculate the health improvement of Canadians, but also to provide a wider base from which to recruit future elite athletes.

In the absence of a Federal Government delivery system for sport participation Sport Canada is working with three different partners and networks. First, it is supporting national sport organisations which have developed sport participation strategies in collaboration with partners including community clubs, schools and municipalities. Fifteen projects were supported in 2002/2003 with funding of over $Can 0.5 million and a further fifteen identified in 2003–2004. Sports that have received support include alpine skiing, athletics, baseball, rugby, cycling and swimming with youth and aboriginal people among the target groups. For example, in 2003 $Can 40,000 was given to Hockey Canada to enhance aboriginal and inner-city youth participation in hockey and $Can 65,000 given to the Canadian Table Tennis Federation schools programme to increase participation among the 8–12 year age group, aboriginal youth, girls and persons with disabilities. However, not all national sport organisations are involved in these programmes and the budget represents only a small part of the total federal funding for the sport organisations.

A second set of partnerships is between Sport Canada and multi-sport organisations especially those for women and aboriginal groups. Part of this initiative was the announcement in 2005 by the minister of sport of a sport policy to increase aboriginal people's participation in sport to which the government has committed $Can 12 million over 5 years. Partners in this policy development included the Aboriginal Sport Circle, provincial and territorial governments and aboriginal sport bodies with the programme covering coaching, athlete development and sport participation.

A third set of partnerships are bilateral agreements between the federal government and the provinces/territories. This initiative has echoes of the previous federal–provincial cost-sharing partnerships and while not restricted to sport participation projects most fall into this category. The criteria for the provision of federal funding are a sport focus, an action orientation, at least matching funding from provincial/territorial government, and a commitment from future funding partners to secure sustainability at the completion of federal funding. The programme was launched in 2002/2003 and in February 2004 a total federal support of $Can4,740,000 was allocated to 10 provinces/territories, covering a wide range of school and community projects targeting, *inter alia* children and youth, aboriginal people and communities with limited access to sport participation. In April 2004 it was announced by the sport minister that the government would fund ParticipAction to conduct a feasibility study of how Canadians participation in organised sport could be increased. Injecting federal funds into the programme is symbolic indicating the renewed engagement of the federal government in sport participation policies. ParticipAction was an organisation that played an important role from its establishment in the early 1970s and for many years (Macintosh, 1996) until it ceased operation in 2000 (Canadian Journal of Public Health, 2004). The philosophy behind ParticipAction has, to an extent, been revived by the government. According to the minister, 'The ParticipAction name is one that has an important symbolic meaning for Canadians', and 'ParticipAction has tremendous potential to tie together all the work that has been done in the area of sport participation, and get Canadians moving' (Sport Canada, 2004b). The overall cost of these three sets of initiatives is approximately $Can 10 million which, out of a total budget of $Can 140 million is, at best, a modest endorsement of the revived priority for participation.

In summary, in recent years the federal government has been reviving its support for sport including its support in the area of sport participation fostering the impression of a renewal of interest in participation after many years of explicit prioritisation of elite sport. However, the renewed modest enthusiasm for participation programmes is driven as much by the emerging health concerns with the consequences of an increasingly sedentary lifestyle as by a commitment to any intrinsic attributes of sport. An instrumental attitude still dominates federal thinking regarding sport.

In Canada the development of sport and recreation policy as part of an emerging welfare state has its origins in the economic crisis of the 1930s. In this early phase the promotion of sport was mainly orientated towards developing healthy young people and citizens. Only gradually did the idea of access to sport and recreation as a social right emerge. The main momentum for this idea was generated at the provincial and municipal levels which have a constitutional responsibility for recreation (Harvey, 2002).

The current framework for recreation policy was specified in a National Recreation Statement agreed by the Inter-provincial Sport and Recreation Council in September 1987. The concept of recreation refers not only to physical activity and sport, but also to culture, arts and related spare time activities. In addition to formulating policy the provinces and territories are responsible for funding specific programmes and their coordination and delivery, often in conjunction with local voluntary organisation. However, the responsibility enjoyed by the provinces for sport and recreation has been interpreted in a variety of ways with some prioritising high performance sport and others emphasising grass-root development. Quebec, for example, has, to a large degree, been concerned to promote elite sport while Ontario, in contrast, has emphasised a broader interpretation of recreation and the Northern Territories have tended to give especial emphasise to fitness.

Alberta is a good example of the variations in policy over time. In the 1960s and 1970s recreation was conceived of as an essential service, and was strongly supported by the provincial government. By the early 1980s the new revenue stream from gaming was allocated mainly to sport, recreation, culture and the arts. However, the economics of the early 1990s led to severe cuts in public finances and diversion of lottery revenues away from recreation and culture to other services resulting in a dramatic decrease in provincial expenditure on recreation and culture between 1989/1990 and 1997/1998. Measured in constant dollars per capita the Government of Alberta's expenditure on recreation and culture declined by about one-third. (Nichols Applied Management, 2005). By the late 1990s not only was there a recovery in the Canadian economy but also a recovery in funding for recreation in Alberta which increased by approximately one-third in real value dollars, increasing from $Can 109 million in 1997 to $Can 158 million in 2001. Although approximately $Can 40 million between 1999 and 2001 was a contribution to the cost of hosting the World Athletics Championships in Edmonton the recovery in public funding was substantial. Nevertheless, when the provincial contribution is compared to that of the municipalities it is clear that it is the latter that make the most substantial contribution at sub-national level. Between 1997 and 2001 municipal expenditure on sport and recreation increased from $Can 287 million to $Can 406 million (Nichols Applied Management, 2005). More importantly, while in 1990/1991 provincial and municipal expenditure on sport and recreation in Alberta was similar, by 2001 municipal expenditure accounted for over 70% of the combined total (Nichols Applied Management, 2005).

England: a government-led approach

Promoting mass participation has been a core element of British sport policy from the early phase of public policy for sport in the 1960s. Although the focus and rationale for government support for sport have changed over the years, the rhetoric of mass participation has remained a relatively constant aspect of the sport policy discourse. However, acknowledging the interruption in the 1980s, the longevity of the mass participation and, from the 1970s, the *sport for all* discourse could be seen as indicating the malleability of the concept rather than the depth of commitment by the government.

The report of the Wolfenden Committee in 1960 provided an important catalyst for a public debate on the role of government in sport development. The Committee was concerned with the decline in sports participation once children left school. The Committee made a number of proposals, some of which, mainly those directed at young people, conceptualised sport as an element of welfare policy while others were concerned to strengthen the performance of the country at elite level. The Committee was also concerned to maintain the role of the voluntary sector as well as encouraging a more active role for government in terms of administrative support and funding. A key suggestion was to establish a Sports Development Council with funding powers. Although this proposal was not accepted immediately an Advisory Sport Council was eventually established in 1965 which was replaced in 1972 by a Sport Council with an executive mandate and a budget to support its activities.

The Sport Council identified, as one of its main tasks, the expansion of the facility base which was achieved in part by providing financial support for voluntary sector facilities but mainly by providing funding to enable the construction of public facilities at the municipal level. Between 1971 and 1981 more than 500 swimming pools and 450 new indoor centres were constructed (Houlihan and White, 2002). In this early phase sports policy was mainly demand led. By developing a network of facilities across the country there was a dramatic increase in participation opportunities which met the substantial latent demand from the grassroots participant as well as the needs of the elite performer. The rapid growth in the facility base certainly played a role in increasing participation levels up to the mid-1980s.

Sport participation received rather less attention in the 1980s. The Thatcher government downgraded traditional welfare policies and through the restructuring of government, budget-cuts, privatisation and the introduction of compulsory competitive tendering in the leisure area, the government diverted attention away from discussion of the future development of *sport for all* policy. However, this is not to argue that government policy stagnated, rather it is to suggest that the focus of sport policy narrowed substantially during the Thatcher period. Besides supporting elite sport, the policy emphasis shifted to the targeting of under-represented and marginalised groups prompted sharply by the riots in the early 1980s which led the government to support Action Sport, a programme coordinated and funded by the British Sport Council in cooperation with Manpower Services Commission. This programme was based on a proactive and interventionist approach towards groups in inner cities, like youth and ethnic minorities. Leadership and motivation for sport and recreation, leadership training, together with cooperation with local authorities and networking with other partners to sustain the programme, were central components. The Action Sport programme was complemented by a series of demonstration projects targeting different groups and working with different partners designed to encourage greater sport participation and included outreach work towards women in rural areas together with the Women's Institute, health and exercise promotion in cooperation with regional health authorities in Liverpool, and projects linked to the school system (Houlihan and White, 2002).

In the late 1980s the British Sport Council introduced the influential pyramid model of the sports development continuum, which was both an ideological and a practical guide for sports development. The continuum provided a diagrammatic representation of the linkages whereby basic skills were acquired at the Foundation level which enabled children to progress to the Participation level and possibly on to Performance and Excellence levels. The idea was to point to the mainly positive and dynamic relationships between the different activity segments and corresponding sport policy areas. However, although the continuum model and the associated rhetoric emphasised harmonisation and linkages between the different areas of sport, shifts in sport policy from 1990 onwards emphasised increasing specialisation and segmentation of interests.

The 1990s was a period during which sport policy moved higher up the central government political agenda. After a temporary relocation from the Department of Environment to the Department of Education and Science, sport was moved to the new Department of Heritage created in 1992, which gave sport a higher profile within government (Houlihan, 1997). The enhanced political status of sport was reinforced by the creation of new sources of income, first through the introduction of the Foundation for Sport and the Arts in 1991 and second by the establishment of the National Lottery in 1994. The introduction of the National Lottery was significant not simply because it added about £200 million per year to overall public investment in sport, but also because the money was 'new' in the sense that it was unencumbered by prior spending commitments and could therefore be used more strategically by distributing bodies to enable progress towards governmental goals.

However, according to Houlihan and White (2002) the focus for much of the 1990s, at least until 1997, was not on mass sport and participation but on performance/elite sport and school sport/youth sport. In 1989 the British Sport Council gave priority to long-term funding of Olympic sports and significantly increased the funding of high-performance athletes. These priorities were articulated in its first national sport policy document for 20 years, *Sport: Raising the Game*, in 1995. In addition to prioritising elite sport and school sport the document sought to define the responsibilities of key actors while the sports continuum was dropped as a conceptual reference. Governing bodies were considered to be involved in talent development and youth development, as well as high-performance sport while schools were given a particular role in the introduction and promotion of traditional sports for young people.

In contrast to the increased attention given to elite and school sport, *sport for all* was neglected. Part of the explanation lay in the removal of responsibility for sport from the Department of Environment, the ministry with oversight of local authorities, and the consequent weakening of links with the main providers of sport and recreation opportunities. More significantly, the neglect of *sport for all* reflected deeply entrenched suspicion of local authorities, especially those controlled by the Labour Party, which had a history of opposition to central government initiatives. According to Houlihan and White (2002, p. 111) the government policy document *Sport: Raising the Game*, failed to acknowledge the contribution of local authorities to sport, not only regarding basic participation, but also as important contributors to pathways to excellence. Although some local authorities did develop effective sport development strategies many experienced a period of policy drift due to shortage of resources and the absence of clear strategic objectives for sport. Local capital expenditure on sport and recreation fell significantly at the beginning of the 1990s although revenue expenditures remained fairly stable. Despite the neglect of *sport for all* by the government important policy development was taking place within the British Sports Council in relation to equity. The development of equity policies concerning gender, race and level of ability and the Brighton Declaration in 1994 on gender equity in sport (White, 2003) provided a solid foundation for the revival of interest in *sport for all* under the 1997 Labour government.

The election of a Labour government in 1997 with a strong commitment to social inclusion helped to return *sport for all* to the national agenda. However, rather than displacing the existing commitment to elite development and school sport, *sport for all* was presented as complementing current policy. Indeed, school sport remained located at the heart of the Labour sport policy partly because it was seen as contributing to both excellence and participation objectives. In *A Sporting Future for All* (DCMS, 2000) the government launched an ambitious plan to upgrade sport in education. Lottery money was allocated to improve the quality of school facilities and equipment and to support the creation of a number of specialist sport colleges. The role of the specialist sport colleges was to act as focal points for the development of expertise which could be shared with other schools in the locality, especially primary schools. In addition, the specialist sports colleges working in conjunction with School Sport Partnerships were to increase the provision of 'out of school hours sport', particularly competitive sport, and to support the talent development programme. Between 1996 and 2004 the government had allocated almost £1 billion for new capital sports development projects on education sites and to support the employment of specialist staff (Carter report, 2005). The emphasis on school sport was not only to increase sport participation, but also to create a firmer foundation and pathway for the development of sport excellence. As such it is interesting to note how the concept of *sport for all* was not interpreted as referring only to the promotion of mass participation, but interpreted more literally to include the pursuit of excellence.

In its policy document, *A Sporting Future for All* (DCMS, 2000) the Labour government emphasised the role of local authorities and acknowledged that their control of facilities and employment of sport development officers gave them a central role to play in delivering *sport for all*. Local authorities were expected to fulfil a dual role of, on the one hand supporting lifelong and grassroots sport participation through access to their own facilities and services and, on the other, supporting and developing the voluntary club structure.

National governing bodies (NGBs) of sport (England's national sports organisations) have traditionally focused on performance and elite sport development. Their involvement in the achievement of wider sports development objectives has primarily been linked to youth sport, as part of basic skills development, talent identification and talent development. Recently, NGBs have also been required by the government to contribute to *sport for all* policy in a wider sense. In *A Sporting Future for All* the NGBs of commercially successful sports were encouraged to set aside at least 5%, and preferably 10%, of television income for investment in grassroots facilities and activities, to involve professional elite sportsmen and women in school and community sport programmes and to develop strategies to attract under-represented groups. One example of the implementation of this policy is the establishment of the Football Foundation as a result of cooperation between the government, the Football Association (FA) and the FA Premier League.

The publication of *Game Plan* (DCMS/Strategy Unit, 2002) represented a further endorsement of objectives associated with sports participation. However, the government was keen to emphasise that the increased commitment to participation did not imply a downgrading of its priority towards high-performance sport. The government argued that its goal was Scandinavian levels of participation and Australian levels of elite success. The increased emphasis on participation was in part justified by growing public health concerns in relation to rising obesity levels. 'Game Plan' was followed by *The Framework for Sport in England* (Sport England, 2004) which set the ambitious 'goal' of increasing the number of people regularly taking part in sport and recreation activities by an average of 1 percentage point per year until 2020.

Increasing participation is currently an integral part of government sport policy. However, it is also clear that the enthusiasm of governments for raising participation levels extends beyond an acceptance of the personal satisfaction and pleasure to be gained from sport. Increased participation is seen as contributing to the achievement of a range of broader social issues 'like health and community safety, education benefits, ... social benefits ... sport is an instrument delivering those other benefits' (Sport England interviewee). The emphasis in current policy on the social and especially health benefits of sports participation overlaps and reinforces many of the objectives which underpin recent investment in school sport, but does not indicate a decline in commitment to elite success. Indeed, since the announcement that London was to host the Olympic Games in 2012 it is clear that public investment in elite sport will increase substantially. As yet there is no evidence that increased spending on preparations for 2012 will result in budget cuts in either *sport for all* or school sport although there is a concern that any budget overspend on the Olympic Games may result in the diversion of funds from mass participation programmes.

Germany: sport-led policies with strong government support

Sport for all has been an important part of German sport policy for many years and has been the product of the close relationship and harmony of interests between the German sport organisations at different levels on one side and the German government at national, *land* and local levels on the other. *Sport for all* as an idea and strategy was promoted by the post-war German sport confederation almost from its establishment. The German Sport Federation began, in the early 1950s, to reflect on, and establish, objectives for the wider social role of the sport movement (Hartmann-Tews, 1996). Its tasks were not only to support the sport clubs and federations, but also to serve the wider society. Against the background of the misuse of sport during the Third Reich period it was important for sport organisations to rebuild the legitimacy and social acceptance of sport. The General Assembly of the German Confederation in 1959 approved as its objective the inclusion of the whole nation in the sport system often referred to as the 'second path' of sport development, alongside that of competitive sport.

The German Sport Federation was very successful in achieving its objective. Between 1950 and 2003 the number of memberships increased more than 4 times. The sport movement had developed from being a competitive arena for mainly young people in the 1950s to being an inclusive movement drawing participants from a broad cross-section of German society. Much of the impetus for the success of the German mass sport participation came from within the voluntary sport sector. The *land* sport confederations, being umbrellas organisation for all sport within a *land*, accepted the promotion of *sport for all* as their primary responsibility and many of the sport clubs, in particular the smaller- and medium-sized, focused almost exclusively on mass sport activities. Even the national sport federations, despite having a strong focus on competitive and high-performance sport, gradually adapted their organisational structures to support and promote *sport for all* (Hartmann Tews, *op.cit.*; Tiemann, 2000).

However, the impressive growth in the number of clubs and in club membership would not have been possible without government support. Of particular importance was the support of municipalities for the rebuilding of club facilities in the early post-war period (Eulering, 2000). Many sports facilities had been destroyed during the war and others were outdated and in poor repair. A broad partnership for facility development between the organised voluntary sport sector and the government was established. The *'Golden Plan for health, play and recreation'* was presented to the government by the German Olympic Society (DOG, not to be confused with the National Olympic Committee, NOK), which, in close cooperation with the *Deutscher Sportbund* (DSB), had prepared a detailed memorandum about the poor state of sports facilities in Germany (Hartmann-Tews, 1996, pp. 157ff). DOG provided estimates regarding the different types of communities' need for basic level sport facilities such as children's playgrounds, school sport grounds and sport halls. It specified the investment needs and encouraged government at different levels to share the costs. DOG advocated a plan for cost sharing with national government (20%), *land* governments (30%) and local governments (50%). This plan attained cross-party support and approval from government actors at different levels. During the following 25 years a massive construction of sport facilities took place. It was accepted that the government (at various levels) would take responsibility for construction and maintenance of facilities, while the sport organisations and clubs took responsibility for developing and promoting sports programmes and general management (Roskam, 2002).

The growth in mass sport was also supported by a series of programmes introduced by the national government aimed at youth sport. Youth sport had been given support from shortly after the Second World War, not because of a commitment to sport, but because of a concern with the socialisation of youth. The Allied occupying powers were concerned with the socialisation of young people into democratic and civic values and considered sport to be a suitable vehicle. Youth and sport organisations formed a close partnership in order to obtain financial support from the Ministry of Family, Seniors, Women and Youth and in 2001, for example, they received about DM6 million from the national government.

In addition to specific programmes such as those targeting youth, the national and state governments have done much to stimulate general sport activity. *Sport for all* has, according to Engelhardt and Heinemann (2003), not only been a programme objective for sport in Germany, but has also been a guiding principle of (welfare) state support of sport. It is stressed that everyone must have the opportunity to participate in sport within a suitable sport facility, which should be within easy commuting distance, at a reasonable cost, and adapted to individual needs, interests and abilities. To accomplish these goals, the government has provided financial support for facility development, thus securing low-cost access to facilities. However, it has also provided revenue funding to employ sports teachers in public schools and help pay for coaches, trainers and services within the voluntary clubs.

Although state funding is important in supporting *sport for all* activity additional funding came from the national lottery. The lottery, *Glücks Spirale*, was originally launched to finance of the Olympic Games in Munich in 1972 and the World Championship in football in 1974. The German Sport Confederation lobbied successfully for the continuation of the lottery (Hartmann-Tews, 1996) and it is currently one of the main sources of income for the Confederation itself, the state sport confederations, the German Sports Aid Foundation, and the NOK and, as such, contributes substantially to the implementation of *sport for all* policies.

Currently, the German welfare system is under pressure, and affecting the economic conditions for *sport for all*. A slow growing economy linked to global restructuring of industry, the cost and economic consequences of the unification of Germany, poor public finances and shrinking lottery revenues are threatening many aspects of the German welfare system, including sport. Although changes are taking place German *sport for all* policy is still characterised primarily by continuity rather than change. The reasons for this inertia are linked to the complex organisational structure of sport, as well as the corporatist system within which German sport organisations and German government actors operate.

One indication of stability is the pattern of German grants for sport in the period 1992–2002 (see Table 7.1). The figures include funding from all government levels, and as can be seen, the amounts are fairly stable over time. However, if inflation is taken into consideration there has been a decrease in government support for sport during the period 1992–2002. Poor public finances in general and the particular financial burden created by unification, are reasons for the real terms negative growth.

The unification issue in itself became an important object of sport policy. The East German Sport System with its extensive focus on elite sport more or less neglected *sport for all* issues and most public sporting facilities were in very poor condition (Roskam, 2002). Only 11.3% of the sport grounds were in accordance with guideline standards used in West Germany. The German Sport Confederation attempted to repeat its past success and suggested a *Golden Plan East* to renew and reconstruct facilities in the eastern parts of Germany. The plan, although supported verbally by the Standing Conference of Sport Ministers of the *Länder* and, from 1999, receiving some support from the national government, has only been partially successful. The DSB proposed a federal contribution of 50%, with the remaining 50% financed by the *länder* and local government. However, the contribution from national government has been very small.

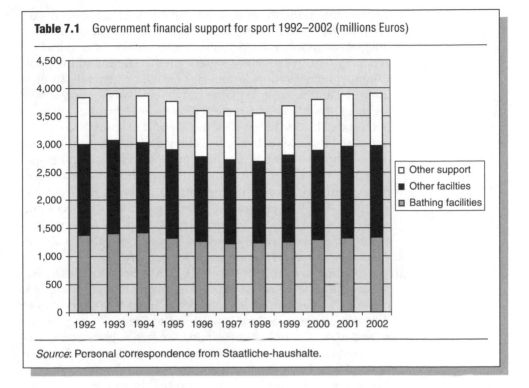

Table 7.1 Government financial support for sport 1992–2002 (millions Euros)

Legend:
- □ Other support
- ■ Other facilties
- ▨ Bathing facilities

X-axis: 1992 1993 1994 1995 1996 1997 1998 1999 2000 2001 2002

Source: Personal correspondence from Staatliche-haushalte.

In the period 1999–2005 the national government allocated €63 million out of a total investment of more than €300 million (BMI, 2005). Compared to a total estimated cost in 1992 of DM24 billion, €63 million was a tiny contribution. The argument of the federal government was that this was not a national responsibility, but a task for the *länder*. The main national responsibility was for elite sport and consistent with this position, the federal government has contributed additional funding of €246 million for the *Golden Plan East* but earmarked it for the modernisation of the *Olympiastadion* in Berlin and the football stadium in Leipzig, both of which were to be arenas in the World Football Championship in 2006.

Despite the current financial pressures the German Sport Confederation continues to organise large nationwide campaigns to encourage active participation in sport activities. The current campaign *Sport tut Deutschland gut. Beweg dich* is promoted through brochures, TV and other media partnerships and emphasises not only the advantages of sport for the individual, but also the advantages for society as a whole. The German Sports

Confederation identifies a number of areas where sport makes an important social contribution including health, community integration, childhood and youth, women, senior citizens and the economy. This represents a significant broadening of the Sport Confederation's rationale for *sport for all*, or generalisation of interests, and may be explained in several ways. First, it may serve as a political and rhetorical device to develop alliances and establish a broad basis for the support of sport. Secondly, it may also be seen as a *de facto* broadening of the scope of *sport for all* in terms of targeting separate groups and developing specific policies. With regard to the latter, over time, German sport does seems to have broadened its scope with, for example, sport for the older generation emerging as a new concern and receiving some admittedly limited funds from the national government. Similarly, family sport as a specific category is also an example of a recently emerged policy concern.

According to a representative of German Sport Confederation the organisation has never received as much project funding as at present. The German Sport Confederation receives support from different national federal ministries to deliver programmes related to, for example, family sports, women's sports, senior citizen sports and the integration of minority sports. There is a clear upward trend in public expenditure on specific sport projects. According to our interviewee this trend can be seen in the broader context of welfare policy restructuring. When restructuring or downsizing the health system, the retirement system or the employment system, national funding for specific sport projects within the area of mass sport, may in part be conceived as an alibi if not quite a substitute. 'When government is reducing certain support systems for the whole population, they have a tendency to support projects that are perceived as "good projects." We have never received so much money for projects as currently'.

The main administrative level for delivery of mass sport (*breiten-sport*) is at the *länder* level. According to the constitution sport as well as culture and education are responsibilities of the *länder*, not the federal government. However, we find some of the same policy development pressures at *länder* level as at the national level. In particular, financial pressures are making it difficult for *länder* to maintain historic levels of financial support and are consequently becoming increasingly selective in the programmes they support. According to the 2002 budgets the *länder* were supposed to give €668 million to sport of which 58% was allocated to sport facilities (including swimming facilities). However, while aggregate *länder* level support for sport remained fairly stable in nominal terms it decreased in real terms from 1992 to 2002 mainly affecting facility development and refurbishment.

In terms of priorities, representatives of the *land* government in Nordrhein-Westfalen (NRW) pointed to two main changes taking place in recent years. One, a stronger focus on talent development and elite sport and two, increased focus on children and youth designed to get this group more involved in the sport system. A less dramatic trend is the increased focus on health-related sport which has been slowly developing for some years.

Table 7.2 below from the largest German *land*, NRW, indicates some of the problems facing *land* government sport policy. On the one hand the government seems to give priority to the education sector, not least with regard to physical education. On the other hand the building of sport facilities has received less priority and sport clubs and organisations as well have problems in maintaining their budget allocations. However, although organisations receive support from state budgets they also receive lottery money. In Brandenburg, for example, decreased support from *land* budgets was, to an extent, compensated for by increasing sport's share of lottery money from 25% to 36%.

In NRW there has been disagreement between the *land* government and the *land* sport confederation (NRW-LSB) concerning cut-backs and redistribution of money. In 2000 the NRW

Table 7.2 Sport budget for Nordrhein-Westphalen 2003

	1998 (million DM)	2003 (million Euros)	Approximate change
Education sector (excluding physical education teachers)	58	46	Growth
Sport clubs and federations	31	14	Small decrease
Building of sport facilities	86	24	Decrease
Other sport promotion measures	9	16.5	Growth
Sport budget – total	184	100	Stability
Expenses of physical education teachers at all types of school	819	900	Strong growth

Source: Ministerium für Städtebau und Wohnen, Kultur und Sport des Landes Nordrhein-Westfalen.

government established a foundation to support talent identification and elite sport thus replacing lottery money and the tasks that had previously been delegated to the LSB. It also tried to reduce the financial support for LSB coaches, but after political intervention from the *land* sports confederation the proposal was dropped. One area where there has been a significant change concerns support from the *land* government to the municipalities for investments in sport facilities. Previously the municipalities had to apply to the *land* sport confederation for public money to support investments whereas under the new system they receive a per capita allocation which they are free to use on sport as they see fit thus substantially reducing the strategic role of the LSB.

Norway: a strengthened policy area

Governmental support for sport is almost as old as organised sport itself in Norway. The government has supported sport almost continually since 1863 when it gave money to the central sport association (Goksøyr, 1992). An analysis of central government sport funding policy and of the government's relationship with the central sport confederation are essential for an understanding of contemporary sport policy in general, and *sport for all* policy in particular (Bergsgard, 2005).

Popular and voluntary-based movements, like the temperance movement, the religious layman movement and the New Norwegian linguistic movement, constitute important elements in the history of Norwegian nation building. Since the Second World War sport has grown to become the largest voluntary-based movement (Wollebæk *et al.*, 2000), whereas other, traditional popular movements have lost members. A combination of significant state support, a strong voluntary sport confederation and sport organisations' accommodation to popular trends, are important factors for this development.

A major base for this development has been the gaming lottery, which was established in the mid-1940s to support sport and science. Initially, the main lottery priority with regard to sport was facility development. Swimming halls were a prioritised area, but football grounds, ski-jumping hills, floodlit tracks for skiing, etc. all received substantial support. Strong growth in lottery income created the opportunity for a substantial increase in facility construction, not least in rural districts and the more remote areas (Goksøyr *et al.*, 1996).

Defence, health and socialisation of youth were important reasons for supporting sport in the first 100 years of government involvement (Goksøyr, M. (ed.), E. Andersen and K. Asdal (1996). Central government's motives for supporting sport were to a large extent, founded on the instrumental value of sport in relation to wider social issues and were less concerned with sport in its more narrow sense of competition and excellence. In the early period of facility development after the war there were no significant tensions between elite sport interests and mass sport interests partly because the major user group of the new facilities, young men, were often involved in competitive sport activities and partly because the facilities were able to meet the needs of both.

During the 1970s and 1980s a revised rationale for government involvement in sport began to emerge and was reflected in *Reports to the Parliament* on culture in which sport was deemed of value in its own right especially in providing pleasure. Sport was consequently considered part of an extended concept of culture in which individual involvement in cultural activities (which included sport and physical activity) was seen as being as important as performance by public officials (Mangset, 1992), a perspective that was consistent with the *sport for all* idea. The revised rationale for government involvement in sport led to the relocation of sport within government. In 1981 the sport and youth office was transferred from the Ministry of Church Affairs and Education to the new Ministry of Culture. The extended culture view of sport was maintained in the first *Report to the Parliament* that specifically dealt with sport which was published in 1991. In the same year sport policy was separated from youth policy and a distinct department of sport was established within the Ministry of Culture which is now part of the Ministry for Culture and Church Affairs.

Sport for all as a specific concept which included physical activity in general and was not limited to competitive and performance sport became popular with politicians in the 1960s and the 1970s. The expansion of the welfare state, the increase in leisure time, the reduction in manual work and the increase in the number of women working outside the home were among factors that contributed to an acceptance of sport as a participation activity for the many. The sport umbrella organisation (NIF/NOC) took the initiative to promote the trim-movement based on fitness practices developed in Germany among other countries.

The period between 1965 and 1985 was one of tremendous growth in sport with the number of sports clubs increasing 4.5 times and sports club memberships increasing by a factor of almost 4. The growth continued into the next decade, but at a slower rate. The growth in participation was supported by, and encouraged, a rapid growth in lottery-supported sport facilities from 1970 to 1990 (Sundbergutvalget, 2003). For example, in this period more than 1000 football pitches and between 400 and 600 multi-use sports halls were developed.

The last government White Paper on *sport for all* policy was published at the turn of the century (St.meld. nr. 14 (1999–2000)). Maintaining continuity with past sport and physical activity for all programmes was identified as the overall vision for government sport policy. The intrinsic value of sport was still specified as a major element in the rationale for government support. In part, this is founded on a citizen perspective; that all have a right to participate in sport and all should be given the opportunity to do so. However, governmental support for sport is also legitimated by a series of wider social values related to health, social integration and the promotion of democratic values. In practice, the health aspect is evident in sport policies to only a limited extent whereas promotion of social integration and democratic values are much more explicit objectives and are particularly obvious in relation to the support for, and development of, local clubs.

This most recent *Report to Parliament* can be interpreted as demarcating more precisely, and sharpening, the focus of *sport for all* policies. An important context for the policy document was the increasing commercialisation of sport, elite sport as well as fitness studios and the like, and it underlined a principle that government money should not go to commercial enterprises or contribute to private profit. In addition to promoting sport and physical activity among the general population some specific target groups were designated such as children (6–12 years), youth (13–19 years) and people with disabilities. The White Paper also signalled, albeit weakly, that support for sport may be given to activities outside formal sport organisations and settings. Moreover, elite sport was given support for reasons associated with national identity whereas competitive sport at national or regional level was excluded as a priority for government policy.

The sharpening of the policy focus on children and youth did not result in a reduction in support for other areas of sport and physical activity: on the contrary, government sport funding has increased significantly across the board. From 1990 to 2000 lottery revenues for sport increased by 40% in real terms and from 2000 to 2005 by a further 14%. As mentioned earlier in Chapter 5 part of the explanation for the increase in lottery funding for sport was successful lobbying by NIF/NOC. However, while the government has been willing to allocate increasing lottery funds to sport it has also sought to increase its control over how those funds are used. Thus by specifying how funds should be distributed to sport, namely through NIF/NOC, and later establishing specified sub-funds and by distributing specific grants which by-passed the central sport confederation the government, in a variety of ways, has taken a firmer grip on how money for sport is to be used (Bergsgard, 2002a; Bergsgard and Opedal, 2002).

Growing administrative costs at the central level of NIF/NOC and the concern to increase support for children and youth have been main reasons for stronger government direction of sport funding. Consequently, the government has sought to divert funds from the national level of sport organisations to local level clubs which deliver participation services. The government in cooperation with NIF/NOC has developed several instruments to pursue its participation strategy. Following a government White Paper on support of the voluntary sector (St.meld. nr. 27 (1996–1997)) the Parliament decided to give lottery money directly to organisations at the local level in order to stimulate local activity among children and youth. Two different grant systems were created, one for sport in particular (Opedal and Nødland, 2004), and the other for children and youth activity and clubs operating within cultural and other settings (Berg *et al.*, 2002). In 2006 120 million NOK was given to local level sport activity and 135 million NOK to other local level culture and youth activity through these grant systems. Furthermore, until 2006 the government provided NIF/NOC with a block grant that it could distribute among its member organisations as it saw fit. In 2006, however, 54 million NOK out of the total grant of 348 million NOK was ring-fenced and could only be used for projects aimed at children, youth and mass sport.

Policy implementation

In contrast to the development of *sport for all* policy where the central/federal level of government plays a crucial role implementation of *sport for all* policy is located more firmly at the sub-national level. However, as will be clear from the subsequent discussion implementation is often a complex process involving different levels of sub-national government and a variety of governmental and non-governmental organisations.

Canada

Although there is some variation between provinces a study of Alberta provides a sharp insight into the general trends in the role of the provinces in sport policy implementation in Canada. The Alberta Sport, Recreation, Parks & Wildlife Foundation (ASRPWF) is the government agency responsible for recreation and sport, and is located within the Ministry of Community Development. Programme delivery is coordinated by the Foundation and in 2002/2003 $Can 15.9 million was allocated to various programmes. Currently, the Foundation is funding more than 100 organisations, many of which are affiliated to national sports organisations. However, the Foundation supports a broader range of organisations than Sport Canada as its mandate is much broader than that of Sport Canada covering not only sport, but also recreation and fitness/lifestyle. Within the Foundation the key priority is to increase physical activity with the consequence that it funds activities which, at federal level, would come within the remit of Health Canada. Thus the Foundation not only supports hockey, football, athletics and other sport disciplines, but also the boy scouts, girl guides, cadets and similar youth organisations. Despite the broad scope of the Foundation activities sport and recreation organisations received, in 2002/2003, more than $Can 6 million.

Operational grants are a relatively stable funding mechanism as the associations receive approximately the same level of funding from one year to another and, if there are changes in funding levels, they tend to be uniform across the sector. Provided associations fulfil certain criteria, such as being the recognised provincial body for its particular activity, having a board of directors, and a minimum of 500 members, they have discretion regarding the use of grant funding. In addition to direct funding associations receive other forms of support. For example, the province participates in a coaching programme delivered by Canadian Coaching Association to develop volunteer coaches. The province is responsible for delivery of the general theoretical element while sport associations are responsible for adapting the theory to the needs of their particular sport.

It is extremely difficult to identify the proportion of provincial funding that is allocated to mass participation. However, approximately 20 of the organisations receiving provincial support are recreational and are focused on recreation and lifestyle activities and issues. In addition, more than 70 organisations define themselves as sport organisations, many of which seem to have as their main focus competitive and elite sport, while also making some provision for general participation. An example is Swim Alberta, which works with a small number of competitive swimmers all the year round, but offers participation opportunities to many youngsters during summer camp activities. There is also a separate performance stream of money, which the Foundation uses to support athlete development and to send talented athletes to national competitions. Moreover, the Alberta government provides financial support to provincial, national and international games taking place in the province. However, the new bilateral provincial–federal programme introduced in 2002/2003 has a clear participation approach. Sport organisations are encouraged to ask for money for development and operations to enhance participation in sport for under-represented groups such as girls and women, aboriginal people, economically disadvantaged groups and persons with disabilities.

The Foundation also funds other programmes and initiatives outside the voluntary sector. For example, in 2002 it started a campaign 'Outside the Box,' directed at youth and those who influence them to encourage young people to adopt a more balanced lifestyle between physical activity and computers/television. The Foundation owns and manages parks and wildlife ventures, and it has an international sport exchange programme and a future leader's programme where, through partnerships, it seeks to reach aboriginal people in communities across the province. Finally, it administers an active lifestyle portfolio in cooperation with a number of active lifestyle partners designed to reflect Health Canada's priorities.

Although the Provinces have significant responsibility for sport and recreation, actual delivery of sport and recreation services mainly takes place at the local level. Municipalities, communities, schools, clubs and leagues are main operators of facilities and activities. Local government is mainly involved in three areas: sport programme administration and operation; facility maintenance and development; and hosting events. Given the extensive service delivery responsibilities of local government a recent trend causing concern is the reduction in funding from the provinces. Many municipalities are struggling financially and recreation has become one of the casualties. In the late 1990s many towns and smaller communities had recreation staff but rural depopulation has weakened the local tax base. Facilities in smaller communities have closed with the consequence that not only do some people have to travel further to the larger towns and cities for sport opportunities, but also that the larger towns and cities are providing opportunities for people who make no tax contribution to revenue costs.

As regards meeting the capital costs of facility provision infrastructure developments are normally achieved through partnerships. The city of Edmonton, for example, has for many years followed a strategy of not building facilities itself. A new indoor soccer centre, Edmonton Soccer Centre South, was completed in March 2004, but while the city of Edmonton provided the land, and a loan at a reasonable rate, the local voluntary soccer organisation, the Edmonton Soccer Association, underwrote the loan. Legally the city of Edmonton owns the facility and leases it back at zero cost while the soccer club runs and maintains the facility (i.e. covers the revenue costs). Although provincial funding has declined in recent years provincial governments will generally make some contribution to the cost of facility development from their lottery income. For smaller facilities there is a basic 50/50 cost-sharing programme between provinces and communities. The Federal government may also contribute to a facility development partnership with the contribution coming not from Sport Canada but from an infrastructure department under the Canada Industry Ministry.

Organising major competitions is one way for communities to acquire new sports infrastructure. The Canada Games, which take place every second year and alternate between summer and winter games, has become a way that many medium-sized communities obtain better facilities through cost sharing with different government levels. Other types of competitions may also leave behind a valuable infrastructure legacy. For example, the World Championship in Athletics in Edmonton in 2001 led to the renewal of Alberta University sport facilities. It is important to note that the momentum for hosting major sports events comes not only from sport organisations, but also, and sometimes primarily, from the local business community.

England

The dominant themes in any consideration of policy implementation in England are first devolution and regionalisation of power and second the government sport funding and delivery system.

At the national level the Great Britain Sports Council was established as an arm's length agency and had a substantial degree of freedom in strategy development. More recently, particularly since the mid-1990s, central government intervened more directly in the operation of the GB Sports Council and its successor bodies insisting that they 'deliver' according to objectives set by the government or, as expressed by an interviewee from Sport England (the most recent successor agency to the GB Sports Council), commenting on the arm's length principle: 'It is not a principle that exists any more. It is a symbiotic relationship, they need us and we need them. But you have to work to their agenda'.

The recent *Review of National Sport Effort and Resources* (Carter Report, 2005) provides a broad overview of the situation of sport in England/UK at different levels and within different sectors paying particular attention to sport participation and community sport, the use of resources and the overall efficiency of the sport system. It recognised that progress has been made in school sport and elite sport, but less in the wider area of sport participation. The Report discussed the deficiencies, imbalances and complexities of the local sports funding and delivery system and also noted that much physical activity is informal, while government policies tend to be directed towards the formal organisations involved in the delivery of physical activity. Among the actions proposed were stronger coordination of community sport and particularly a better linking of schools to community settings, the integration of pathways for aspiring performers, and greater investment in clubs, coaches and volunteers. Better government coordination of existing investment streams and the possible creation of a National Investment Fund with both public and private sector finance were also options mentioned in the Report. The overall aim was a 'single system for sport in the community from Government to grassroots' (Carter Report, 2005, p. 28).

On the one hand the systematic approach to the coordination of the sport system appears to reflect Britain's centralist traditions and is consistent with the underlying assumptions of sports development which stress the interconnection between forms or levels of participation. On the other hand there is a counter trend of decentralisation, at least at an administrative level, which has resulted in many of the activities of Sport England being devolved to the regions, resulting in a substantial reduction in staffing levels in the London headquarters. The enhancement of the role of the regional offices of Sport England and the creation of independent Regional Sport Boards was in part prompted by a perception that Sport England had become detached from the public it was established to serve. Consequently, while the regional offices of Sport England are responsible for implementing the centrally determined policy objectives in their area each region develops its own regional plans. For example, in the East Midlands, the regional office has developed a planning document for 2004 to 2008, 'Change 4 Sport' (Sport England East Midlands, 2004) which incorporates *Game Plan*'s (DCMS/Strategy Unit, 2002) sharper focus on health and physical activity but, according to regional officers attempts to maintain a balance between regional and national priorities. However, the focus on youth participation and creating pathways for participation for the adult population which are current regional priorities sit comfortably alongside the priorities expressed in *Game Plan*. The enhanced role of the region is not only due to the reduction in headquarters capacity, but also due to Regional Sports Boards being given responsibility for the distribution of substantial sums from the national lottery. However, as one regional officer observed the capacity for extensive regional autonomy is constrained by the fact that 'you either deliver government's objectives or you don't get resources to deliver your objectives'.

Thus while the regions have developed sport planning documents which depart from *Game Plan* the extent of deviation is limited. In the East Midlands region for example, it is suggested that *Game Plan*'s focus on physical activity and health has had an impact on regional priorities although there is still a focus on aspects of excellence and mass sport. The regional plan produced in the East Midlands (Sport England East Midlands, 2004) specified a number of desired outcomes including: a 4 percentage point increase in sport participation; to be the most successful region in terms of sport excellence; to reduce inequalities, improve health, achieve stronger and safer communities, improve education and lifelong learning, strengthen the local economy; and to produce a better sports system. At the regional level sport is placed within a broad development framework with the plan being part of a wider integrated strategic framework developed by the Regional Assembly which encompasses economic, social, environmental and spatial objectives. Sport contributes to the achievement of social objectives which include aspects of education, culture, health, leisure, discrimination, community safety and especially the long-term reduction in social exclusion. In addition, physical activity, exercise and sport contributes to 5 (out of 18) strategic priorities in the regional public health strategy as well as being a part of the Regional Tourism Strategy.

Although the strategic importance of the regional level has increased the primary level for service delivery is the local level. Most resources for sport and physical activity are provided at the local level, either by local authorities (municipalities and counties) or the voluntary sector. Almost 90% of total government expenditure on sport is delivered via local authorities and not by the sports councils (DCMS/Strategy Unit, 2002). There was a perception at both national government and regional Sport England levels that many local authorities were failing to integrate the range of service providers operating in their area and that not only were more opportunities for synergy and economies of scale being missed but that pathways for progression and talent development were often absent or partial. Consequently, the recent establishment of County Sport Partnerships (CSPs) was intended to achieve greater coordination of local provision, capacity building and contribution by sport to the wider social agenda. CSPs involve stakeholders from public, voluntary and private sectors, and to receive continued funding from Sport England they must demonstrate success in developing a single high-quality system for sport within their area. In the East Midlands County Sports Partnerships have been established in five counties: Nottinghamshire, Derbyshire, Leicestershire, Lincolnshire and Northamptonshire. The Partnerships are generally strong on the public side, and have involvement from the voluntary sector and government bodies involved, but are less successful in involving commercial providers. Although CSPs are in the very early stage of their development they face substantial challenges even within counties such as Nottinghamshire which has a 30-year history of successful sports development, at least by comparison to many other counties. The current County budget for sports development is about £1.5 million most of which is spent on staff rather than facilities. Indeed the county does not own any major leisure facilities and it is this dispersed ownership, often involving independent trusts, that indicates some of the problems of coordination facing the CSP. Furthermore, the County is divided into nine administrative units, the city which is a unitary authority, and eight district councils. Once the need to work with clubs and schools is added to the district councils and various trusts it is easy to see both the need for a CSP and also the challenges it faces in coordinating such a disparate range of organisations.

Germany

Implementation of *sport for all* policies takes place at all government levels, but with a relatively limited contribution from the national level, balanced by a more substantial contribution from the *land* level and particularly from the municipalities and districts at the local level.

At national level the main initiatives are taken by the national sports federations rather than by the government. Although most national sports federations have elite sport as their main focus they do promote *sport for all*, though with varying degrees of enthusiasm. The German Gymnastics Federation is one of the exceptions as it concentrates primarily on mass sport through its club system. To support its activities it received 4–500,000 DM annually between 1998 and 2001 from the federal government for its work with children, youth and seniors, and also for more general work related to nutrition, fitness and health (*Sportbericht des Bundesregierung*, 2002). The German Table Tennis Federation has strengthened its approach towards grassroots sport as part of a strategy to half the decline in membership. It has a programme '*Weisser Fleck*' (White Spot) which aims to establish new clubs in areas of under provision. The Federation organises mini-championships for children (below 12 years of age) and school championships, which are organised at city, regional and national levels. Every year 40–50,000 participate, many of whom subsequently join a local club.

At the *land* level the role of government is significantly stronger and is based on two pillars: school sport and voluntary sport. Regarding voluntary sport, the main model is one of partnership between the *land* government and the *land* sport confederation in relation to programmes aimed at elite sport and *sport for all*. For example, in Brandenburg one of the smaller *länder*, €15–16 million was allocated to sport in 2003–2004 of which a quarter was for investment in facilities. Of the remainder, €5.8 million was allocated to mass sport and €5.2 million to elite sport. Most of the operational support, €8 million, was transferred to the Land Sport Confederation which has the responsibility to support activities of the regional and local sport federations and clubs who receive finance on a per capita basis for coaching, travel costs for competitions, etc. The *land* administration also provides finance for a number of programmes which are of indirect benefit to participation objectives, including funding directed to schools and to organisations working with people with disabilities. The bulk of public support for sport is thus distributed by the sport itself.

The most important contributions to policy implementation especially with regard to *sport for all* are made at the local level (Heinemann, 1996). The municipalities have a core role as owners and operators of facilities. About two-thirds of public money for sport is distributed by municipalities. In 2002 the municipalities expended more than €3 billion on sport. Of the total public investment in facilities the municipal sector contributed 85.5%, the *länder* 13% and the national level only 1.5%.

The municipalities differ substantially with regard to the sports opportunities available. Variation is influenced by the local economic situation, the possibility of partnership with the commercial sector and the nature of the local infrastructure of sports clubs. The City Sport Council of Potsdam, located in the *land* of Brandenburg, has about 120 clubs with 18,000 members (14% of the population). Interviewees in both the local government and the City Sport Council, which is at the most local level of the German Sport Confederation, agreed that cooperation between the two sets of organisations was close and mutually beneficial. In the city there is a municipal committee responsible for both education and sport mainly because the 54 sport facilities are used both by schools and sports clubs. Sport services are viewed as contributing to municipal objectives not only in education, but also in welfare, leisure and health. Sport is seen as making a major contribution to the youth plan aimed at the avoidance of segregation and the reduction in crime. The local government administration offers a broad range of facilities for sports use including specific facilities for water sport, canoeing and football. Almost all sport facilities are run by the municipality with the exception of fitness studios which remain the preserve of the commercial sector. In Brandenburg the use of most facilities is free of charge, the major exception being the use of swimming pools where an entrance fee is charged. Potsdam spends approximately €3.2 million per year on direct sport service provision and distributes a further €160–170,000 in grants to local sports organisations and for special events hosted by the city. Recent research by Beck and Rode (2002) indicated that about two-thirds of people in Potsdam were physically active, that informally organised sport was clearly the most important activity, and that many of the publicly owned facilities were in a poor state of repair and required about €70 million in order to bring the facilities up to an acceptable standard. The accumulating cost of refurbishment is consequently putting the strong commitment to *sport for all*, via free access to facilities, under intense pressure.

Sport is also a politically important service in Paderborn in Nordrhein-Westfalia. In 2001 the *land* government and the *land* sport confederation launched a project, 'cities of sport', and Paderborn was among those designated as a 'city of sport', reinforcing the importance of sport to the city's image. Paderborn has 130 clubs in 70–80 different sport disciplines. Its sport policy is based on two pillars: (i) mass sport, health and children and (ii) elite sport and talent development. The local sport administration traces its roots back to the early 1950s when a unit for youth (which included sport) was created within the city government. The local sport administration looks upon itself as working in partnership with the clubs and, consequently, does not run activities of its own, but rather provides support for clubs and the city's Sport Council. Within the city council the committee for sport and leisure issues consists of five elected politicians and five representatives from sport. This committee has a degree of independent decision-making authority with regard to policy and the allocation of financial support. Moreover, it discusses all sport issues before they are passed to the city council for decision.

The city Sports Council serves as a mediator between sport clubs and the local government, for instance regarding use of current sport facilities and future facility development. Several local government members are also members of the sport committee. The city has athletes and teams of national and international standard in a number of sports including squash and basketball. Its football team has moved to the second division and a new football stadium was inaugurated in 2006. The stadium was built to standards set by the German Football Federation with the city providing one-third of the expected total cost of €12 million raised by the sale of publicly owned gas and water utilities. Further evidence of the city's commitment to sport is its support for a system operated in cooperation with the education system, which involved third year school children being tested to identify those with a talent for sport and also those with physical motor problems. In summary, Paderborn has a substantial infrastructure for sport which partly reflects the strong local economy and partly the high level of political support for sport among elected members of the city government.

Norway

The municipal level is the main focus for the delivery of *sport for all* policies in Norway. The national and county levels of government and the national sport organisations are more concerned with setting broad policy objectives and distributing resources. Consequently, it is sport clubs that are the main vehicles for organising sport activities at the local level and which are the main instrument for implementation of government *sport for all* policies.

National government support for *sport for all* can be divided into support for activity programmes and support for facilities. The two major instruments of activity programme support are both directed towards the club level, one delivered through national sport organisations and the other through geographical sport structures. The most recent support programme delivered through national sport organisations has yet to be evaluated, but is intended to strengthen the relationship between the central organisation (national federation) and the clubs. The money may not necessarily be given direct to local clubs, but can be used to stimulate the local activity level, for instance by supporting regional level staff in their efforts to recruit clubs and members in areas where participation and provision are weak. The other funding stream is channelled through the local sport councils at municipal level who distribute funding to the clubs with the clubs having considerable discretion over its use. According to an evaluation by Opedal and Nødland (2004) this funding stream has resulted in a broadening of the range of activities available for children and youth.

Lottery financed facility support is channelled by central government through the county level to the municipalities and the clubs. In 2005 the national government allocated 666 million NOK to sport facilities, most of it to local facilities. The system is application based and each year the ministry decides the distribution of money between counties related to need, population, existing facilities and economic circumstances. The sports department of the Ministry of Culture and Church Affairs, which has a special unit concerned with facilities, will decide the distribution of funding between different types of facilities and may also influence facility design. It is the responsibility of county level government to coordinate applications and to decide how money should be distributed among the municipalities' sport clubs or other types of club that are eligible to apply for facility support.

Despite the significant contribution of central government through lottery funding to local activities, children and youth sport and to facility development the main provider of resources and the major actors in *sport for all* policy implementation are at the local level. Local government is the major funder of sport and sport-related activities that overlap with culture, children and the youth services. According to financial data for 2003 364 of the 435 municipalities gave 350 million NOK to clubs within sport and culture. By comparison, national level support for the whole country amounted to just below 200 million NOK. Municipalities also provide substantial additional support. For example, close to half of all sport halls are free of charge for children and youth, and the average fee for those who have to pay is fairly modest due to substantial local subsidy (Sundbergutvalget, 2003). Local government also gives financial support, for instance for facility investment, as a co-financer or by giving a site for new facilities at no cost (Heinzerling and Rommetvedt, 2002). By giving 1 billion NOK to facility development in 2005 local government allocated approximately 50% more funding than the national government. Many facilities have been developed in this way with national and local government providing the finance and the clubs contributing voluntary work to cover revenue costs. The underlying rationale for this financial pattern is that facility financing should be a partnership between the state, municipality and club albeit substantially supported by lottery income.

Sport is not a statutory task for the municipalities. The organisation of municipal policy structures of sport as well as for other service sectors has changed over time (Opedal and Rommetvedt, 2006). The national government has influenced the organisation of sport at municipal level, first by encouraging the formation of local sport committees shortly after the Second World War (Goksøyr et al., 1996) and soon after by promoting the transformation of these committees into sport and youth committees. Later on, from 1970 when the national government developed the idea of sport as part of an extended concept of culture, these committees were combined with culture in their own administrative units and political boards at municipal level (Mangset, 1992). In 1992 the municipalities were given greater liberty to choose their organisational structures. To avoid sector-dominated policy, changes have taken place during the last decade where a number of local services and tasks, including sport, have been combined in larger administrative structures and committees. Consequently, sport has to compete for attention and resources with other tasks and objectives. In spite of this sport has maintained a fairly stable share of municipal budgets since the early 1990s. Moreover, municipal sport expenditure increased with 17% (measured in fixed prices) from 2001 to 2005. However, it should be borne in mind that there may be large variations among municipalities as to how much money is given to sport. An analysis of municipal revenue expenditure for sport in the period 1991–1997 showed that the upper quartile of municipalities gave almost 4 times more support to sport per capita than the lowest quartile.

The national government has also contributed to linkages between local sport organisations and local government in other ways apart from funding. For example, local sport councils comprising all NIF/NOC clubs in the municipality are increasingly becoming an important link between municipalities and local sport clubs because of their authority to distribute national government funding to local sport activity. Moreover, in 1988 the ministry decided that, each municipality had to prepare plans for sport and outdoor life in order. Local sport clubs and sport councils are active partners in this public planning process.

Factors influencing variations in *sport for all* policy

Do *sport for all* policies become more similar across countries, as was the case with elite sport policies, or does this policy area, with its stronger local focus and without the strong links to global competitive arenas, vary due to the endogenous features of each country? The empirical evidence presented earlier in this chapter points to a number of differences which, in part at least, reflect the different sport structures and values across the four countries. However, there are also similarities in terms of policy content and patterns of change that may indicate the emergence of common developmental features of *sport for all* policies. In the discussion that follows we will summarise and comment on the major features of *sport for all* policies in the four countries and discuss how these features may be linked to the different types of welfare system and the analytical dimensions discussed earlier.

Continuity and discontinuity of *sport for all* policies

From the late 1970s/early1980s *sport for all* policies have followed, to a limited extent at least, different tracks with regard to overall national government policy. As the following review indicates one difference concerns the continuity or lack of continuity of national *sport for all* policy.

In Canada the federal government's main concern was with elite sport, whereas the provinces, in line with their constitutional responsibility, took the lead in the development of *sport for all*. Federal government involvement in policy for sport participation and recreation decreased significantly from the early 1970s and was mainly limited to the promotion of individual fitness and an active lifestyle. More recently, however, as a consequence of the formulation of the *Canadian Sport Policy* (Sport Canada, 2002), a more active *sport for all* policy has been adopted by the federal government.

In the 1970s the British government promoted participation through the broad development of the facility base across the country. During the Thatcher period general welfare and *sport for all* policies received less attention and although the government of John Major was more committed to promoting and supporting sport priority was given to school sport and elite sport rather than to mass participation leaving local level actors to develop and promote *sport for all*. However, the publication of *A Sporting Future for All* in 2000 and *Game Plan* in 2002, raised sport participation higher on the national political agenda.

In Germany, by the late 1970s *sport for all* policies were already well established. Mainly run by the local voluntary sector, municipal sport organisations and sport clubs, sport participation and membership rates in the voluntary German sport system have been high for some time and are still increasing. But the cost of unification and financial pressure on welfare services seems to have put a degree of strain on national sport policy and funding, as well resulting in a real term decline in *land* and municipal support for sport over the 10 years since the early 1990s.

Norway is distinctive because of its generally favourable economic situation. *Sport for all* has been consistently identified in government policy documents as the main objective of Norwegian sport policy. During the last 10–15 years sport has received increasing funds from government, almost exclusively from the lottery. Not only has government sought to maintain a high level of financing for facilities, but special government funding has also been allocated to stimulate mass sport and local sport.

To some extent Canada and England are similar insofar as the priority of *sport for all* has varied considerably over time with the most substantial fluctuations in support evident in Canada. In Germany and Norway the *sport for all* policy area has been marked by greater stability. In terms the allocation of government resources Germany is characterised by nominal stagnation and real, though slight decline, while the pattern in Norway has been one of growth. It is tempting, at least in part, to explain these dissimilarities by the different conceptualisations of welfare prevalent in the liberal nations of Canada and England as compared to conservative Germany and social democratic Norway.

Machinery of government and the delivery of *sport for all*

In the federal states of Canada and Germany the main responsibility for *sport for all* policies follows the subsidiarity principle and is located at the provincial/*länder* level, as is the case for education and culture. The only exceptions relate to some sport-related functions where the locus is at national level within non-sports Ministries. For example in Canada the promotion of a healthy lifestyle and in Germany the promotion of family sport, rest with health and welfare ministers respectively.

In the unitary states of England and Norway the main responsibility for *sport for all* policy development is at the national level. In England there is a division of labour between the Department of Culture, Media and Sport and Sport England, the quango responsible for participation sport in England. In the unitary state of Norway the picture is simpler, however, with the Ministry for Culture and Church Affairs being responsible for national sport policies for mass as well as elite sport.

With regard to implementation of *sport for all* policies, local government is the main agent for implementation in all countries and, as was made clear above, the main provider of resources, especially for revenue-based programmes. However, there are some variations in the infrastructure of service delivery. Until recently Canadian federal government support for sport was mainly directed through the provincial level for allocation to a range of voluntary, educational and municipal delivery organisations. In the new Canadian sport policy a greater proportion of federal funding is channelled through national sport and multi-sport organisations as well through the traditional provincial government route. Similarly, in England, there has been a gradual expansion in the number of organisations delivering *sport for all* with an increasing role for the education sector and a greater expectation of co-operation between voluntary, commercial and public agencies. In contrast, in both Germany and Norway the voluntary sport system and the municipalities retain their dominant role. In Germany most money is distributed through the *länder* and local government levels, even though national ministries are increasingly providing project funding for sport. In Norway, the national government has, since 2000, strengthened its influence, by introducing significant revenue-based and development funding programmes aimed at children and youth at the local club level. Government funding is allocated through local sport councils and national sport organisations, respectively with the consequence that less is channelled through the national voluntary organisation, NIF/NOC.

Structural features and continuity and discontinuity

Can different emphasis over time on *sport for all* policies be related, in part at least, to different policy structures and values? Figure 7.1 suggests a possible set of interrelationships.

The degree of continuity and discontinuity in *sport for all* policies as demonstrated by our four case countries can, in part, be explained by two sets of interrelated factors characterising the sport policy system. First, *sport for all* may be understood in relation to the strength of emphasis given to health and social

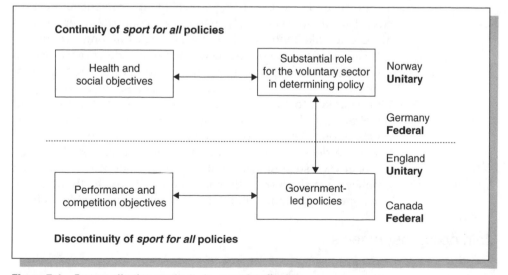

Figure 7.1   Factors affecting continuity in *sport for all* policy

objectives of sport versus performance and competitive success objectives. Secondly, non-government and independent sport interests especially voluntary clubs and their national organisations will vary in the influence they exert over government sport policy formulation as well as implementation. Conversely, the government may be more or less dominant in policy development with voluntary interests and structures having only a weak impact on sport policy. It may be argued that the health and social function concept should mobilise more support within the political system than a policy benefiting the small numbers involved in high-performance sport. A large and well-organised voluntary sector would be able to influence public policy and successfully challenge government dominance of the policy process and influence, for example, the level of monetary support.

The evidence presented in this chapter provides support for these hypotheses with there being significant differences between Norway and Germany on the one hand, and England and Canada on the other. The former two countries adopted a wider concept of *sport for all* than the latter and in both countries the voluntary sector is larger and coordinate their interests more effectively and have arguably more influence on policy than in Canada and England. It may also be hypothesised that the higher growth of *sport for all* funding in Norway by comparison to Germany, and the apparently less severe fluctuations in national government support for *sport for all* in England than in Canada can be understood by reference to the different state systems. More specifically, unitary states, with their greater concentration of policy development and funding powers, may be able to maintain a more uniform and possibly stronger level of government support for *sport for all* more effectively than federal countries where there is a greater likelihood of different strategies among provinces/ *länder*. It may therefore be concluded that differences in overall policy systems in general appear to lead to different degrees of continuity in *sport for all* policies. In turn, these differences appear to be linked to different understandings of welfare goods and welfare distribution systems in social–democratic and conservative countries compared to neo-liberal ones. The evidence we provide does not strictly conform with the Esping–Andersen model as we suggest that a unitary state will adopt a more focused policy towards *sport for all* than a federal state even though both are operating within a similar conceptualisation of public welfare.

Main policy instruments

Regarding the policy instruments used to promote *sport for all* there are some significant similarities between countries as well as differences. The most significant commonality is the use of facility development in all countries mainly in the 1970s and 1980s as a major instrument in the promotion of 'sport for all'. However, the heavy reliance on facility development to promote participation has been difficult to maintain with all countries, with the exception of Norway, experiencing funding difficulties. For example, in Germany the government has not been able to repeat the *Goldener Plan* of the 1950s and 1960s, which was so successful in the west, for the former states of East Germany. In contrast, Norway, because of its favourable economic situation due to increasing state revenues and lottery money for sport, has been able to sustain a high level of financial support for local facility development. A second common instrument for promoting *sport for all* has been the use of campaigns targeted at the general public or specific groups. While targeted campaigns were common in all four countries in the 1970s there was a general lack of continuity with the exception of Germany which has maintained a continuous cycle of campaigns. In the 1970s and during the Thatcher government in England targeting became an important part of *sport for all* policies often aimed at motivating marginalised groups, such as youth and ethnic minorities, to increase their participation in sport. In Germany, a number of specific groups, for example ethnic minorities and senior citizens, have been regularly targeted and the number of different groups subject to targeting is increasing. In Canada, the new sport policy of 2002 includes projects directed at specific groups under-represented in sport, such as women and aboriginal people. Finally, in Norway, there have for some years been projects directed at young ethnic minority groups in cities and also programmes targeted more broadly at children and youth. While targeting strategies seem to be important in all four countries the motives are, in most cases not only, or even not primarily, to increase overall sport participation or to secure equal access to sports opportunities, but to achieve social welfare goals such as community integration, stability and higher levels of employment.

Alternative arguments for sport for all • • •

The understanding of participation in sport as an individual right, as an activity for pleasure and personal benefit, adapted to individual aspirations, are important aspects of the concept of *sport for all* as expressed in the European Charter. However, in recent years the social consequences related to mass sport activity, are becoming as important as the intrinsic personal benefits of sport. In particular, health arguments were identified by many of our interviewees as a major rationale for promoting sport participation. Increased obesity and diseases like diabetes are put forward as justification for investment for *sport for all* policies. Health arguments are increasingly central in Canada and England not only among government interviewees, but also among those representing voluntary sport interests. In Germany health is one of a bundle of societal arguments utilised by the German Sport Confederations to sustain the campaign of *Sport tut Deutschland gut* (Sport is good for Germany). The health rationale seems to be least evident in Norway, but even there the issue is identified as a priority in the proposed new strategy of the sport confederation.

In a situation where sport and recreation activities are situated in competition for people's attention it may be argued that policy actors (government as well as sport organisations) use arguments external to sport's primary functions to generate support for government policy. This way of interest generalisation is evident in all countries, and it may be argued that this process for legitimating *sport for all* policies is a major point of cross-country similarity.

Pushing responsibilities downwards • • •

In all four countries there are indications of the regional/local levels becoming increasingly important with regard to their role in implementation and the maintenance of policy support. In Canada, as part of the new sport policy, the provinces are more willing to co-operate with the national level in pursuit of participation objectives while in England, local authorities have been 'rediscovered' as important actors in delivering sport participation. Responsibilities are also being pushed downwards to regional Sport England offices and to the recently established County Sports Partnerships. In Norway, the government has established a support programme with state funding directed towards the local club level and, in NRW, the largest *land* of Germany, municipal government now receive investment funds from the *land* government without the requirement of making project specific applications.

The reasons for the increased role of sub-national government vary. One important explanation may be the increased pressure on national and state level government funding with the result that in the Canadian state of Alberta local government financing of sport and recreation has become about as important as that from the provincial government. A further explanation might be that it is considered more effective to transfer money direct to the final user, as is the case in England with the increasing financial role of the regional sport boards. However, devolution of responsibility for funding and service delivery does not always reflect a transfer of strategic responsibility. In England responsibility for the strategic direction of policy on *sport for all* remains firmly in the hands of Sport England and the DCMS.

A new policy focus? • • •

In the 1960s and 1970s when facility development and mass participation were clear political priorities in all four countries, political support for *sport for all* was underpinned by powerful social trends such as increased leisure time, greater disposable income and the changing status of women which caused a *demand-led growth*. Individual needs and wants went together with growth in voluntary sport and the development of government-supported services and facilities. The consumption society developed in parallel to a welfare state, with sport participation as one component.

Hartmann-Tews (1999) argues for the importance of *supply factors* particularly in explaining why German sport clubs, until the mid-1980s, were recruiting more members than English ones. The German sport confederation mounted a vigorous campaign in support of mass participation that involved lobbying at government level, as well as public campaigning to attract new club members and public support. A similar analysis can be applied in Norway where sport interests repeatedly lobbied politicians to increase sport's share of lottery incomes (Bergsgard, 2005). In contrast, the English Central Council of Physical Recreation (CCPR) failed to unify its heterogeneous membership and act as an effective pressure group on behalf of the voluntary sector as was also the case in Canada, where sport participation until the recent new sport policy was largely excluded from federal policy due, partly at least, to the failure of the development of an effective lobby for mass sport (Bercovitz, 1998).

In summary, we have argued that supply explanations may contribute to the different policy trends of Germany and Norway in comparison to Canada and England in the 1980s and 1990s. The voluntary sport sectors of the first two countries were able to argue for their general cause, while in the latter sport participation interests seem to have had difficulties articulating and promoting their interests. However, in recent years there is less talk of a rapidly increasing demand for sport and recreation. In fact participation rates have remained broadly static in all four countries and there is evidence that a significant proportion of participation growth, where it has taken place, has been in the commercial sector (fitness centres) rather than in the voluntary or public sector.

Finally, the increasing prevalence of linking *sport for all* with non-sport concerns, in particular health, may possibly be considered a new and strengthening trend in all four countries. Increasingly, the growth in demand for access to fitness and recreation opportunities by individuals is being incorporated into the rationale adopted by sports organisations for greater public investment in facilities and in their own development activities. In other words they adapt to the principle of generalisation of interests to strengthen their leverage in the competition for public resources.

In this chapter we have shown that there has been a strong, though not always consistent, interest in *sport for all* in the four countries. Even in countries like Canada and England which, at times, have experienced a marginalisation of *sport for all* there has been a recent revival of government interest. It may be argued that there are two powerful factors that can lead to convergence in *sport for all* policies: first, when there is strong demand, as in the 1960s, there was a broadly uniform response of facility development and second, when governments co-opt sport in order to pursue non-sport social welfare objectives as was the case in all four countries in the late 1990s. Conversely, during periods of stable demand and/or government inattention it is more probable that factors on the supply side will lead to a differentiation of policy trajectories between countries.

CHAPTER 8

Sport policies compared

The major aims of this study have been to identify characteristics of sport policies in Canada, England, Germany and Norway and to see how sport policies are affected by general attributes of the domestic political systems and transnational influences. Comparative studies of sport policies tend to focus on the evaluation of policy outputs. In this study we have analysed not only the outputs but also the interactions between policy actors that generate the policy inputs and the processes that produce the policy outputs.

Strict tests of theories require representative large n reviews and statistical analyses. Our ambition in this respect has been more modest. Instead we have chosen the four countries for theoretically informed in-depth studies and comparisons. Our qualitative approach makes it possible to capture not only differences and similarities but also the dynamics of policy processes. The study is limited to Western democratic and economically developed countries, but the cases we have selected vary with regard to cultural traditions, political institutions and welfare regimes. However, in what is frequently perceived as an era of globalisation one may expect differences in cultural and political values to decrease and consequently we have raised the question of whether policies converge or not.

In this chapter we will summarise our findings on the basis of theoretical perspectives discussed in Chapters 1–3, and particularly the analytical dimensions outlined in Chapter 2. Hopefully, our comparative study contributes to a richer understanding of sport policies and sport policy-making processes in a wider political and institutional context.

Cultural differences and welfare regimes

In our study we have focused on two Anglo-American and two Continental/Northern European countries, a distinction based on underlying assumptions regarding cultural differences. We suppose the cultures of Canada and England to be more individualistic, commercialised and competitive than the more collectivist and egalitarian cultures of Germany and, in particular, Norway. Furthermore, cultural differences are related to variations in political systems and policy styles. The four cases represent three different types of welfare state regimes. The liberal welfare regime is represented by Canada and England/UK, the conservative regime by Germany, and finally the social democratic welfare regime by Norway.

The overall impression with regard to welfare state regimes and variations in *sport* policies is that our assumptions need to be modified. In all four countries voluntary sport organisations have played important roles in the historic development of modern sport and they still play prominent roles as organisers of sport activities. However, in all four cases we also find that government is strongly involved with sport. This is not only the case in the 'state friendly' social democratic welfare state of Norway. Public policies are important for sport in the conservative welfare regime of Germany and the liberal welfare regimes of Canada and England as well.

Even more surprising is the variations with regard to the roles played by government. With certain reservations, one could expect the Norwegian state to play the most comprehensive role with regard to sport, that is to be engaged in both the organisation and funding of sport activities, but this is not the case. In general, Norwegian central and local government is not directly involved with the organisation of sport, they act more as facilitators for the voluntary sport organisations and clubs and they contribute substantially to the funding of sport activities. In fact, the role played by government in liberal England can be considered to be more comprehensive than in social democratic Norway. Central and local government in England are more directly involved with the organisation of sport. Physical education and school sport are important elements in the English sport delivery system as are the publicly financed sport development officers. Similar tendencies, although to a more limited degree, are found in Canada. In Germany on the other hand, the role of government is more of a facilitator and financial contributor as is the case in Norway. The organisation of sport activities is the responsibility of German sport organisations.

Our study reveals a particular aspect of the role of government in sport that should be related to differences in the systems of sport organisations. The organisational systems of sport in Canada and England are much more fragmented than in Germany and Norway. On the one hand, German and Norwegian confederations of sport play central roles in the coordination of sport and sport policies. The absence of strong coordinating bodies within the Canadian and English sport movements on the other hand, seems to give government a more significant role to play in this respect.

Cultural differences with regard to elite orientation and competitiveness can be traced in the voluntary sport organisations and in public policies. England on the one hand and Norway on the other represent the two extremes. In Norway we find the strongest *sport for all* values and the strongest ambivalence in relation to elite sport. A concern with the 'dark side' of elite sport (doping, etc.) is found in all countries, but England does not hesitate to emphasise explicit elite sport performance indicators in its public sport policy.

Although we have not conducted in-depth studies of the most commercialised segments of sport, we nonetheless, see that commercial interests are growing. Commercialisation manifests itself in a rapidly growing fitness industry and professionalisation of competitive sports. Individual physical activities in training studios have grown more than membership in traditional sport organisations in all four countries. Professional sports are more widespread in England and Canada, but Germany and Norway are moving in the same direction. However, differences with regard to the degree of professionalisation and commercialisation are larger between various sport disciplines than between the countries in our study.

State systems

Cultural variations and welfare regime differences should be analysed in relation to the formal state systems of the respective countries. Consequently, we have chosen two federal systems, Canada and Germany, and two unitary states, England/UK and Norway. Furthermore, we expected the Canadian version of federalism to be more decentralised than the German version, and the UK version of a unitary state to be more centralised than the Norwegian version.

At the outset we expected both Canadian and English sport policy to be limited in scope. Within this limited scope we supposed that central government would dominate sport policy in England while the provinces and local authorities would play more prominent roles in Canada. German and Norwegian sport policies were expected to be more comprehensive. The *länder* and municipalities were assumed to play prominent roles in Germany and Norway respectively. Finally, we expected sport in England and Canada to be highly commercialised, while in Norway and in Germany in particular, we assumed that voluntary sport organisations would be more important.

No doubt, our study shows that state systems have consequences with regard to sport policies. As expected, in the federal states of Canada and Germany the provinces/*länder* play a much more significant role than the sub-national/county level of government in the unitary states of England/UK and Norway. Local government seems to play significant roles in all four countries, especially with regard to *sport for all* policies. Policies regarding elite and high performance sport on the other hand belong primarily within the domain of central government. Provinces and *länder* in the two federal states occupy an intermediate position, being more elite oriented than local government, but also playing important roles in funding and facilitating *sport for all*. Formally, the differences and divisions of responsibilities are fairly clear-cut, but in practice the borderlines between levels of government seem to have become more blurred. In Germany there seems to be a tendency for the federal government to become more involved with *sport for all* and mass participation, areas that traditionally have been the responsibilities of the *länder* and local government. In Canada the coordination between the levels regarding sport policy is rather weak, but some attempts to increase coordination have taken place over the years.

Within the federal-unitary divide, we have also pointed to expectations regarding differences related to centralised, unitary England/UK and decentralised, unitary Norway on the one hand and centralised, federal Germany and decentralised, federal Canada on the other. The importance of central versus local government with regard to sport policy is difficult to measure and our findings are not always in line with expectations. This may be due to the fact that the systems of sport organisations are more fragmented in both England and Canada and more unified in both Germany and Norway. In Germany and Norway, sport organisations seem to be better coordinated and public *sport for all* policies to be characterised by stability and continuity while in Canada and England the systems of sport organisations are fragmented and *sport for all* policies characterised by fluctuations and discontinuity. In fact with regard to sport policies the two decentralised countries, federal Canada and unitary Norway, seem to position themselves on separate extreme points of discontinuity and continuity respectively.

Public policies regarding high performance sport seem less exposed to fluctuations than *sport for all* policies. This could be related to the fact that the major government responsibility for elite sport is located at the national level and *sport for all* at the local level of government. Local government is probably more vulnerable and subject to shifting social and economic conditions than central government. Elite sport policies seem to reflect different nation-specific historical events and developments, like the DDR legacy and unification process of Germany, the Ben Johnson affair in Canada, specific impacts of Olympic successes or failures in all countries. However, in the long run high performance sport policies seem to move more or less in the same direction, that is to become more systematic and scientific and to be included in government responsibilities. In this respect Canada was an early starter and Britain a latecomer.

Executive-legislative relations

An important aspect of democratic political systems and policy-making processes is the relationship between and relative powers of legislatures and executives. In parliamentary systems like the ones we have studied here, the government needs support, or at least acceptance, from the majority of the parliament. The parliamentary bases of governments may vary, depending on the majority or minority status of the governments, and the occurrence of single-party and coalition governments. Consequently, when we analyse executive-legislative power relations we need to take into account the strength of the opposition as well as the governing parties.

Various assessments of the strength of legislatures and/or oppositions indicate that the British Parliament is a relatively weak legislature dominated by single-party majority governments. The Norwegian Parliament used to receive weak evaluations, but since the 1970s the *Storting* seems to have strengthened its position *vis-à-vis* relatively weak minority and coalition governments. The Parliament of Canada seems to be dominated by the executive, while the *Bundestag* plays a more prominent role in German politics.

The question we have asked in this context is whether the general assessments are relevant with regard to sport policy-making as well. If so, we should expect Canadian and English sport policy-making to be dominated by the executive and Norwegian and German sport policy-making to be dominated by parliament. However, by and large our findings show that sport policies in all four countries are dominated by the executive. Most striking is the limited role played by the Norwegian Parliament, which was generally expected to be a relatively strong parliament. As we have seen, the process for dealing with the financing of sport, a crucial element of sport policy in Norway, is subject to rather unusual procedures. Grants for culture, excluding sport, are subject to normal budget procedures in parliament, but the large sums of money that are allocated to sport are not. Allocations to sport are determined by the Ministry of Culture, thus strengthening the power of the executive. Furthermore, sport policy-making has been dominated, not by the Minister, but by prominent civil servants in the Ministry's department of sport.

Specialised parliamentary committees are frequently considered to be of crucial importance with regard to the power of parliaments. In the UK and Germany there are (more or less) specialised sport committees: the Culture, Media and Sport Select Committee of the British Parliament and the *Sportausschuss* of the German *Bundestag*. Neither the Canadian nor the Norwegian parliament have specialised sport committees. It is hard, however, to see any effects of this difference. The British and German parliaments do not seem to play more significant roles in sport policy-making than their Canadian and Norwegian counterparts. Sport policies in all four countries are dominated by the respective ministries and/or the more operative non-governmental sport organisations.

The limited influence on sport policies exerted by legislatures is related to limitations regarding sport legislation as in most countries there are few legal instruments or laws specifically designed to regulate sport. Liberal Canada has a 'Physical Activity and Sport Act', but in otherwise state friendly Norway laws and regulations regarding sport are considered to be part of the private sphere where the development of sport is decided, not by the parliament, but by the sport organisations themselves. Money is a more frequently used public policy instrument than legislation. Substantial portions of the public funding of sport are based on national and provincial lotteries. The allocation of lottery money does not follow ordinary state budget procedures and consequently the influence of parliamentarians and the exchequer is limited.

The limited use of the most powerful policy instruments of parliaments, legislation and budget allocations is, to some degree, compensated by another function of parliaments, namely agenda setting. Every now and then members of parliament raise questions with government ministers and table private members' bills regarding sport, and government reports and white papers outlining major sport policy principles are submitted to, and discussed in, parliament. Over the last decade or so there has been a certain increase in examples of this type of parliamentary intervention, but they seem to be incidental (triggered by specific events) rather than a reflection of a deliberate or systematic expansion of the competence of parliament into the area of sport.

Government–interest group relations

Policy-making is not only a matter of executive-legislative or government-opposition relations. Organised interests and voluntary associations play important roles in the countries we have studied, and sport organisations can show high membership figures. Interest groups may be more or less integrated into the processes of formulation and implementation of public policies. As noted already, voluntary associations are supposed to play a prominent role in the delivery of welfare services in a conservative welfare state regime like that in Germany.

Corporatism is a frequently used term for highly integrated and institutionalised government–interest group relations where certain associations are given privileged access to public policy-making and policy implementation through representation and negotiation in governmental boards, councils and committees. In pluralist systems, on the other hand, government–interest group relations are less institutionalised and there is a multiplicity of organised associations lobbying for their political interests. Furthermore, we have linked corporatism to concentration and pluralism to dispersion of public and private power.

A number of related concepts like policy networks, policy communities and segments, etc. have been introduced in order to capture certain aspects of government–interest group relations. The thesis of a segmented state is related to a sectorised system. Members of the segment represent different public and private institutions and organisations, but they share a common understanding of problems and solutions, as do members of what others prefer to call policy communities. Segments and communities are relatively closed systems with limited access for external actors. They may include formalised corporatist bodies, but close informal relationships between a limited number of actors may have the same function. Policy networks and issue networks in particular are more open and fluctuating with regard to membership and saliency. In open, pluralist systems there is a need for more flexible lobbying strategies.

In general, Norway and Germany are placed on the corporatist side where government–interest group relations are close. England and Canada are placed on the pluralist side with rather more distant relationships between government and interest groups. Viewed against this background, we would expect sport organisations to be more closely integrated into public policy-making and implementation in corporatist Norway and Germany than in pluralist Canada and England. However, in Norway at least there has been a certain move in the pluralist direction, with a greater variety of interest groups and a downsizing of the corporatist apparatus. This may be the case for Germany as well – and for sport and sport policy.

Traditionally, public policies have been highly sectorised and well suited for segmentation and development of policy communities. However, due to modernisation, pluralisation and increased cultural diversity combined with better communications, sectors and segments cannot live their own lives, isolated from the environment. Sectors become more intertwined and 'everything becomes dependent on everything'. Closed segments and communities seem to be opened up for new political actors. On the basis of these general developments we would expect sport to have become a less clearly demarcated political segment or policy community.

As noted above, the systems of sport organisations in Canada and England are more fragmented than in Germany and Norway. In Canada and England we find a plurality of organisations responsible for different tasks related to sport while in Germany and Norway we find more unified and coordinated sports movements. Consequently, the basis for corporatist representation and integration into public decision-making processes is better in Germany and Norway than in Canada and England where the dispersion of power among a variety of sport organisations facilitates more open and less institutionalised strategies of lobbyism in order to influence sport policies.

We see tendencies in this direction, but what is more striking, is the similarities we find. In all four countries there are close relationships between voluntary sport organisations and public authorities at national as well as provincial and local levels. The occurrence of formalised corporatist bodies is limited and, as we have seen, a typical corporatist body like the Norwegian Sport Council, with members from the Ministry and confederation of sport, was closed down in the late 1980s. The highly formalised and institutionalised relationship was replaced by less formalised, but still close contacts. Lottery money is allocated after informal discussions between the Ministry's Department of Sport and the Norwegian Confederation of Sport.

Instead of sport corporatism we may speak more adequately about sport segments and sport policy communities in the four countries we have studied. We have seen that some politicians, for example, members of the *Sportausschuss* of the German *Bundestag*, are perceived as members of the 'sport lobby' or sport policy community, together with civil servants in ministerial sport departments and leaders of sport organisations. They have certain common beliefs regarding the importance of sport and sport policy, even though they represent different institutions. Phrases like 'family-relations' and 'friendship-relations' have been used to describe the character of relationships between public and private actors in the field of sport, in particular in Norway and Germany.

It is difficult to measure, but the sport communities or networks in Canada and England seem to be more open and loosely connected than the corresponding networks in Germany and Norway. This may be due to stronger corporatist traditions in the latter countries and the more fragmented and pluralist sport systems in the first mentioned cases. However, in England sport councils seem to have lost some of their independence and to be perceived more like government agencies. In German and Norwegian sport on the other hand we have noted developments towards increased pluralism and dispersion of power. Outside the voluntary sport movement there is a growing fitness industry and increased commercial interest in sport and inside the voluntary sport organisations there is an ongoing process of professionalisation and specialisation. An indication of the process of specialisation and, to an extent, of the dispersion of power is the fact that the number of national sport organisations within the sport confederations in Germany and Norway have doubled during the post-war period.

In sum, this means that the number of potentially conflicting interests involved with sport increases and to some degree conflicts of interest manifest themselves more clearly in sport policy-making processes. Sport segments and sport policy communities open up for new actors. The greater variety of interests involved with sport may be one of the reasons for the trend towards governmentalisation of sport that can be observed not only in traditionally state friendly Norway, but also in liberal Canada and England and 'voluntaristic' Germany. Governments take on a mediating and coordinating role and they seem more willing to (attempt to) govern sport than before, or at least this willingness has become more apparent. Although, tensions can be observed in government–interest group relations, the relationship is still close within the field of sport.

Generalisation of interest and coalition building

A development towards an increasingly pluralistic society with dispersion of power among a growing number of interest groups combined with a strengthening of parliament *vis-à-vis* the government and downsizing of the corporatist apparatus have strategic implications for political actors who seek to influence policy-making. Political actors need to build alliances in order to gain necessary support.

If one party dominates the scene or if two parties can strike a deal and divide the 'cake' between them, then parties can maintain and pursue their self-interest. In a three-party bargain the players need to build coalitions and the more numerous the participants in the game, the broader the coalitions need to be. The 'common good', general or public interests have a wider appeal than self-interest and consequently generalisation of interests is a way to enhance legitimacy and win support from other actors.

In appealing to the public good, one needs to take into consideration the general cultural and political values of the society. In our study we selected four countries based on the assumption that individualist, elitist and commercialist values are more widespread in the Anglo-American countries while in Northern and Continental Europe we would find more collectivist, egalitarian and non-commercial values. If the general assumptions are equally relevant to sport, then we would expect sports in England and Canada to be more competitive, elite oriented and commercialised and sports in Germany and Norway to be less competitive, more *sport for all* oriented and less commercialised. In the first two cases we would expect sport organisations to emphasise the potential contribution of sport to business development, job creation and the like. In the last two cases we would expect sport organisations to build their strategy of generalisation of interests on the possible contributions of sport to public health, social inclusion and similar values. However, in what is generally believed to be an era of globalisation, commercialisation and neo-liberalism we could expect variations between the four countries to diminish.

Our study clearly demonstrates that sport organisations do apply the strategy of generalisation of interest and appeal to non-sport concerns, and that governments on the other hand use sport for political purposes. Over the years the alleged 'multi-functionality' of sport has been related to a variety of public goods. In the early stages of the development of modern sport, emphasis was put on physical training for military defence and international competitiveness in order to strengthen national identity and pride. In the post-war period attention turned to *sport for all*'s possible contributions to the solution of problems related to public health and social inclusion, and in later years the development of sport arenas and hosting of big events have been perceived as useful instruments for urban development as well as business development and employment.

In a long-term perspective attention with regard to sport's contribution to general public interests seems to have moved from 'basics' like the ability to defend the state's territory to the social concerns of the welfare state and more or less to the commercialised interests of the modern world. There are variations with regard to timing and 'mixes' of concerns expressed in sport policy-making processes in the countries we have studied, but the long-term trend can be observed in all four cases. Welfare state issues are important elements in sport policy discourses in Canada and England, and commercial potential is put on the sport policy agenda more frequently than before in Germany and Norway.

Cultural differences are most clearly expressed in relation to the prioritisation and legitimatisation of policies for high performance sport and *sport for all* respectively. Competitive and elite sport is a more prominent element of sport policies in the more individualist and competitive cultures of Canada and England. In the more collectivist and egalitarian cultures of Germany and Norway sport policies are more concerned with *sport for all*.

However, differences between cultures and countries are matters of degree, they are not at all categorical. Furthermore, there are reasons to believe that some of the differences are rhetorical rather than substantive. As we have seen, social issues play an important role in sport policies in competitive England, as does elite sport in egalitarian Norway. The Olympic and World Championship successes of Norwegian athletes are the result of, among other things, substantial government funding. The way of talking about *sport for all* versus high performance sport differs, however. In simplified terms we may say that in Canada and England the argument is that *sport for all* should be supported in order to increase the pool of talent and to recruit participants to high performance sport. In Norway the argument is reversed, that is, that elite sport should be supported in order to motivate the masses to participate in physical activity and *sport for all*. To exaggerate the point; elite sport is the end and *sport for all* the means in the first mentioned countries while in the latter *sport for all* is the end and elite sport the means.

Variations in means-end relations and ways of arguing may be part of the explanation for the variations we have seen with regard to continuity and fluctuations in public sport policies. As noted, sport policies in Germany and Norway have been more stable than in Canada and England and thus it seems easier to generalise interests and build coalitions with external partners among non-sport public authorities on the basis of *sport for all* than on the basis of elite sport. However, high performance sports may have greater appeal among commercial actors.

Divergence or convergence?

The point of departure for much of the discussion above has been factors that may explain differences between sport policies in the four countries, but we have also noted tendencies towards convergence. In Chapter 3 we discussed some of the transnational forces of change, including globalisation, commersialisation, governmentalisation and politicisation. We assumed that these trends are general and contribute to convergence of policies. On the other hand we expected cultural traditions and institutional constraints to lead to variations in the responses and adaptations to international trends and developments and consequently the degree of convergence in sport policies may vary.

It may seem natural to expect elite and high performance sport to be more exposed to international trends than *sport for all*. Rules of the games and international competitions are decided on and organised by international sport organisations. National sport organisations have to comply with international rules if they want to play international games. There is more room for local variations in less competitive forms of physical exercise and *sport for all* does not necessarily follow strict rules. Consequently, there is a stronger imperative for coordination and for public policies regarding high performance sport to adapt to international trends and thus converge, than is the case for *sport for all* policies. Furthermore, the major responsibilities for *sport for all* policies rest with local government and consequently one may expect a greater variety of adaptations regarding policies for mass participation.

Our study indicates that elite sport systems and policies do converge. A sharp focus on international competitiveness and systematic and professional coaching, the establishment of elite sport centres and the use of scientific methods to improve performance, are common denominators of contemporary high performance sport policies in the four countries we have studied. However, the convergence of elite sport systems is restricted by different national political structures, traditions and values, and different courses of events. There are still differences in the rhetoric regarding elite versus mass sport and early talent identification is another example of persistent differences between the countries. Norway is more cautious and does not expose children to specialisation and intense competition at a very young age while in Canada, England and Germany the search for talent and the best 'pathway to the podium' is more explicit. As we have seen earlier, there have been and still are important variations in *sport for all* policies and delivery systems, not only between countries but also between provinces and municipalities. However, we do find homogenising trends as well. There are long traditions, of course, associated with the promotion of physical exercise in order to strengthen military defence, but in recent years sport in general and *sport for all* in particular has come to be an important instrument in the endeavour to reach a large number of political goals. Governments fund mass participation in sport in order to reduce childhood obesity and improve public health, to avoid juvenile delinquency, and for urban regeneration and social inclusion of immigrants, indigenous people and physically disabled persons, etc. At the same time sport organisations appeal to public goods and general interests like this in order to obtain public support. As a result, *sport for all* has become governmentalised not only in traditionally state oriented countries like Norway, but also in liberal, 'state sceptical' countries like Canada and England. However, somewhat paradoxically and parallel to the process of governmentalisation, we also see a process of commercialisation of *sport for all* and physical exercise in the form of a growing fitness industry.

The systematisation, specialisation and professionalisation of high performance sport and the widening of political concerns and aims to be pursued through *sport for all* have a common implication: a growing need for money. Consequently the traditionally private/voluntary sport organisations seek new sources for funding. In the four countries we have studied, profits from public lotteries and money gaming have become an important source of income for sport. In Norway, the gaming corporation was established in 1946 in order to finance sport and scientific research and over the years lottery money has become the dominant form of state funding of sport. In Canada and Germany, lotteries that include sport as a beneficiary were established in the 1970s in connection with the Munich and Montreal Olympics but today profits from lotteries at the province/*länder* level are used to support sport in general. In Britain lottery funding of sport did not start until the mid-1990s but it has become an important source of finance for the sport councils' new initiatives. Another response to the growing demand for economic resources, and an expression of converging tendencies, is the establishment of new forms of public-private partnerships between local authorities, private investors and voluntary sport organisations. The underlying assumption is that combined facilities with areas for sport as well as shops, offices and housing may attract business developers and thus generate funding for new sport facilities.

Conclusion

Our study clearly illustrates that sport is a multifaceted phenomenon. In a period of time often portrayed as an era of globalisation, neo-liberalism and commercialisation, we find that sport and sport policies reflect not only global trends and developments but at the same time also reflect national and local cultural and political traditions and peculiarities. We have observed a variety of changes in sport and sport policies in the fairly similar cases we have selected for our study, including trends of convergence. However, the duality of the simultaneous processes of commercialisation and governmentalisation in Canada, England, Germany and Norway demonstrate that even in the case of convergence there is a need for nuanced description and comparative analysis of sport and sport policies.

References

Aambø, J. (2005). 'Hvem vil egentlig ha toppidrett?' in: D.V. Hanstad and M. Goksøyr (eds.), *Fred er ei det beste. Festskrift. Hans B. Skaset 70 år*. Oslo: Gyldendal.

Allison, L. (2001). *Amateurism in sport*. London: Frank Cass.

Amis, J. and B. Cornwell (eds.) (2005). *Global Sport Sponsorship*. Oxford: Berg.

Andersen, S.S. and K.A. Eliassen (eds.) (1993). *Making Policy in Europe: The Europeification of National Policy-Making*. London: Sage.

Arbena, J.L. (ed.) (1988). *Sport and Society in Latin America: Diffusion, Dependency and the Rise of Mass Culture*. NY: Greenwood Press.

Augestad, P. (2003a). *Skolering av kroppen. Om kunnskap og makt i kroppsøvingsfaget*. PhD Thesis, Høgskolen i Telemark/ Telemark University College, Norway.

Augestad, P. (2003b). 'Architecture and the education of the body: the gymnasium in Norwegian physical training, 1889–1930', *The International Journal of the History of Sport* 20(3): 58–76.

Augestad, P. and N.A. Bergsgard (2005). *Olympiatoppen mellom barken og veden*. Preliminary manuscript, Telemark University College, Norway.

Augestad. P., Bergsgard, N.A and Hansen, A.Ø. (2005a). *The institutionalisation of an elite sport organisation in Norway – the case of 'Olympiatoppen'*. Chapter 2 of report, preliminary draft.

Augestad. P., Bergsgard, N.A and Hansen, A.Ø. (2005b). *Olympiatoppens posisjon og institusjonelle lokalisering*. Chapter 3 of report. Preliminary draft.

Augestad, P., N.A. Bergsgard and A.Ø. Hansen (2006). 'The institutionalisation of an elite sport organisation in Norway: the case of "Olympiatoppen"', *Sociology of Sport Journal* 23(3): 293–313.

Auld, C. and G. Godbey (1998). 'Influence in Canadian national sports organisations: perceptions of professionals and volunteers', *Journal of Sport Management* 12(1): 20–28.

Beck, J. and J. Rode (2002). *Perspektiven der Sport- und Sportstättenentwicklung der Stadt Potsdam. Institut für Sportwissenschaft.* Universität Potsdam, Stadt Potsdam, Stadtsportbund, Potsdam.

Bennet, B. *et al.* (1975). *Comparative Physical Education and Sport.* Baltimore, MD: Lea and Febiger.

Benson, J.K. (1982). 'Networks and policy sectors: a framework for extending inter-organisational analysis', in: D. Rogers and D. Whitton (eds.), *Inter-organisational Co-ordination.* Iowa, IA: Iowa State University.

Bercovitz, K.L. (1998). 'Canada's active living policy: a critical analysis', *Health Promotion International* 13(4): 319–328.

Berg, C. and H. Rommetvedt (2002a). 'Idrett og politikk i kommunene', in: P. Mangset and H. Rommetvedt (eds.), *Idrett og politikk – kampsport eller lagspill?* Bergen: Fagbokforlaget.

Berg, C. and H. Rommetvedt (2002b). 'Kommunal organisering og bevilgninger til idretten', in: P. Mangset and H. Rommetvedt (eds.), *Idrett og politikk – kampsport eller lagspill?* Bergen: Fagbokforlaget.

Berg, C., S.I. Nødland and S. Opedal (2002). *Hørt om Frifond!? Evaluering av ny støtteordning for lokalt frivillig virke blant barn og unge.* Rapport RF 2002/355. Stavanger: Rogalandsforskning.

Bergsgard, N.A. (1999). *Idrettspolitikkfeltets organisering i 1990-årene.* Arbeidsrapport nr. 5/99. Bø: Telemarksforsking-Bø.

Bergsgard, N.A. (2002a). 'Spillet om spillemidlene', in: P. Mangset and H. Rommetvedt (eds.), *Idrett og politikk – kampsport eller lagspill?* Bergen: Fagbokforlaget.

Bergsgard, N.A. (2002b). 'Nasjonalanlegg for ski – "Ja takk, alle tre"', in: P. Mangset and H. Rommetvedt (eds.), *Idrett og politikk – kampsport eller lagspill?* Bergen: Fagbokforlaget.

Bergsgard, N.A. (2002c). National facility for ski sport – 'Yes please, all three'. From rational and sequential to open and ambigous decision-making process. Paper presented at the *XV World Congress of Sociology*, Brisbane.

Bergsgard, N.A. (2005). *Idrettspolitikkens maktspill. Endring og stabilitet i den idrettspolitiske styringsmodellen.* Dissertation, Dr. Polit., University of Oslo. Rapport 228. Bø: Telemarksforsking-Bø.

Bergsgard, N.A. and S. Opedal (2002). 'Nasjonal politikk for den lokale idretten', in: P. Mangset and H. Rommetvedt (eds.), *Idrett og politikk – kampsport eller lagspill?* Bergen: Fagbokforlaget.

Bergsgard, N.A. and H. Rommetvedt (2004). 'Når idrett og politikk kolliderer: feilskjær eller systemfeil?' in: S. Røyseng and D. Solhjell (eds.), *Kultur, politikk og forskning. Festskrift til Per Mangset på 60-årsdagen*. Bø: Telemarksforsking-Bø.

Bernstein, A and N. Blain (eds.) (2003). *Sport, Media and Culture: Global and Local Dimensions*. London: Frank Cass.

Bhasker, R. (1975). *A Realist Theory of Science*. Brighton: Harvester-Wheatsheaf.

Bhasker, R. (1998). 'Introduction', in: M. Archer, R. Bhasker, A. Collier, T. Lawson and A. Norrie (eds.), *Critical Realism: Essential Readings*. London: Routledge.

Blom-Hansen, J. (1997). 'A "new institutional" perspective on policy networks', *Public Administration* 75(4): 669–693.

BMI (1999). *Neunter Sportbericht der Bundersregierung. Unterrichtung durch die Bundesregierung*. Berlin: Bundesministerium des Innern.

BMI (2002). *Unterrichtung durch die Bundesregierung. 10. Sportbericht der Bundesregierung*. Drucksache 14/9517. Berlin: Bundesministerium des Innern.

BMI (2005). *Bericht zur Situation des Sports, Vereine und der Sportstätten in den neuen Bundesländern, für die 56. Sitzung des Sportausschusses des Deutschen Bundestages am 29 Juni 2005*. Berlin: Bundesministerium des Innern.

BMI (2006). *Leistung fördern. Die Sportpolitik des Bundesministerium des Innern*. Berlin: Bundesministerium des Innern.

Bramham, P., I. Henry, H. Mommas, and H. van der Poel (eds.) (1989). *Leisure and Urban Processes: Critical Studies of Leisure Policy in Western European Cities*. London: Routledge.

Bramham, P., Henry, I., Mommas, H. & van der Poel, H. (eds) (1993). *Leisure policies in Europe*, Wallingford, Oxon.: CAB International.

Bramham, P., I. Henry, H. Mommas, and H. van der Poel (eds.) (1996). *Leisure Policies in Europe*. Wallingford, Oxon: CAB International.

Brown, D.W. (1984). 'Imperialism and games on the playing fields of Canada's private schools', in: N. Müller and J.K. Rühl (eds.), *Olympic Scientific Congress 1984. Official Report*, Niederhausen, Germany: Schors.

Burchell, G. (1993). 'Liberal government and techniques of the self', *Economy and Society* 22(3): 267–282.

Cambridge Econometrics (2003). *The Value of the Sports Economy in England*. London: Sport England.

Cameroun, C., C. Craig and S. Paolin (2004). *Local Opportunities for Physical Activity and Sport*. Ottawa: Canadian Fitness and Lifestyle Research Institute.

Canadian Journal of Public Health (2004). 'ParticipACTION. The mouse that roared. A marketing and health communication success story', *Canadian Journal of Public Health* 95(Suppl 2), May/June.

Carlson, B. (1992). 'The seduction of amateur sport', *Recreation Canada* 50(4): 30–31.

Carter Report (2005). *Review of National Sport Effort and Resources.* London: DCMS. (www.culture.gov.uk/Reference_library/Publications/archive_2005/ carter.htm).

Castles, F. and D. Mitchell (1990). *Three Worlds of Welfare Capitalism or Four?* Public policy discussion paper no. 21. Canberra: Australian National University.

CCPR (2004). *CCPR Challenge 2004–5.* Meeting Westminster, 30 November 2004 (www.ccpr.org.uk).

CCPR (2005). *CCPR Red Book for Sport and Recreation*, March 2005 (www.ccpr.org.uk).

Chaker, A.-N. (1998). *A Study of Laws Affecting Sport in Countries Having Acceded to the European Cultural Convention.* Strasbourg: Council of Europe.

Chalip, L. (1995). 'Policy analysis in sport management', *Journal of Sport Management* 9: 1–13.

Chalip, L., A. Johnson and L. Stachura (eds.) (1996). *National Sport Policies. An International Handbook.* London: Greenwood Press.

Christensen, T. and M. Egeberg (1979). 'Organized group-government relations in Norway', *Scandinavian Political Studies* 2(3): 239–259.

Christiansen, P.M. and H. Rommetvedt (1999). 'From corporatism to lobbyism? Parliaments, executives, and organized interests in Denmark and Norway', *Scandinavian Political Studies* 22(3): 195–220.

CMSC (2003). *The Work of the Committee in 2002.* Second Report of Session 2002–03. House of Commons – Culture, Media and Sport Committee. London: The Stationery Office Limited.

Coakley, J. (2003). *Sport in Society: Issues and Controversies*, 8th edn. Boston, MA: McGraw Hill.

Coakley, J. and P. Donnelly (2004). *Sports in Society. Issues and Controversies.* Whitby, Ontario: McGraw-Hill Ryerson.

Coalter, F. (2004). 'Future sports or future challenges to sport?' in: N. Rowe (ed.), *Driving up Participation: The Challenge of Sport.* London: Sport England.

Collins, M.F. (1991). 'Sport and the state: the case of the United Kingdom', in: F. Landry, M. Landry and M. Yerles (eds.), *Sport … The Third Millennium. Proceedings of the International Symposium*, Quebec, Canada, Sainte-Foy: Presse de l'Université Laval.

Council of Europe (2001 [1992]). *European Sports Charter*. Strasbourg: Council of Europe.

Deacon, B., M. Hulse and P. Stubbs (1997). *Global Social Policy: International Organisations and the Future of Welfare*. London: Sage.

Deloitte & Touche (2003). *Investing in Change – High Level Review of the Modernisation Programme for Governing Bodies of Sport*. London: UK Sport.

Deloitte & Touche (2006a). *Annual Review of Football Finance. Highlights*, 15th edn. London: Deloitte & Touche.

Deloitte & Touche (2006b). *Press Release 24.04.06, Fitness is the Top Sport in Germany and Many Other European Countries*. Düsseldorf: Deloitte & Touche.

Deloitte & Touche (2006c). *Press Release 25.08.06, Steep Drop in Membership of Health Clubs*. London: Deloitte & Touche.

Department of Culture, Media and Sport (DCMS) (2000). *A Sporting Future for All*. London: DCMS (www.culture.gov.uk/default.htm).

Department of Culture, Media and Sport (DCMS) (2002). *Coaching Task Force – Final Report*. London: DCMS, Sport and Recreation Division.

Department of Culture, Media and Sport (DCMS) (2003). *A Sporting Future for All. The Government's Plan for Sport. Annual Report 2002–3*. London: DCMS, April 2003. (www.culture.gov.uk/default.htm).

Department of Culture, Media and Sport/Department for Education and Employment (2001). *A Sporting Future for All. The Government's Plan for Sport*. London: DCMS (www.culture.gov.uk/default.htm).

Department of Culture, Media and Sport (DCMS)/Strategy Unit (2002). *Game Plan: A Strategy for Delivering Government's Sport and Physical Activity Objectives*. London: DCMS/Strategy Unit.

Department of the Environment (1975). *Sport and Recreation*, Cmnd. 6200, London: HMSO.

Department of Finance (2003). *Budget 2003. Investing in Canada's Health Care System*. Ottawa: Department of Finance.

Department of Heritage/Sport Canada (2002). *The Canadian Sport Policy*. Ottawa: Department of Heritage/Sport Canada.

Deutscher Bundestag (2003). *Sportausschuss. Deutscher Bundestag* (A report on the history of the committee). Bonn: Deutscher Bundestag.

Deutscher Sportbund (2003a). *Sport in Deutschland*. Frankfurt am Main: Deutscher Sportbund.

Deutscher Sportbund (2003b). *Sportpolitische Konzeption des Deutschen Sportbundes. Verlage für den Sportausschuss des Deutschen Bundestages Sitzung am 5. November 2003*. (www.dsb.de).

Deutscher Sportbund (2004). *Bestandserhebung 2004*. Frankfurt am Main: Deutscher Sportbund.

DfES/DCMS (2005). *The Results of the 2004–05 School Sport Survey*. London: DfES/DCMS.

Digel, H. (2002). 'A comparison of competitive sport systems', *New Studies in Athletics* 17(1), March.

Digel, H. *et al.* (2002). *Organisation of High-Performance Athletics in Selected Countries. Final Report for the International Athletics Foundation*. Germany: University of Tübingen.

Digel, H., V. Burk and H. Sloboda (2003). *Hochleistungssport in Grossbritannien & Nordirland*. Weilheim/Teck: Brauer.

Dolowitz, D. and D. Marsh (2000). 'Learning from abroad: the role of policy transfer in contemporary policy-making', *Governance: An International Journal of Policy and Administration* 13(1): 5–24.

Dopson, S. and I. Waddington (2003). 'Sport and welfare in Britiain', in: K. Heinemann (ed.), *Sport and Welfare Policies. Six European Case Studies*, Series Club of Cologne, Vol. 3. Schorndorf: Hoffmann Verlag/Schattauer.

Dowding, K. (1995). 'Model or metaphor?: A critical review of the policy network approach', *Political Studies*, 43 (7): 136–158.

Edwards, M. (2001). 'Participatory governance into the future: roles of the government and community sectors', *Australian Journal of Public Administration* 60(3): 78–88.

Egeberg, M., J.P. Olsen and H. Sætren (1978). 'Organisasjon-ssamfunnet og den segmenterte stat', in: J.P. Olsen (ed.), *Politisk organisering*. Bergen: Universitetsforlaget.

Elster, J. (1992). 'Arguing and bargaining in the federal convention and the assemblée constituante', in: R. Malnes and A. Underdal (eds.), *Rationality and Institutions*. Oslo: Universitetsforlaget.

Engelhardt, G.H. and K. Heinemann (2003). 'Sport and welfare policy in Germany', in: K. Heinemann (ed.), *Sport and Welfare Policies. Six European Countries*, Series Club of Cologne, Schorndorf: Hoffmann Verlag/Schattauer.

Enjolras, B. (2004). *Idrett mellom statlig styring og selvbestemmelse. Idrettens bruk av spillemidler*. Rapport nr. 2004:7. Oslo: Institutt for samfunnsforskning.

Enjolras, B. and Ø. Seippel (2001). *Norske idrettslag 2000. Struktur, økonomi og frivillig innsats*. Rapport nr. 2001:4. Oslo: Institutt for Samfunnsforskning.

Enjolras, B., Ø. Seippel and R.H. Waldahl (2005). *Norsk idrett – organisering, fellesskap og politikk*. Oslo: Akilles.

Enzensberger, H.M. (1984). *Norsk utakt*. Oslo: Universitetsforlaget.

Erlinghagen, M. (2003). *Wer treibt Sport im geteilten und vereinten Deutschland. Eine quantitative Analyse sozio-ökonomischer Determinanten des Breitensports*. Graue Reihe des Instituts Arbeit und Technik 2003–2004.

Esping-Andersen, G. (1990). *The Three Worlds of Welfare Capitalism*. Cambridge: Polity Press.

Esping-Andersen, G. (1999): *Social Foundations of Postindustrial Economies*. Oxford: Oxford University Press.

Eulering, J. (2000). 'Die Aufgaben der öffentlichen Hand in der Sportentwicklung', in: DSB (2000). *Der Sport – ein Kulturgut unserer Zeit. 50 Jahre Deutscher Sportbund*. Frankfurt am Main: Deutscher Sportbund.

European Commission (1998). *European Model of Sport*. European Commission.

Farmer, P.J. and S. Arnaudon (1996): 'Australian sports policy', in: L. Chalip, A. Johnson and L. Stachura (eds.), *National Sport Policies. An International Handbook*. London: Greenwood Press.

Featherstone, M. (1991). *Consumer Culture and Postmodernism*. London: Sage.

Finlayson, A. (2003). *Making Sense of New Labour*. London: Lawrence and Wishart.

Fischer, F. (2003). *Reframing Public Policy: Discursive Politics and Deliberative Practices*. NY: Oxford University Press.

Fisher, D. and J. Borms (1990). *The Search for Sporting Excellence*. Schorndorf, FRG: Verlag Karl Hoffman.

Forestiere, C. (2005). The role of opposition activity in evaluating legislative behavior. Paper, *ECPR Joint Sessions of Workshops*, Granada, Spain, April 14–19.

Fox, K. and L. Richards (2004). *Sport and Leisure. National Statistics*. London: TSO.

Franks, C.E.S. and D. Macintosh (1984). 'The evolution of federal government policies toward sport and culture in Canada: a comparison', in: N. Theberge and P. Donnelly (eds.), *Sport and the Sociological Imagination*. Fort Worth, TX: Texas Christian University Press.

Geertz, C. (1973). 'Thick description: towards an interpretive theory of culture', in: C. Geertz (ed.), *The Interpretation of Culture*. NY: Basic Books.

Giddens, A. (1984). *The Constitution of Society. Outline of the Theory of Structuration*. Cambridge: Polity Press.

Goksøyr, M. (1992). *Staten og idretten 1861–1991*. Oslo: Kulturdepartementet.

Goksøyr, M. (1996). 'Phases and functions of nationalism: Norway's utilisation of international sport in the late nineteenth and early twentieth centuries', in: J.A. Mangan, (ed.), *Tribal Identities: Nationalism, Europe and Sport*. London: Frank Cass.

Goksøyr, M. (2005). 'Idrettspolitikk fra Rolf Hofmo til Hans B. Skaset', in: D.V. Hanstad and M. Goksøyr (eds.), *Fred er ei det beste. Festskrift. Hans B. Skaset 70 år*. Oslo: Gyldendal.

Goksøyr, M. and F. Olstad (2002). *Fotball! Norges Fotballforbund 100 år*. Oslo: Norges fotballforbund.

Goksøyr, M. (ed.), E. Andersen and K. Asdal (1996). *Kropp, kultur og tippekamp. Statens idrettskontor, STUI og idrettsavdelingen 1946–1996*. Oslo: Universitetsforlaget.

Goodin, R.E. and H.-D. Klingemann (1996). 'Political science: the discipline', in: R.E. Goodin and H.-D. Klingemann (eds.), *A New Handbook of Political Science*. Oxford: Oxford University Press.

Granovetter, M. (1985). 'Economic action and social structure: the problem of embeddedness', *American Journal of Sociology* 91(3): 481–510.

Gratton, C. (1999). *Compass Report*. London: UK Sport.

Gratton, C. and P. Taylor (2000). *Economics of Sport and Recreation*. London: E & FN Spon.

Green, M. (2003). *An Analysis of Elite Sport Policy Change in Three Sports in Canada and the UK*. PhD Thesis, Loughborough University, UK.

Green, M. (2004). 'Changing policy priorities for sport in England: the emergence of elite sport development as a key policy concern', *Leisure Studies* 23(4): 365–385.

Green, M. (2006). *Policy Transfer, Lesson Drawing and Perspectives on Elite Sport Development Systems*. Unpublished manuscript, Loughborough University.

Green, M. and Houlihan, B. (2006). 'Governmentality, Modernisation and the "Disciplining" of National Sporting Organisations: The Cases of Athletics in Australia and the United Kingdom', *Sociology of Sport Journal*, 23 (1), 47–71.

Green, M. and B. Houlihan (2005). *Elite Sport Development. Policy Learning and Political Priorities*. London: Routledge.

Green, M. and B. Oakley (2001). 'Elite sport development systems and playing to win: uniformity and diversity in international approaches', *Leisure Studies* 20: 247–267.

Haas, P.M. (1992). 'Introduction: epistemic communities and international policy coordination', *International Organisation* 46(1): 1–35.

Hall, M.A. (2003). 'Girls and women's sport in Canada: from playground to podium', in: I. Hartmann-Tews and G. Pfister (eds.), *Sport and Women Social Issues in International Perspective*. London: Routledge/ISCPES.

Hall, P. (1986). *Governing the Economy: The Politics of State Intervention in Britain and France*. Oxford: Oxford University Press.

Hall, A., T. Slack, G. Smith and D. Whitson (1992). *Sport in Canadian Society*. Toronto, Ontario: McClelland & Stewart Inc.

Hanstad, D.V. (2002). *Seiern'n er vår. Men hvem har æren? En bok om det norske idrettseventyret*. Oslo: Schibsted.

Hardman, K. (2002). *European Physical Education/Sport Survey.* Strasbourg: Council of Europe.

Hardman, K. and J. Marshall (2000). 'The state and status of physical education in schools in international context', *European Physical Education Review* 6(3): 203–229.

Hardmann, K. and R. Naul (2002). 'Sport and physical education in the two Germanies, 1945–90', in: K. Hardmann and R. Naul (eds.), *Sport and Physical Education in Germany.* London: Routledge.

Hartmann-Tews, I. (1996). *Sport für alle!? Schriftenreihe des Bundesinstituts für Sportwissenschaft*, Bind 91, Schorndorf: Verlag Karl Hoffmann.

Hartmann-Tews, I. (1999). 'The idea of sport for all and the development of organised sport in Germany and Great Britain', *Journal of European Area Studies* 7(2): 145–156.

Harvey, J. (1999). 'Sport and Quebec nationalism: ethnic or civil identity?' in: J. Sugden and A. Bairner (eds.), *Sport in Divided Societies.* Achen: Meyer and Meyer.

Harvey, J. (2002). 'Sport and citizenship policy: a shift toward a new normative framework for evaluating sport policy in Canada', *Isuma – Canadian Journal of Policy Research* 3(1): 160–165.

Hay, C. (1999). *The Political Economy of New Labour: Labouring Under False Pretences.* Manchester: Manchester University Press.

Hechter, M. (1975). 'Review essay', *Contemporary Sociology* 4: 217–222.

Heclo, H. (1978). 'Issue Networks and Executive Establishment', in: A. King (cd.), *The New American Political System.* Washington: AEI.

Heidenheimer, A., H. Heclo and C. Teich Adams (1990). *Comparative Public Policy: The Politics of Social Choice in America, Europe and Japan*, 3rd edn. NY: St. Martin's Press.

Heinemann, K. (1996). 'Sports policy in Germany', in: L. Chalip, A. Johnson and L. Stachura (eds.), *National Sport Policies. An International Handbook.* London: Greenwood Press.

Heinemann, K. (1997) 'Sport for all in Germany – a social movement or a political power', in: A. Mussino, N. Porro and P. De Nardis (eds.), *Sport: Social Problems, Social Movements: Contributions to the 12th International Seminar*, 19–22 July, 1995, Rome. Rome: Edizioni Seam.

Heinemann, K. and M. Schubert (1999). 'Sports clubs in Germany', in: K. Heinemann (ed.), *Sports Clubs in Various European Countries*, Series Club of Cologne, Vol. 1. Schorndorf: Hoffmann Verlag/Schattauer.

Heinemann, K. (ed.) (1999). *Sport Clubs in Various European Countries.* Series Club of Cologne, Vol. 1. Schorndorf: Hoffmann Verlag/Schattauer.

Heinz, J.P., E.O. Laumann, R.L. Nelson and R.H. Salisbury (1993). *The Hollow Core. Private Interests in National Policy Making.* Cambridge, MA: Harvard University Press.

Heinzerling, G. and H. Rommetvedt (2002). 'Utbygging av idrettsanlegg – planer, penger og partnerskap', in: P. Mangset and H. Rommetvedt (eds.), *Idrett og politikk – kampsport eller lagspill?* Bergen: Fagbokforlaget.

Held, D. and A.G. McGrew (2002). *Governing Globalisation. Power, Authority and Global Governance.* Cambridge: Polity.

Henry, I.P. (2001). The governance of sport and leisure. The roles of the nation-state, the European Union and the City. Paper presented at a *Conference on Sports Policy*, Bø, Norway, 3 December 2001.

Héretier, A. (1998). 'Institutions, interests and political choice', in: R.M. Czada, A. Héretier and H. Keman (eds.), *Institutions and Political Choice. On the Limits of Rationality.* Amsterdam: VU-University Press.

Higgins, J. (1981). *States of Welfare. Comparative Analysis in Social Policy.* Oxford: Basil Blackwell.

Hill, J. (2002). *Sport, Leisure & Culture in Twentieth-Century Britain.* Basingstoke: Palgrave.

Hirst, P. and G. Thompson (1999). *Globalization in Question. The International Economy and the Possibilities of Governance.* Cambridge: Polity.

Holt, R. (1992 [1989]). *Sport and the British. A Modern History.* Oxford: Clarendon Press.

Holt, R. and T. Mason (2000). *Sport in Britain 1945–2000.* Oxford: Blackwell.

Horna, J.L.A. (1989). 'Trends in sports in Canada', in: T.J. Kamphorst and K. Roberts (eds.), *Trends in Sports. A Multinational Perspective.* Culemborg, The Netherlands: Giordano Bruno.

Houlihan, B. (1994). *Sport and International Politics.* London: Harvester-Wheatsheaf.

Houlihan, B. (1996). 'Sport in the United Kingdom', in: L. Chalip, A. Johnson and L. Stachura (eds.), *National Sport Policies. An International Handbook.* London: Greenwood Press.

Houlihan, B. (1997). *Sport, Policy and Politics. A Comparative Analysis.* London/NY: Routledge.

Houlihan, B. (2003). 'Sport and globalisation', in: B. Houlihan (ed.), *Sport and Society. A Student Introduction.* London: Sage.

Houlihan, B. and M. Green (2006). 'The changing status of school sport and physical education: explaining policy change', *Sport, Education and Society* 11(1): 73–92.

Houlihan, B. and A. White (2002). *The Politics of Sport Development: Development of Sport or Development Through Sport?* London: Routledge.

Innst. S. nr. 132 (1984–1985). *Innstilling fra kirke- og undervisningskomiteen om kulturpolitikk for 1980-åra og nye oppgaver i kulturpolitikken (St.meld. nr. 23 for 1981–1982 og St.meld. nr. 27 for 1983–1984).* Oslo: Stortinget (Parliament).

Innst. S. nr. 147 (2000–2001). *Innstilling fra familie-, kultur- og administrasjonskomiteen om idrettslivet i endring – om statens forhold til idrett og fysisk aktivitet.* Oslo: Stortinget (Parliament).

Institute of Youth Sport (2005a). *Monitoring and Evaluation of the Specialist Sports College Initiative: Report on the 2004 National Survey of Specialist Sports Colleges.* Loughborough: Loughborough University, Institute of Youth Sport.

Institute of Youth Sport (2005b). *Monitoring and Evaluation of School Sports Partnership, 2004.* Loughborough: Loughborough University, Institute of Youth Sport.

Interprovincial Sport and Recreation Council (1987). *National Recreation Statement*, Quebec: Interprovincial Sport and Recreation Council.

Jenkins-Smith, H. and P. Sabatier (1994). 'Evaluating the advocacy coalition framework', *Journal of Public Policy* 14(3): 175–203.

John, P. (1998). *Analysing public policy*, London: Pinter.

John Hopkins University (2006). *The Comparative Nonprofit Sector Project.* Findings by Country. (www.jhu.edu).

Kamphorst, T.J. and K. Roberts (1989). *Trends in Sports: A Multinational Perspective.* Culemborg, The Netherlands: Giordano Bruno.

Kassim, H. (1994). 'Policy networks, networks and European Union policy-making: A sceptical view', *West European Politics*, 17 (4), 15–27.

Keech, M. (2003). 'England and Wales', in: J. Riordan and A. Krüger (eds.), *European Cultures in Sport. Examining the Nations and Regions.* Bristol: Intellect books.

Keman, H. (2002). 'The comparative approach to democracy', in: H. Keman (ed.), *Comparative Democratic Politics.* London: Sage.

Kidd, B. (1996). *The Struggle for Canadian Sport.* Toronto: University of Toronto Press.

Kidd, B. and Macfarlane, J. (1972). *The death of hockey*, Toronto, ON.: New Press.

Kikulis, L., T. Slack and C.R. Hinings (1995). 'Towards an understanding of the role of agency and choice in the changing structure of Canada's national sports organisations', *Journal of Sport Management* 9: 135–152.

Klages, A. (2004 [2002]). *Mitgliederentwicklung im Deutschen Sportbund – Die Grösste Personenvereinigung Deutschland vor neuen Hearusforderungen*, Note (www.dsb.de).

König, T. (ed.) (1998). 'Modelling Policy Networks'. Special Issue of *Journal of Theoretical Politics* 10(4).

Krüger, A. (1999). 'Strength through Joy. The culture of consent under Fascism, Nazism and Francoism', in: J. Riordan and A. Krüger (eds.), *The International Politics of Sport in the Twentieth Century*. London: Routledge.

Krüger, A. (2003). 'Germany', in: J. Riordan and A. Krüger (eds.), *European Cultures in Sport: Examining the Nations and Regions*. Bristol: Intellect.

Kvavik, R.B. (1976). *Interest Groups in Norwegian Politics*. Oslo: Universitetsforlaget.

Landman, T. (2000). *Issues and Methods in Comparative Politics*. London: Routledge.

Lange, B. (2003a). 'Bruk av flerbruks- og svømmehaller', *Idrett & Anlegg* 1: 6–9.

Lange, B. (2003b). 'Hvordan brukes fotball- og ishaller', *Idrett & Anlegg* 3: 10–11.

Langkaas, L, (ed.) (1997). *Nasjonalatlas for Norge: Idrett*. Hønefoss: Statens kartverk.

Leibfried, S. (1990). 'The classification of welfare state regimes in Europe', Paper, *Social Policy Association Annual Conference*, University of Bath.

Leibnitz Universität Hanover (2000). *Press Release 08.11.00, 'Økonomie des Profisports'*. Hanover: Leibnitz Universität.

Lewis, P.A. (2002). 'Agency, structure and causality in political science: a comment on Sibeon', *Politics* 22(1): 17–23.

Lichbach, M. and A. Zuckermann (eds.) (1997). *Comparative Politics: Rationality, Culture and Structure*. Cambridge: Cambridge University Press.

Lichbach, M.I. (1997). 'Social theory and comparative politics', in: M. Lichbach and A. Zuckermanm (eds.) (1997), *Comparative Politics: Rationality, Culture and Structure*. Cambridge: Cambridge University Press.

Lijphart, A. (1971). 'Comparative politics and the comparative method', *American Political Science Review* 65: 682–693.

Lijphart, A. (1999). *Patterns of Democracy*. New Haven, CT: Yale University Press.

Lovesey, P. (1979). *The Official Centenary History of the AAA*. Enfield: Guiness Superlatives.

Lunden, K. (1993). *Nasjon eller union? Refleksjonar og røynsler*. Oslo: Samlaget.

Macintosh, D. (1996). 'Sport and Government in Canada', in: L. Chalip, A. Johnson and L. Stachura (eds.), *National Sport*

Policies. An International Handbook. London: Greenwood Press.

Macintosh, D., T. Bedecki and C.E.S. Franks (1987). *Sport and Politics in Canada. Federal Government Involvment since 1961.* Kingston/Montreal: McGill-Queen's University Press.

Maguire, J. (1999). *Global sport: Identities, Societies and Civilisations.* Cambridge: Polity Press.

Mangset, P. (1992). *Kulturliv og forvaltning. Innføring i kulturpolitikk.* Oslo: Universitetsforlaget.

Mangset, P. (2004). *Mange er kalt, men få er utvalgt. Kunstnerroller i endring.* Rapport No. 215/2004. Bø: Telemarksforsking-Bø.

Mangset, P. and H. Rommetvedt (eds.) (2002). *Idrett og politikk – kampsport eller lagspill?* Bergen: Fagbokforlaget.

Marchand, J. (1990). *Sport for All in Europe.* London: HMSO/Council of Europe.

Marsh, D. and R.A.W. Rhodes (eds.) (1992). *Policy Networks in British Government.* Oxford: Clarendon Press.

Metcalfe, A. (1974). 'Some background influences on nineteenth century Canadian sport and physical education', *Canadian Journal of Sport and Physical Education* 5(1): 62–73.

Mills Report (1998). *Sport in Canada: Everybody's Business. Leadership, Partnership and Accountability.* Standing Committee on the Study of Sport in Canada.

Minton, J. and K. Roberts (1989). 'Trend in sport in Great Britain', in: T.J. Kamphorst and K. Roberts (eds.), *Trends in Sports: A Multinational Perspective.* Culemborg, The Netherlands: Giordano Bruno.

Munk, M. and J. B. Lind (2004). *Idrættens kulturelle pol. En analyse av idrætsfeltets autonomi belyst med Pierre Bourdieus metode.* København: Museum Tusculanums Forlag.

National Audit Office (2005). *UK Sport: Supporting Elite Athletes* (HC 182 – SE/2005/9 Session 2004–2005). London: The Stationery Office.

Naul, R. and K. Hardman (2001). *Sport and Physical Education in Germany.* London: Routledge.

Naul, R. (2002). *Physical Fitness, Sporting Lifestyles and Olympic Ideals: Cross-cultural Studies on Youth Sport in Europe.* Schorndorf: Hofmann.

Nichols Applied Management (2005). *The Public Financing of Recreation and Culture in Alberta,* a historical review prepared for ARPA, April 2002, revised January 2005. Edmonton, Alberta: Nichols Applied Management.

Nichols, G. (2003). *Citizen in Action. Voluntary Sector, Sport and Recreation.* Executive Summary. Sheffield: University of Sheffield.

NIF/KKD (2003). *Tilstandsrapport 2003. Om idrett of fysisk aktivitet i Norge.* Oslo: Akilles.

Norberg, J.R. (1997). 'A mutual dependency: Nordic sports organisations and the state', *The International Journal of the History of Sport* 4(3): 115–135.

Nordby, T. (2000). *I politikkens sentrum. Variasjoner i Stortingets makt 1814–2000.* Oslo: Universitetsforlaget.

Norges Idrettsforbund og Olympiske Komité (NIF/NOC) (2000 [1987]). *Bestemmelser om barneidrett, med utfyllende kommentarer. Revidert pr. 1.* April 2000.

Norges Idrettsforbund og Olympiske Komité (NIF/NOC) (2003). *Idrettspolitisk dokument.* Tingperioden 2003–2007.

Norges Idrettsforbund og Olympiske Komité (NIF/NOC) (2005). *Søknad om spillemidler 2006.*

Norges Idrettsforbund og Olympiske Komité (NIF/NOC) (2006). *Årsrapport 2005.*

Norton, P. (ed.) (1990). *Legislatures.* Oxford: Oxford University Press.

Oakley, B. and Green, M. (2001) 'The production of Olympic champions: International perspectives on elite sport development systems', *European Journal of Sport Management* – Special issue 2001.

Ohr, F. and N.H. Solum (2000). *Tippeligaen 2000. Økonomiske nøkkeltall.* (Arbeidsrapport M0112) Molde: Møreforsking.

Olsen, J.P. (1983). *Organized Democracy. Political Institutions in a Welfare State – the Case of Norway.* Oslo: Universitetsforlaget.

Olsen, J.P. (1998). 'Political science and organisation theory: parallel agendas but mutual disregard', in: R.M. Czada, A. Héretier and H. Keman (eds.), *Institutions and Political Choice: On the Limits of Rationality.* Amsterdam: VU-University Press.

Opedal, S. and S.I. Nødland (2004). *Bedre kår for lokalidretten? Evaluering av Kultur- og kirkedepartements tilskuddordning til lokale idrettslag.* Rapport RF 2004/224. Stavanger: Rogalandsforskning.

Opedal, S. and H. Rommetvedt (2006). 'Politikk for norsk lokalidrett', in: *Idrottshistoriskt symposium 2005.* Stockholm: Sveriges Centralförening för Idrottens Främjamnde.

Østerud, Ø. (1986). 'Nasjonalstaten Norge – en karakteristisk skisse', in: L. Alldén, N.R. Ramsøy and M. Vaa (eds.), *Det Norske Samfunn.* Oslo: Gyldendal.

Østerud, Ø., F. Engelstad and P. Selle (2003). *Makten og demokratiet.* Oslo: Gyldendal Akademisk.

Ostrom, E., R. Gardner and J. Walker (1994). *Rules, Games and Common Pool Resources.* Ann Arbor: University of Michigan Press.

Ot. prp. nr. 75 (2000–2001). *Lov om organisert kampaktivitet som tillater knockout.*

Paraschak, V. (1989). 'Native sports history: pitfalls and promise', *Canadian Journal of Sport History* 20(1).

Peppard, V. and Riordan, J. (1993). *Playing politics: Soviet sports diplomacy to 1992*, Creenwich, Conn.: JAI Press Inc.

Pitsch, W. and E. Emrich (2000). *Veränderungen des Umfangs hauptamtlicher Tätigkeit in Sportvereinen im Vergleich verschiedener empirischer Erhebungen.* DVS-Informationen , 15(2): 15–20.

Pitter, R. (1996). 'The State and Sport Development in Alberta: a struggle for public status', *Sociology of Sport Journal* 13: 31–50.

Polsby, N.W. (1990 [1975]). 'Legislatures', in: P. Norton (ed.), *Legislatures.* Oxford: Oxford University Press. Originally published in F.I. Greenstein and N. W. Polsby (eds.), *Handbook of Political Science.* Reading, MA: Addison-Wesley.

Pontusson, J. (1995). 'From comparative public policy to political economy: putting political institutions in their place and taking interests seriously', *Comparative Political Studies* 28(1): 117–147.

Power, M. (1997). *The Audit Society: Rituals of Verification.* Oxford: Oxford University Press.

Przeworski, A. and H. Teune (1970). *The Logic of Comparative Social Enquiry.* New Jersey: Wiley.

Putnam, R.D. (2000). *Bowling Alone.* NY: Simon & Schuster.

QCA (Qualification and Curriculum Authority) (2004). *High Quality PE and Sport for Young People.* London: DfES/DCMS.

Raco, M. and R. Imrie (2000). 'Governmentality and rights and responsibilities in urban policy', *Environment and Planning A* 32: 2187–2204.

Ragin, C. (1994). 'Introduction to qualitative comparative analysis', in: T. Janoski and A. Hicks (eds.), *The Comparative Political Economy of the Welfare State.* Cambridge: Cambridge University Press.

Ravenscroft, N. (2004). 'Sport and Local Delivery', in: N. Rowe (ed.), *Driving up Participation: The Challenge of Sport.* London: Sport England.

Rhodes, R. A. W. (1981). *Control and power in central-local government relations*, Aldershot, Gower.

Richardson, J.J. and G. Jordan (1979). *Governing Under Pressure.* Oxford: Basil Blackwell.

Ridley, F.F. (1987). 'Tradition, change, and crisis in Great Britain', in: M.C. Cummings, Jr. and R.S. Katz (eds.), *The Patron State. Government and the Arts in Europe, North America, and Japan.* NY, Oxford: Oxford University Press.

Riordan, J. (ed.) (1978). *Sport Under Communism*. London: Hurst.

Rodger, B. (1978). *Sport in Its Social Context: International Comparisons*. Strasbourg: Council of Europe.

Rokkan, S. (1966). 'Norway: numerical democracy and corporate pluralism', in: R.A. Dahl (ed.), *Political Opposition in Western Democracies*. New Haven, CT: Yale University Press.

Rommetvedt, H. (2000). 'Private and public power at the national level', in: H. Goverde, P.G. Cerny, M. Haugaard and H.H. Lentner (eds.), *Power in Contemporary Politics*. London: Sage.

Rommetvedt, H. (2002a). *Politikkens allmenngjøring og den ny-pluralistiske parlamentarismen*. Bergen: Fagbokforlaget.

Rommetvedt, H. (ed.) (2002b). *Matmakt. Politikk, forhandling, marked*. Bergen: Fagbokforlaget.

Rommetvedt, H. (2002c). Pluralisation and parliamentarisation, and their strategic implications. Paper presented at the *RCLS/ IPSA and TPSA Conference on Political Parties, Parliamentary Committees, Parliamentary Leadership and Governance*, Istanbul, 23–26 June, 2002.

Rommetvedt, H. (2003). *The Rise of the Norwegian Parliament*. London: Frank Cass.

Rommetvedt, H. (2005). 'Norway: resources count but votes decide? From neo-corporatist representation to neo-pluralist parliamentarism', *West European Politics* 28(4): 740–763.

Rose, N. (1999). *Powers of Freedom: Reframing Political Thought*. Cambridge: Cambridge University Press.

Rose, N. and P. Miller (1992). 'Political power beyond the state: problematics of government', *British Journal of Sociology* 43(2): 172–205.

Rose, R. (2005). *Learning from Comparative Public Policy: A Practical Guide*. London: Routledge.

Roskam, F. (2002). 'Sport Facilities', in: R. Naul, and K. Hardman (eds.), *Sport and Physical Education in Germany*. London: Routledge/ISCPES.

Ross, M.H. (1997). 'Culture and identity in comparative political analysis', in: M. Lichbach and A. Zuckermann (eds.) (1997), *Comparative Politics: Rationality, Culture and Structure*. Cambridge: Cambridge University Press.

Rowe, D. (2003). *Sport, Culture and the Media: The Unruly Trinity*, 2nd edn. Maidenhead: Open University Press.

Sabatier, P. and H. Jenkins-Smith (1993). *Policy Change and Learning: An Advocacy Coalition Process*. Boulder: Westview Press.

Sabatier, P. (1998) 'The advocacy coalition framework: revisions and relevance to Europe', *Journal of European Public Policy* 5(1): 98–130.

Sabatier, P. A. (ed.) (1999). *Theories of the policy process: Theoretical lenses on public policy*, Boulder, CO.: Westview Press.

Salter, M. (1977). The Indian athlete: exploiting or exploited? *Proceedings of the Society on the History of PE and Sport in Asia and the Pacific Area 1976.* Natanya, Israel: Wingate Institute for PE and Sport.

Sayer, A. (1992). *Methods in Social Science. A Realist Approach.* London: Routledge.

Scambler, G. (2005). *Sport and Society. History, Power and Culture.* Maidenhead: Open University Press.

Schmidt, M.G. (2002). 'The impact of political parties, constitutional structures and veto players on public policy', in: H. Keman (ed.), *Comparative Democratic Politics.* London: Sage.

Schmitter, P.C. (1979). 'Still the Century of Corporatism?' in: P.C. Schmitter and G. Lehmbruch (eds.), *Trends Toward Corporatist Intermediation.* London: Sage.

Scholte, J.A. (2003). *Globalization: A Critical Introduction.* Basingstoke: Palgrave.

Searle, M.S. and R.E. Brayley (2002). *Leisure Services in Canada. An Introduction.* State College, PA: Venture Publishing, Inc.

Selle, P. (1995). 'Idretten og det offentlige: Ein familie?' in: K.K. Klausen and P. Selle (eds.), *Frivillig organisering i Norden.* Bergen: TANO and Copenhagen: Jurist- og Økonomiforbundets Forlag.

Siaroff, A. (1994). 'Work, women and gender equality: a new typology', in: D. Sainsbury (ed.), *Gendering Welfare States.* London: Sage.

Siaroff, A. (1999). 'Corporatism in 24 industrial democracies: meaning and measurement', *European Journal of Political Research* 36: 175–205.

Sibeon, R. (1999). 'Agency, structure and social change as cross-disciplinary concepts', *Politics* 19(3): 139–144.

Silk, M., D. Andrews and C.L. Cole (eds.) (2004). *Sport and Corporate Nationalisms.* Oxford: Berg.

Simri, U. (1979). *Comparative Physical Education and Sport.* Natanya, Israel: Wingate Institute for PE and Sport.

Skirstad, B. and K. Felde (1996). 'Sport Policy in Norway', in: L. Chalip, A. Johnson and A. Stachura (eds.), *National Sports Policies.* London: Greenwood Press.

Skirstad, B. (1999). 'Norwegian sport at the crossroad', in: K. Heinemann (ed.), *Sport Clubs in Various European Countries.* Series Club of Cologne, Vol. 1. Schorndorf: Hoffmann Verlag/Schattauer.

Skirstad, B. (2002). 'Norske idrettslag: Oversikt og utfordringer', in: Ø. Seippel (ed.), *Idrettens bevegelser. Sosiologiske studier av idrett i et moderne samfunn.* Oslo: Novus.

Slack, T. (1999). 'An outsider looking in or an insider looking out, reflections on changes in sport clubs in Europe and some North American comparisons', in: K. Heinemann (ed.), *Sports Clubs in Various European Countries*. Series Club of Cologne, Vol. 1. Schorndorf: Hoffmann Verlag/Schattauer.

Slack, T. (2003). 'Sport in the United States and Canada', in: Barrie Houlihan (ed.), *Sport & Society. A Student Introduction*. London: Sage.

Slack, T. (ed.) (2004). *The Commercialisation of Sport*. London: Routledge.

Slack, T. and C. Hinings (1992). 'Understanding change in national sports organisations: an integration of theoretical perspectives', *Journal of Sport Management* 6: 114–132.

Slagstad, R. (1998). *De nasjonale strateger*. Oslo: PAX.

Smith, M. J. (1993). *Pressure, power and policy: State autonomy and policy networks in Britain and the United States*, Hemel Hempstead: Harvester-Wheatsheaf.

SMK (2001). *SMK. Ständige Konferenz der Sportminister der Länder in der Bundesrepublik Deutschland. Beschlüsse und Empfehlungen 1977–2000*. Potsdam: Ministerium für Bildung, Jugend und Sport des Landes Brandenburg.

Sport Canada (1998). *Sport Participation in Canada*. Ottawa: Sport Canada.

Sport Canada (1999). *Canadian Sport Centres*. Position Paper. Ottawa: Canadian Olympic Association, Coaching Association of Canada, Sport Canada.

Sport Canada (2002). *The Canadian Sport Policy*. Ottawa: Sport Canada.

Sport Canada (2004a). *National Roundtable on Future High Performance Sport Funding*. Discussion Paper (2 April, 2004). Ottawa: Sport Canada.

Sport Canada (2004b). *Government of Canada Seeks to Boost Participation in Sport*. Press Release, 7 April.

Sport England (2002). *Higher Education and Sport in England*. Executive Summary. London: Sport England.

Sport England (2003). *Young People and Sport in England. Trends in Participation 1994–2002*. London: Sport England.

Sport England (2004). *The Framework for Sport in England. Making England an Active and Successful Sporting Nation: A Vision for 2020*. London: Sport England.

Sport England Annual Report (2001–2002). Part 1. London: Sport England, 2002.

Sport England East Midlands (2004). '*Change 4 Sport*' in *England's East Midlands. A regional Plan for Sport 2004–2008*. Nottingham: Sport England EM.

Sport Matters Group (2006). *Fulfilling Canada's Promise of Becoming A Leading Sport Nation.* 2006 Pre-Budget Consultation Brief, 19 April, 2006. Ottawa: Sport Matters Group.

Sport: The Way Ahead (1992), *The Report of the Minister's Task Force on Federal Sport Policy,* (chair J.C. Best), Ottawa: Minister of Supply and Services Canada.

Stamm, H.-P. and M. Lamprecht (2001). 'Sydney 2000 – The best Games ever? World sport and relationships of structural dependency', *Proceedings of the 1st World Congress of Sociology of Sport,* Seoul, Korea, 20–24 July.

Statistics Canada (2004a). *Cornerstones of Community: Highlights of the National Survey of Nonprofit and Voluntary Organisations.* Ottawa: Statistics Canada.

Statistics Canada (2004b). 'Arts, entertainment and recreation services', *The Daily,* 30 April, 2004. Ottawa: Statistics Canada.

Statistics Canada (2005). 'Arts, entertainment and recreation services', *The Daily,* 12 May, 2005. Ottawa: Statistics Canada.

Statistics Canada (2006). 'Arts, entertainment and recreation services', *The Daily,* 8 May, 2006. Ottawa: Statistics Canada.

Statistics Norway (SSB) (2003). *Statistisk Årbok 2002.* Oslo/ Kongsvinger: Statistisk sentralbyrå [SSB = Statistics Norway].

Statistics Norway (2003). *Kulturstatistikk 2003.* Oslo/Kongsvinger: Statistics Norway.

Statistics Norway (2004). *Kulturstatistikk 2004.* Oslo/Kongsvinger: Statistics Norway.

St.meld. nr. 8 (1973–1974). *Om organisering og finansiering av kulturarbeid.* Oslo: Kyrkje- og undervisningsdepartementet.

St.meld. nr. 52 (1973–1974). *Ny kulturpolitikk. Tillegg til St.meld. nr. 8 for 1973–1974. Om organisering og finansiering av kulturarbeid.* Oslo: Kyrkje- og undervisningsdepartementet.

St.meld. nr. 23 (1981–1982). *Kulturpolitikk for 1980-åra.* Oslo: Kyrkje- og undervisningsdepartementet.

St.meld. nr. 27 (1983–1984). *Nye oppgåver i kulturpolitikken. Tillegg til St.meld. nr. 23 (1981–1982) Kulturpolitikk for 1980-åra.* Oslo: Kultur- og vitenskapsdepartementet.

St.meld. nr. 41 (1991–1992). *Om idretten. Folkebevegelse og folkeforlystelse.* Oslo: Kulturdepartementet.

St.meld. nr. 14 (1999–2000). *Idrettsliv i endring. Om statens forhold til idrett og fysisk aktivitet.* Oslo: Kulturdepartementet.

Sundbergutvalget (2003). *Finansieringen av statlig idrettspolitikk.* Oslo: Kultur- og kirkedepartementet, Idrettsavdelingen.

Szalai, A. (1972). *The Use of Time.* The Hague: Mouton.

Tangen, J.O. (2004). *Hvordan er idrett mulig? Skisse til en idrettssosiologi.* Kristiansand: Høyskoleforlaget.

Tavis Consulting, Caminata Consulting, WillowBridge Consulting (2003). *An Alberta Recreation Industry Labour Market Analysis. Phase 1. Setting the Stage*, made for Alberta Recreation & Parks Association. Edmonton: Tavis Consulting, Caminata Consulting, WillowBridge Consulting.

Thelen, K. and S. Steinmo (1992). 'Historical institutionalism in comparative politics', in: K. Thelen, S. Steinmo and F. Longstreth (eds.), *Structuring Politics: Historical Institutionalism in Comparative Analysis*. Cambridge: Cambridge University Press.

Theodoraki, E. (1999). 'Structural change in Britain and its implications for sport', in: K. Heinemann (ed.), *Sport Clubs in Various European Countries*. Series Club of Cologne, Vol. 1. Schorndorf: Hoffmann Verlag/Schattauer.

Thibault L., M. Kikulis, and W. Frisby (2004). 'Partnerships Between Local Government Sport and Leisure Departments and the Commercial Sector; Changes, Complexities and Consequences', in: T. Slack (ed.), *The Commercialisation of Sport*. London: Routledge.

Tiemann, B. (2000). 'Die Spitzenverbände – eine Säule der Sportbewegung', in: DSB: *Der Sport – ein Kulturgut unserer Zeit. 50 Jahre Deutscher Sportbund*. Frankfurt am Main: Deutscher Sportbund.

Tønnesson, S. (1986). 'Folkehelse, trim, stjerner 1939–1986. Bind 2', in: F. Olstad and S. Tønnesson (eds.), *Norsk idretts historie, Bind 1 og 2*. Oslo: Aschehoug.

UK Sport (2002). *Summary financial statements of UK Sport's Exchequer and Lottery accounts 2001/2002* (www.uksport.gov.uk)

UK Sport (2003). *Europeans Sporting Success. A Study of the Development of Medal Winning Elites in Five European counties*. London: UK Sport/Sheffield Hallam University.

Vaage, O. F. (2004). 'Trening, mosjon og friluftsliv. Resultater fra levekårsundersøkelsen 2001 og Tidsbruksundersøkelsen 2000', Statistisk Sentralbyrå, rapport 2004/13.

Vaage, O.F. (2005). 'Nordmenn har mest fritid – men ser lite på TV', *Samfunnsspeilet* 1/2005.

Van Bottenburg, M., B. Rijnen and J. van Sterkenburg (2005). *Sports Participation in the European Union: Trends and Differences*. Nieuwegein, The Netherlands: Arko Sports Media.

Veltins (1999). *Veltins-Sportsstudie*. Brauerei C. & A. VELTINS in cooperation with DSB. Meschede-Grevenstein: Veltins.

Vig, N.J. and S.E. Schier (1985). *Political Economy in Western Democracies*. NY: Holmes and Meier.

Vrijman, E.N. (1995). *Harmonisation: Can It Ever Really be Achieved?* Strasbourg: Council of Europe.

WBI (2001). *Governance: A Participatory, Action-Oriented Program*. World Bank Institute (www.worldbank.org/wbi/governance).

White, A. (2003). 'Women and sport in the UK', in: I. Hartmann-Tews and G. Pfister (eds.), *Sport and Women Social Issues in International Perspective*. London: Routledge/ISCPES.

Wilson, J. (1988). *Sport and Leisure*. London: Unwin-Hyman.

Wollebæk, D., P. Selle and H. Lorentzen (2000). *Frivillig innsats. Sosial integrasjon, demokrati og økonomi*. Bergen: Fagbokforlaget.

Index